Magnus Magnusson is an Icelander who has spent nearly all his life in Scotland. Educated at Edinburgh Academy, he won an Open Scholarship to Jesus College, Oxford (1948–53), from where he graduated in English and Old Icelandic literature.

He became a journalist in Scotland before moving to current affairs television on programmes like *Tonight*. He is best-known for his 25 year reign as Quizmaster of *Mastermind*. His main interest, however, was in making historical documentaries. He was the founder-presenter of *Chronicle* (1966–80), a monthly series on world archaeology and history.

As a writer and historian, Magnus has published thirty books, dealing with archaeology, Iceland, Scottish History, Irish history and Lindisfarne, as well as translating Icelandic sagas and modern novels and editing the 1995 *Chambers Biographical Dictionary*.

Magnus was the founder chairman of Scottish Natural Heritage (1992–99), the government's environmental agency in Scotland. He has been awarded honorary doctorates by five universities, and the honorary Fellowship of his old college. But his proudest honour is the honorary knighthood (KBE) he was awarded for services to the heritage of Scotland.

Also by Magnus Magnusson

INTRODUCING ARCHAEOLOGY
VIKING EXPANSION WESTWARDS
THE CLACKEN AND THE SLATE
HAMMER OF THE NORTH
BC: THE ARCHAEOLOGY OF THE BIBLE LANDS
LANDLORD OR TENANT? A VIEW OF IRISH HISTORY
ICELAND
VIKINGS!
MAGNUS ON THE MOVE
TREASURES OF SCOTLAND
LINDISFARNE: THE CRADLE ISLAND
READER'S DIGEST BOOK OF FACTS (Editor)
ICELAND SAGA
CHAMBERS BIOGRAPHICAL DICTIONARY (Editor-in-Chief)
THE NATURE OF SCOTLAND (Editor)
RUM: NATURE'S ISLAND
SCOTLAND: THE STORY OF A NATION

Magnus Magnusson's Quiz Book

Magnus Magnusson

Researcher
Christine Moorcroft

WARNER BOOKS

A *Warner* Book

First published in Great Britain in 2000
by Warner Books

Copyright © Magnus Magnusson

The moral right of the author has been asserted.

The author gratefully acknowledges permission to quote from the following:
Under Milk Wood by Dylan Thomas published by JM Dent.
Brewer's Dictionary of Phrase and Fable 16th edition,
edited by Adrian Room published by Cassel & Co.
'Sunday Morning' by Louis MacNeice, from *Collected Poems*
published by Faber & Faber.
'The Waste Land' from *Collected Poems* 1909–1962 by T.S. Eliot
published by Faber & Faber.

Every effort has been made to trace the copyright holders
and to clear reprint permissions for the following:
'The Fog' by Carl Sandburg from *Oxford Dictionary of*
Phrase, Saying and Quotation;
'From a Railway Carriage', *Read Me: A Poem a Day for*
the National Year of Reading (1998);
Wind In the Willows by Kenneth Grahame, published by Penguin;
Subaltern's Love-Song, *New Bats in Old Belfries 1945*,
The Best of Betjaman selected by John Guest published by Penguin;
'Tarantella' by Hilaire Belloc and 'The Mosquito' by D.H. Lawrence
from *Sounds Good* published by Faber & Faber.

A CIP catalogue record for this book is
available from the British Library.

ISBN 0 7515 3065 4

Typeset in Sabon by M Rules
Printed and bound in Great Britain by
Clays Ltd, St Ives plc

Warner Books
A Division of
Little, Brown and Company (UK)
Brettenham House
Lancaster Place
London WC2E 7EN

Contents

Foreword   1

ABC 1
A is for Art   5
A is for Art: General Knowledge   7
B is for Birds   9
B is for Birds: General Knowledge   11
C is for Cities   13
C is for Cities: General Knowledge   15
D is for Drama   17
D is for Drama: General Knowledge   19
E is for Exploration   21
E is for Exploration: General Knowledge   23
F is for Football   25
F is for Football: General Knowledge   27
G is for Geography   29
G is for Geography: General Knowledge   31
H is for Human Body   33
H is for Human Body: General Knowledge   35
I is for Inventions   37
I is for Inventions: General Knowledge   39
J is for Jewellery   41
J is for Jewellery: General Knowledge   43
K is for Kings   45
K is for Kings: General Knowledge   47
L is for London   49
L is for London: General Knowledge   51

M is for Mountains   53
M is for Mountains: General Knowledge   55
N is for Norse Mythology   57
N is for Norse Mythology: General Knowledge   59
O is for Olympics   61
O is for Olympics: General Knowledge   63
P is for Perfume   65
P is for Perfume: General Knowledge   67
Q is for Quizzes   69
Q is for Quizzes: General Knowledge   71
R is for Railways   73
R is for Railways: General Knowledge   75
S is for Saints   77
S is for Saints: General Knowledge   79
T is for Time   81
T is for Time: General Knowledge   83
U is for Universe   85
U is for Universe: General Knowledge   87
V is for Variety   89
V is for Variety: General Knowledge   91
W is for Words   93
W is for Words: General Knowledge   95
X is for Xmas   97
X is for Xmas: General Knowledge   99
Y is for Yorkshire   101
Y is for Yorkshire: General Knowledge   103
Z is for Zoology   105
Z is for Zoology: General Knowledge   107

ABC 2
A is for Architecture   109
A is for Architecture: General Knowledge   111
B is for Business   113
B is for Business: General Knowledge   115
C is for Cricket   117
C is for Cricket: General Knowledge   119
D is for Dance   121
D is for Dance: General Knowledge   123
E is for Engineering   125
E is for Engineering: General Knowledge   127
F is for Films   129

F is for Films: General Knowledge   131
G is for Games   133
G is for Games: General Knowledge   135
H is for Humour   137
H is for Humour: General Knowledge   139
I is for Information Technology   141
I is for Information Technology: General Knowledge   143
J is for Japan   145
J is for Japan: General Knowledge   147
K is for Kitchen   149
K is for Kitchen: General Knowledge   151
L is for Literature   153
L is for Literature: General Knowledge   155
M is for Mathematics   157
M is for Mathematics: General Knowledge   159
N is for Natural History   161
N is for Natural History: General Knowledge   163
O is for Operas   165
O is for Operas: General Knowledge   167
P is for Pop and Rock Music   169
P is for Pop and Rock Music: General Knowledge   171
Q is for Quotations   173
Q is for Quotations: General Knowledge   175
R is for Religions   177
R is for Religions: General Knowledge   179
S is for Ships and Shipping   181
S is for Ships and Shipping: General Knowledge   183
T is for Textiles   185
T is for Textiles: General Knowledge   187
U is for United States of America   189
U is for United Statesof America: General Knowledge   191
V is for Villains   193
V is for Villains: General Knowledge   195
W is for Weather   197
W is for Weather: General Knowledge   199
Y is for Yesterdays   201
Y is for Yesterdays: General Knowledge   203

Foreword

Why tease me with pedantic themes,
Predicaments and enthymemes,
My mental storehouse vainly stowing
With heaps of knowledge not worth knowing?[1]

Why, indeed? Incidentally, since this is the Foreword to a quiz book, what *is* an enthymeme? (It means a condensed syllogism, and derives from the Greek *enthumeisthai*, to consider or infer, from *en* plus *thumos*, 'mind'.)

All the world's a quiz, and all the men and women merely players (as Jaques might have said in *As You Like It*). Everything in the world is matter for a quiz. What happened? When and why did it happen? Where was it? Who did it, and to whom was it done? Who invented what (human ingenuity being infinite and unfathomable)? Ever since Socrates, people have been asking questions about the world and their place in it.

That seems to me to answer the question I posed at the start – 'Why, indeed?' Why tease people with 'pedantic themes' and 'heaps of knowledge not worth knowing'? To my mind, there is no such thing as knowledge not worth knowing. All knowledge, however esoteric or trivial-sounding, is worth knowing; and quizzes celebrate that knowledge and stimulate the quest for further knowledge.

[1] Translation of an epigram of Anacreon, by Thomas Love Peacock, in *The Halliford Edition of the Works of Thomas Love Peacock*, edited by H. F. B. Brett-Smith and C. E. Jones, 10 vols., 1924–34.

Quizzes are what I like to call 'serious entertainment' as opposed to 'light entertainment': they are a pastime whose purpose can be as serious or light-hearted as one wishes.

All quiz books (unless they are mere compilations of stock pub-quiz fodder) are to a large extent personal, and reflect the interests and preoccupations of the quiz-setters. This book is no exception. Apart from my own concerns, such as archaeology, history, natural history, Norse mythology, Scotland and words, it also reflects the enthusiasms of Christine Moorcroft (*Mastermind*, 1988 and 1996), who checked and researched all the questions and inspired so many of them. She has a vivid personal and professional interest in all sorts of subjects such as art and architecture, chess, clocks, education, football, games of all kinds, IT, jewellery, Liverpool, mathematics, perfumes, recipes, science, textiles and Yorkshire. This quiz book is just as much Christine's as mine.

All the questions and, more importantly, the *answers* in this quiz book were exhaustively researched in a variety of sources, in an attempt to make them as accurate and up-to-date as possible. We made judicious use of the Internet (which can be sadly inaccurate and out-of-date) and all the 'usual suspects': dictionaries, reference books, specialised publications of all kinds as well as original publications wherever possible. We have delved into topics suggested by excellent TV quiz programmes like *Mastermind*, *University Challenge*, *15 to 1* and *100% Gold*. Brewer, Britannica, Larousse and Oxford have been constant companions.

We have not been content merely to dip into the shallower reaches of the ever-expanding reservoir of 'General Knowledge' expected of quiz-contestants; instead, we have sought out questions which have unusual or unexpected answers, or intriguing stories behind them. We have used *Mastermind*'s classic twin formula of specialised questions and general knowledge. The questions in each set are graded into four invisible bands ranging from 'family easy' to 'professional stinker'; each general knowledge set echoes the theme of the preceding specialised set in its first and last question.

Many of the questions will strike a chord with *Mastermind* devotees, for I have included not a few which had particular significance for me and for the programme – Guernica, for instance (Art General Knowledge); the name of the highest mountain in Canada, which I used as a rehearsal question so often that it is permanently engraved on my memory (Mountains General Knowledge); the capital of Mongolia (Geography); and – oh, the shame of it! – the name of Hamlet's father (Drama).

We owe thanks to a host of friends and helpers – many of them from the Mastermind Club (living proof that there is life after *Mastermind*) – over specific questions and answers. They are too numerous to name, but I cannot resist mentioning just a few of them. My publisher Alan Samson of Little, Brown (*Mastermind* 1985) took time during a visit to Stockholm to check on the name of Gustav II Adolf's horse (Kings); he also challenged me to find out the identity of the baby held by Olivia de Havilland in *Gone with the Wind* (Films); Stuart Almond, of the Derbyshire Training and Enterprise Council in Sheffield, started me off on a quest for the original of 'the Sillitoe Tartan' (London General Knowledge); Penny Silva, senior editor of the *Oxford English Dictionary*, with whom I shared the 'Dictionary Corner' on *Countdown*, sought out the details of a textile called 'maud' (Textiles); Fred Housego (*Mastermind* champion, 1980) challenged me to try 'the Knowledge', the exam which London taxi drivers have to pass (Textiles General Knowledge); another taxi driver stumped me by asking what the initials of the BMW car company stood for (Textiles General Knowledge).

They and so many others have all contributed to making this *not* the ultimate quiz book (no one can claim that) but a very special, very favourite quiz book – *Magnus Magnusson's Quiz Book*.

Magnus Magnusson KBE
May 2000

A is for Art   Questions

1 As what is the painting *La Gioconda* better known?

2 Which artist painted the portrait of Sir Winston Churchill which was destroyed on Churchill's orders shortly before he died?

3 About which painting, sold for £24,750,000 in March 1987, did the artist write to his brother '. . . if our Monticelli bunch of flowers is worth 500 francs to a collector, and it is, then I dare swear to you that my — are worth 500 francs too, to one of these Scots or Americans'?

4 From what is Carl André's 1966 work *Equivalent VIII* (displayed in the Tate Modern, London) made?

5 What term describes a work of art, originally with a religious theme and used as a portable aid for private devotion, consisting of a central panel with two hinged side panels which fold over it to protect it?

6 Which ancient cinerary urn of transparent blue glass in the British Museum was attacked and smashed to pieces in 1845, but was repaired and put back on display there, where it remains?

7 Of what did the Japanese artist Hokusai make a series of 36 prints in the nineteenth century?

8 Which seventeenth-century artist painted the portrait *Charles I in Three Positions*?

9 What is the term used to describe ghostly images (painted out when the artist changed his or her mind) which begin to show through paint?

10 For which genre of painting are the sixteenth-century artists Nicholas Hilliard and Isaac Oliver chiefly known?

11 The work of which twentieth-century artist includes many compositions made up of maps, photographs and text, such as *A Hundred Mile Walk*?

12 Which artist painted *The Ambassadors*, a double portrait of two young men: Jean de Dinteville (French Ambassador to England) and Georges de Selve (Bishop of Lavaur in France)?

13 The word for which genre of painting or drawing comes from the French for 'line for line'?

14 Which Royal Academician, in 1830, anonymously slipped one of his own paintings (*Landscape, a Study: Watermeadows near Salisbury*) into the selection panel for an exhibition – only to have it rejected by his colleagues?

15 Two of which kind of animal are depicted in Edwin Landseer's *Dignity and Impudence*?

16 On whose sculptures were the tall thin figures based which moved in time to Benjamin Britten's *Playful Pizzicato* (from *Simple Symphony*) in a Royal Bank of Scotland television commercial?

17 In David Hockney's painting *Mr and Mrs Clark and Percy*, who is Percy?

18 In 1504 Michelangelo completed a marble sculpture, *David*; which other Renaissance artist cast a bronze *David* in 1433?

19 In *Son of Man* (1964) by René Magritte, what hides the subject's face?

20 Who was the sculptor of *Liverpool Resurgent*, immortalised by The Spinners in these lines from the folk-song *In My Liverpool Home*: 'They speak with an accent exceedingly rare/Meet under a statue exceedingly bare'?

A is for Art

1 *Mona Lisa*. It was painted by Leonardo da Vinci in 1503–6. The subject was Lisa Gherardini (the wife of a Florentine official, Francesco di Zanobi del Giocondo).

2 **Graham Sutherland**. Churchill was unhappy about the painting even before it was finished in 1954; on one occasion Sutherland returned to the version he had left at Chartwell to find that Churchill had altered it.

3 *Sunflowers*. It was painted by Vincent van Gogh in 1888 and that version is now owned by the Yasuda Fire & Marine Insurance Company of Tokyo.

4 **Firebricks**. It is a floor piece made up of bricks arranged in two rectangular layers.

5 **Triptych**.

6 **The Portland Vase**. It is also known as the Barberini Vase, after the Barberini Palace, from which Sir William Hamilton bought it and from whom it came into the possession of the Duke of Portland, one of the Trustees of the British Museum, who placed it there for exhibition. It was originally found in a tomb (assumed to be that of Alexander Severus) near Rome in the seventeenth century.

7 **Mount Fuji**.

8 **Sir Anthony van Dyck**. The painting was commissioned by Queen Henrietta for the sculptor Bernini to use as a model from which to make a marble bust. It was painted between 1635 and 1637 and remained with the Bernini family in Rome until 1802, when it entered the collection of Walsh Porter. It was acquired for the Royal Collection in 1822.

9 **Pentimenti**. Pentimento (singular) is from the Italian *pentirsi* (to repent).

10 **Miniature**.

11 **Richard Long**. *A Hundred Mile Walk* is based on a walk he took over New Year 1971 on Dartmoor. He walked the same path about fourteen times to clock up 100 miles. The area in which he walked is circled on the map and a photograph shows the way ahead as he walked. The text is a seven-day log with a phrase entered for each day – phrases which came into his head while he was walking.

12 **Hans Holbein** (1497–1543). It was painted in 1533 and is now in the National Gallery, London.

13 **Portrait** (*trait pour trait*).

14 **John Constable**. When Constable told the selection council (of which he was a member) that the painting was his, adding, 'I had a notion that some of you didn't like my work', the President wanted it to be admitted. In spite of apology and entreaty, Constable refused: 'No! It must not! Out it goes!'

15 **Dogs**. 'Dignity' is a bloodhound called Grafton; 'Impudence' is a Scots terrier called Scratch.

16 **Alberto Giacometti** (1901–66).

17 **A cat**. Mr and Mrs Clark are the fashion designer Ossie Clark and the textile designer Celia Birtwell.

18 **Donatello** (*c* 1386–1466).

19 **An apple**. The green apple hovers in the air with its stalk just above the rim of the sitter's bowler hat.

20 **Jacob Epstein**. The statue, of a huge naked man, was commissioned by the directors of Lewis's store to symbolise the struggle of the city to rehabilitate itself after it was blitzed in the Second World War.

General Knowledge

1 During the Spanish Civil War, which town in the Basque region was destroyed by German bombers, an event which Picasso commemorated in a painting in 1937?

2 What was the title of Art Garfunkel's 1979 theme song for the animated film *Watership Down*?

3 Who created the *Teletubbies*?

4 What is the name for a hole in the side of a volcano which gives off volcanic gases?

5 On which Scottish island is the stone circle known as the Ring of Brogar?

6 Which metal comes from the ore cinnabar?

7 Mathematically, for what is π (pi) the symbol?

8 What does the musical term 'pizzicato' mean?

9 Which bird, whose scientific name is the onomatopoeic *crex crex*, has a cry which can be imitated by moving two notched bones across one another?

10 What does the name Agnes symbolise?

11 Which boxer became known as 'the Punchin' Preacher' after a ten-year absence from the sport during which he had become a church minister?

12 Which plant is also known as 'burning bush'?

13 Whose law is summarised as 'bad money drives out good'?

14 Which Hindu deity has the head of an elephant?

15 Who composed the following quatrain:
Sir Christopher Wren
Said, 'I am going to dine with some men.
If anyone calls
Say I'm designing St Paul's.'

16 Who was the first person to be confined in the Bastille?

17 Which royal palace, built during the last decade of Henry VIII's reign, was given by Charles II to his mistress, the Duchess of Cleveland, who sold it for building materials?

18 Which sixteenth-century alchemist and physician (still regarded as the patron of alternative medicine) pronounced that he would not use the teachings of Hippocrates and Galen, since experience alone would disclose the secrets of disease?

19 What was the name of George Stephenson's first locomotive (built in 1814)?

20 How did Admiral Sir William James acquire the nickname 'Bubbles'?

General Knowledge   Answers

1 **Guernica**, in 1937. 'Guernica' was the subject of the very first question asked on *Mastermind*, and I wanted to make the very *last* question echo it. Before the 1997 final we rehearsed the ploy, secretly, and decided that if the outcome of the final did not depend on it, I would get a cue in my earpiece just before the end of the last general knowledge round.

2 *Bright Eyes*.

3 **Anne Wood**. She also created Roland Rat and Rosie and Jim. In 1984, after getting a commission from Channel 4 to make the programme *Pob*, she set up her own company, Ragdoll Productions.

4 **Fumarole**.

5 **Mainland Island** in the Orkneys.

6 **Mercury**.

7 **The symbol of ratio of the circumference to the diameter of a circle** ($^{22}/_7$, or 3.14, when reduced to two decimal places).

8 **Plucked** (literally 'pinched': the notes on a stringed instrument are to be plucked, not bowed).

9 **Corncrake**.

10 **Purity**, from the Greek *agnos* (pure) and the Latin *agnus* (lamb). Agnes is the patron saint of young virgins. She was said to have been martyred in the Diocletian persecution (*c* 304) at the age of 13.

11 **George Foreman** (b 1949).

12 **White dittany** (*Dictamus albus*). In strong heat the oil in this plant can vaporise and catch fire without harming the plant itself.

13 **Gresham's Law**. Sir Thomas Gresham (1519–79) was the founder of the Royal Exchange in 1537, when he also became Lord Mayor of London. He gave Queen Elizabeth of England the advice that the state should borrow money from London merchants instead of foreigners, making an observation, known as 'Gresham's Law': of two coins of equal exchange value, the one of the lower intrinsic value would tend to drive the other out of use.

14 **Ganesha**. A legend tells how the goddess Parvati made Ganesha from flakes of her own skin into which she breathed life. The god Shiva cut off Ganesha's head but, after seeing Parvati's distress and hearing her story, promised to kill the first creature he came across and give its head to Ganesha: it was an elephant.

15 **E. Clerihew Bentley** (1875–1956). He gave his name to the 'clerihew'.

16 **Hugues Aubriot**, provost of Paris, who had built the Bastille (*c* 1369). He was imprisoned there on a charge of heresy.

17 **Nonsuch Palace** (at Cuddington in Surrey, close to Cheam and Ewell). The Duchess (Barbara Villiers) made an agreement with George, Lord Berkeley, keeper of the palace to demolish it for building materials in return for £1,800.

18 **Paracelsus** (Philippus Aureolus Theophrastus Bombastus von Hohenheim), who took the name Paracelsus, which means 'better than Celsus' (the Roman physician).

19 **Blücher**. Blücher was a dialect word from Tyneside, where Stephenson lived, for a clumsy, awkward thing.

20 **From his childhood portrait, known as** *Bubbles*. It was painted in 1886 by Sir John Everett Millais, and became well known when it was used by Lever Brothers for an advertisement for Pears' soap.

B is for Birds

1 Which bird is also known as 'Cuddy's duck' because St Cuthbert protected it and gave it his blessing during his residence in the Farne Islands, where it nests?

2 The whooper, mute and Bewick's are what kind of bird?

3 'Merrythought' is one of the popular names for which bony structure on a bird, properly named the furcula?

4 Which bird is named after its feeding habit of up-ending stones to look for small creatures such as shellfish?

5 Which bird is featured in the name of the pub in the song *Pop goes the Weasel*?

6 Which bird, which re-established itself in Suffolk in the late 1940s, is featured on the logo of the RSPB?

7 The first two Bird Reserves were acquired by the RSPB in 1931. One was at Dungeness in Kent – where was the other?

8 Which bird's name, derived from Old English, can be translated, in birdwatchers' parlance, as 'a little brown job'?

9 What kind of bird is stuffed and displayed in the MCC Museum at Lords, where it had been killed by a cricket ball?

10 What is the collective noun for larks?

11 On which island off Iceland was the last known great auk killed, in 1844?

12 Which bird is known in Gaelic as 'the eagle with the sunlit eye'?

13 Which bird, popular as a cage-bird, symbolised the Passion of Christ in medieval religious paintings?

14 *Puffinus puffinus* sounds as if it should be the Latin name for a puffin, but it isn't. What is it?

15 Which bird was the symbol of the goddess Athene (Minerva)?

16 What is the name given to a male falcon?

17 From which wild species is the London pigeon descended?

18 Thoth, the ancient Egyptian god of wisdom, was usually depicted with the head of which bird?

19 Which is the only endemic species of bird confined entirely to Britain?

20 Who wrote the short story *The Song of the Wren*, published in 1972?

B is for Birds

1 **Eider.** St Cuthbert lived as a hermit on Inner Farne from 676 to 687.

2 **Swan.** Bewick's was named after Thomas Bewick (1753–1828), who made the woodcuts for *History of British Birds* (1804).

3 **Wishbone.**

4 **Turnstone.**

5 **Eagle:**

> *Up and down the City Road,*
> *In and out the* Eagle,
> *That's the way the money goes,*
> *Pop goes the weasel!*

6 **Avocet.** Avocets bred regularly on the east coast of England until the early nineteenth century; the last records dated from Kent in the 1840s. A century later, in 1941, avocets from the Netherlands started nesting at a site in Norfolk, and in 1947 they recolonised two sites in Suffolk – Minsmere, and Havergate Island, both of which are now RSPB Reserves.

7 **Eastwood**, at Stalybridge, Manchester.

8 **Dunnock** (*Prunella modularis*). 'Dun' means 'brownish-grey', and '-ock' is a diminutive suffix indicating smallness. The dunnock was formerly known as the accentor, or hedge sparrow, but it is not related to the house sparrow or the tree sparrow. (The similarity in their names dates from when people called *any* 'little brown job' a sparrow.)

9 **House sparrow** (*Passer domesticus*). A ball from Jehangir Khan, bowling for Cambridge University to Tom Pierce of MCC on 3 July 1936, hit the unfortunate bird and killed it.

10 **Exaltation.**

11 **Eldey** ('Fire Island'). The last two of these flightless birds were caught and killed by an expedition financed by a Danish museum; no sighting has been recorded since.

12 **Sea-eagle**, or **white-tailed eagle**. Its name in Gaelic is *iolaire sùil na grèine*.

13 **Goldfinch.**

14 **Manx shearwater.**

15 **Owl.**

16 **Tiercel.** It was given the name from the Latin *tertius* (third) because it is usually a third of the size of the female. The male goshawk is often called a 'tassel-gentle', which is a corruption of tiercel.

17 **Rock dove.**

18 **Ibis.** Thoth was occasionally depicted with the head of a baboon. He was the patron of scribes and magicians; he was the secretary of the gods, and at the judgement of the dead he weighed the heart.

19 **Scottish crossbill.**

20 **H. E. Bates.** In the story a Miss Shuttleworth feeds the birds in her large garden on carefully prepared sandwiches. She knows their tastes well: the chaffinches always ate the Gentleman's Relish, the blue tits the cream cheese, the robin the tomato and the sparrows first the anchovy paste and then the blackberry jam; but the wren never ate any of them – it just sang.

General Knowledge Questions

1 Where do British swallows spend the winter?
2 Which Grand National winner in 1991 shared its name with the race's sponsors?
3 What does 'tandoori' mean?
4 Who played the part of Manuel in the 1975–9 BBC2 series *Fawlty Towers*?
5 What is the name for the part of a church (east of the crossing) which contains the main altar, sanctuary and, in larger churches, the choir?
6 After what is the Exchequer named?
7 Which essential herbs are used to flavour béarnaise sauce?
8 In a suit of armour, which part of the body was protected by a sabaton?
9 Which opera, originally entitled *La Maledizione* (the curse), was based on *Le Roi s'amuse*, a play by Victor Hugo?
10 What was the former name of Tokyo?
11 Who was the first (British) Princess Royal?
12 What is an opsimath?
13 Which Shakespearean character has a dog named Crab, which he describes as 'the sourest-natured dog that lives'?
14 What is a *vade mecum*?
15 Kinloch Castle is on which Hebridean island?
16 German attacks on British cities (in reprisal for British raids on Cologne and Lübeck) in the Second World War were named after whose books?
17 Which Welsh-language poet wrote *The Gododdin* in about AD 600?
18 Which Scottish physicist wrote *Treatise on Electricity and Magnetism* in 1873 – a mathematical treatment of Michael Faraday's theory of electrical and magnetic forces?
19 Which American architect developed 'geodesic domes'?
20 What kind of bird is the 'Liver Bird' featured on the coat of arms of Liverpool?

General Knowledge Answers

1 **Africa.**
2 **Seagram.** Ivan Straker, the chairman of Seagram, had been offered the chance to buy the horse, but turned it down.
3 **Cooking over a charcoal fire in a** *tandoor*, a cylindrical clay oven traditionally used in India.
4 **Andrew Sachs.**
5 **Chancel.**
6 **The chequered cloth** on which the reckoning of revenues took place. Henry I (1100–35) set up the Exchequer as a government agency to deal with the income of the Crown. It was abolished in 1833, although Exchequer is still the unofficial name of the Treasury.
7 **Chervil** and **tarragon.** Béarnaise sauce is also flavoured with spices such as mace and pepper. Sometimes parsley is added but this is not essential.
8 **The foot.**
9 *Rigoletto* by Giuseppe Verdi (1813–1901) which was first performed at the Fenice Opera House, Venice, in 1851. Censors objected to the plot, saying that 'it was filled with debauchery'. The Fenice Opera House negotiated some changes with Verdi and Francesco Maria Piave (the librettist), including that 'the action will be transposed from the Court of France to one of the independent duchies of Burgundy or Normandy, or one of the small Italian principalities'.
10 **Edo** or **Yedo** ('estuary'). It was renamed in 1868 when it became the residence of the emperor and replaced Kyoto ('western capital') as the capital. Tokyo means 'eastern capital'.
11 **Princess Mary** (1631–60), daughter of Charles I, who was given this honorary title for the eldest daughter of the sovereign in *c* 1642. The title is conferred at the monarch's discretion and retained for life even if there is another monarch with a daughter.
12 **One who learns late in life** (from the Greek *opse* and *math*). When one gets to a certain age, it is an extremely comforting word.
13 **Launce**, servant of Proteus, in *The Two Gentlemen of Verona*.
14 **A handy reference book** (literally 'come with me').
15 **Rum.** The castle was built (between 1897 and 1900) by George Bullough, a Lancashire textile machinery manufacturer who bought the island, which is now a National Nature Reserve owned by Scottish Natural Heritage.
16 **Karl Baedeker** (1801–59). 'Baedeker Raids' (a term which originated in 1942) targeted cities of historical or cultural importance, like those listed in the *Baedeker* Guidebooks.
17 **Aneirin** (*c* sixth–seventh century). The poem commemorates the 360 men who died during a heroic raid (*c* 600) led by the king of the Gododdin, Mynyddog Mwynfawr, from his stronghold of *Din Eidyn* (Edinburgh) to *Cattraeth* (Catterick), North Yorkshire, which was occupied by the Angles.
18 **James Clerk Maxwell** (1831–79).
19 **Richard Buckminster Fuller** (1896–1983). A geodesic dome is a half-spherical framework which can resist forces in any direction and can enclose huge volumes.
20 **Cormorant.** The bird depicted on Liverpool's first corporate seal, shortly after the city was granted its charter by King John in 1207, was an eagle, but it was a poor drawing and was later mistaken for a cormorant.

C is for **Cities**

1 What is the Italian name for the city of Florence?
2 Which British city's airport is at Rhoose?
3 What name, meaning 'mid-water settlement', did the Romans give to Paris?
4 On which Japanese island is Tokyo?
5 What was the meaning of the word Dublin, the Norse name for the city?
6 In Thomas Hardy's *Jude the Obscure*, which city did he call 'Christminster'?
7 In the centre of which English city are the large outdoor sculptures *The River*, *Youth* and *The Guardians* by Dhruva Mistry?
8 On the site of which ancient city is Bodrum in Turkey built?
9 Which city had the original ghetto in the sixteenth century?
10 If you were at longitude 24° 55′ east and latitude 60° 15′ north, in which capital city would you be?
11 In which European city is there a lake called the Tjörn?
12 Which Asian city (other than the walled section of Beijing which contains the Imperial Palace) was known as the Forbidden City?
13 About which city did William Dunbar (*c* 1460–*c* 1520) write:
> *May nane pass through your principal gates*
> *for stink of haddocks and of skates,*
> *for cries of carlings [old women] and debates [arguments] . . .*
> *tailors, souters [shoemakers], and craftis vile*
> *the fairest of your streets does fyle [defile] . . .'*
14 Which city was the capital of Timur's (Tamerlane's) empire?
15 In the centre of which South American city is the Square of Three Powers?
16 After which city is mayonnaise said to be named?
17 The prophet Muhammad was born in Makkah (Mecca); in which city did he die?
18 On which city did Charles Darrow base his original game of Monopoly, which he patented in the early 1930s?
19 According to classical legend, which city was the home of the original Palladium?
20 The name of which African capital city is the corruption of a word for ants?

C is for **Cities**

1 **Firenze**.

2 **Cardiff**.

3 **Lutetia**. Paris was in existence by the end of the third century BC as a settlement on an island, the modern Île de la Cité in the River Seine, and was inhabited by a Gallic tribe known to the Romans as the Parisii.

4 **Honshu**. Japan has four main islands: Hokkaido, Honshu, Kyushu and Shikoku, and numerous smaller ones.

5 **Black Pool**. The dark bog water made a 'black pool' – Dubh Linn in Irish, Dyflinn in Norse – which gave the city its name. The vikings, or Norsemen, came in the ninth century (c 831) and built upon the ridge above the river's south bank, on the spot where Dublin Castle was later constructed.

6 **Oxford**.

7 **Birmingham**. The sculpture group (unveiled in 1993 and soon dubbed 'The Floosie in the Jacuzzi' by local wags) is in Victoria Square.

8 **Halicarnassus**. The Mausoleum, numbered among the Seven Wonders of the World, was built by Artemisia, the widow of Mausolus (d 353/2 BC).

9 **Venice**. The Venetian word ghetto, probably derived from an iron foundry in the neighbourhood, was first used in Venice in 1516. In that year an area for Jewish settlement was set aside, shut off from the rest of the city, and superintended by Christian watchmen. It became a model for ghettos in Italy. The practice of confining Jews within walled quarters, locked at night, became a common social practice, at least in the central and eastern parts of the continent.

10 **Helsinki** (Finland).

11 **Reykjavík** (Iceland).

12 **Lhasa**, the capital of Tibet. It was closed to Westerners until the beginning of the twentieth century.

13 **Edinburgh**.

14 **Samarkand** (east-central Uzbekistan).

15 **Brasilia**. The Three Powers are represented by three buildings which dominate the square: the Palaço do Planalto (the Executive), the Palaço do Congresso (Congress) and the Palaço da Justiça (the Justiciary).

16 **Port Mahon**, the capital of Minorca. The story goes that when the Duc de Richelieu landed there in 1756 and demanded a meal, his chef (having little left in the larder) took whatever food he could find and beat it together to make a sauce: the yolks of eggs, olive oil, vinegar, pepper and salt. He named it 'mahonaise'.

17 **Madina** (Medina), now in Saudi Arabia. The Arabic forms are: Al-Madinah (formally Al-Madinah Al-Munawwarah), meaning 'The Luminous City', and Madinat Rasul Allah, meaning 'City of the Messenger of God'. It is the ancient city of Yathrib.

18 **Atlantic City**, New Jersey.

19 **Troy**. It was a huge wooden statue of Athene in the citadel of Troy which was said to have fallen from heaven. The statue had to be kept safe to ensure the safety of the city. The word palladium is now applied to any type of safeguard.

20 **Accra**. It is a corruption of the Akan word *nkran* for the black ants which are common in the vicinity.

General Knowledge

1 What did the Romans name the town upon which the city of Carlisle was founded?

2 Who wrote the ballad *Paul Revere's Ride*?

3 What is the meaning of Sinn Fein?

4 By what name was the music-hall entertainer Matilda Wood known?

5 The story of whose return from exile is celebrated by the Hindu festival of Divali?

6 Which Rugby player was known as 'the Peer of Wigan'?

7 Which artist and self-taught anatomist painted the race-horses *Molly Longlegs* in 1760–62 and *Whistlejacket* in 1762?

8 What is the name for the symbol, consisting of two dots, which is placed above a letter in Germanic languages?

9 In Roman mythology, what was the name of the god of fire and metal-working?

10 To what period, in law, does the term 'time immemorial' refer?

11 Which Scottish king was known as 'Toom Tabard'?

12 What kind of animal is *Rana esculenta*?

13 Who was the last Earl of Wessex before the title was conferred upon Prince Edward in 1999?

14 What is a 'Pyrrhic' victory?

15 Which member of the *Plumiera* family of trees, unusually, was named after a perfume rather than the other way round?

16 Which town is the capital of the Orkneys?

17 For which profession did Mohandas Gandhi train when he first went to London in 1888?

18 Which art critic wrote the fairy-tale *The King of the Golden River* – the tale of Gluck and his greedy brothers?

19 Which ancient body controls the grazing rights in the New Forest?

20 Which African capital city's name means 'rope matting', and came about when fifteenth-century Portuguese colonists asked the local inhabitants the name of the place? (They thought they were being asked what they were doing.)

General Knowledge   Answers

1 **Luguvalium**.

2 **Henry Wadsworth Longfellow** (1807–82). Paul Revere (1735–1818) was the principal rider for Boston's Committee of Safety. On 18 April 1775 he and William Dawes set off from Boston to warn Revolutionary leaders John Hancock and Samuel Adams of an impending attack by the British. Revere, Dawes and Samuel Prescott then set off for Concord, but were stopped by a British patrol; only Prescott got through. Revere was released and returned on foot to Lexington. Because of Revere's warning, the Minutemen were ready the next morning on Lexington Green for the battle, which launched the American War of Independence.

3 **We ourselves**. Sinn Fein was formed in 1905 and in 1919 set up the Irish Republic under Éamon de Valera.

4 **Marie Lloyd** (1870–1922). One of her most popular songs was *My Old Man Said, 'Follow the Van'*.

5 **Rama and Sita**. They were banished from the Ayodha by Rama's father, the King of Ayodha, on the insistence of one of his wives to whom he had once promised a wish and who wanted her own son to be the next king.

6 **Billy Boston** (b 1934). He was signed (from Neath) for Wigan for a fee of £3,000 in 1953 and played for them until 1968; after that he played for Blackpool until he retired in 1970 to become landlord of the Griffin, a pub near Wigan's ground.

7 **George Stubbs** (1760–1806). *Molly Longlegs* is in the Walker Art Gallery, Liverpool and *Whistlejacket* is in the National Gallery, London.

8 **Umlaut**. For example, in *Männer*, the German word for men, it gives the 'a' the sound of 'e'.

9 **Vulcan**, son of Jupiter and Juno.

10 **Before the reign of Richard I** (1189–99). The first Statute of Westminster of 1275 fixed this as the time limit for bringing certain types of action.

11 **John Balliol**. He was appointed King of Scots by Edward I of England in 1292. 'Toom Tabard' means 'empty tabard', referring to the stripping of the royal insignia from his surcoat by Edward in July 1296.

12 **The edible frog**.

13 **King Harold Godwinsson** (d 1066).

14 **A victory whose cost is so great as to negate its value**. Pyrrhus was a warrior king of Epirus in the third century BC. He fought and beat the Romans at the Battle of Asculum in 279 BC, but his casualties were so heavy that the tag 'Pyrrhic' was applied to a costly victory.

15 **Frangipani**. The perfume is made from orris, spices, civet and musk and named after the Italian family who created it in the fifteenth century.

16 **Kirkwall**.

17 **Law**. Gandhi's eldest brother, Laxmidas, paid for him to study in England when he left school in the state of Rajkot in India.

18 **John Ruskin** (1819–1900). Ruskin was also a moralist. The story's moral is 'good triumphs over evil'.

19 **The Court of Verderers**. In English forest law, which dates from Saxon times, a verderer has official jurisdiction in the royal estates, with especial charge of trees and undergrowth. William I of England placed the New Forest under forest law.

20 **Banjul**, the capital city of Gambia.

D is for Drama

1 Where in Bavaria has the biennial Passion Play been held since 1634?

2 In Shakespeare, who gives his son the advice 'neither a borrower nor a lender be'?

3 Of which theatre is Alan Ayckbourn the artistic director?

4 From which play, first performed in 1956, was the term 'Angry Young Men' derived?

5 In traditional English drama, who was Columbine's lover?

6 What was the name of the *Jew of Malta* in the play by Christopher Marlowe?

7 What is a 'closet drama'?

8 Who wrote *An Ideal Husband*?

9 Which English poet and dramatist was jailed for murder after killing the actor Gabriel Spencer in a duel in 1598?

10 From a play by which Greek comedy dramatist does the expression 'Cloud-Cuckoo-Land' come?

11 During the opening of which play by J. M. Synge, in 1907, were there riots named after the play?

12 Which London theatre, opened in 1818, was originally called the Royal Coburg?

13 Who founded the Royal Academy of Dramatic Arts in 1904?

14 In Greek mythology, who was the muse of tragedy?

15 What name is given to the group of people said to have first been organised at a theatre, by a certain Monsieur Sauton in Paris in 1820, as paid 'applauders'?

16 What is the setting of Jean-Paul Sartre's play *Huis-clos* ('Vicious circle' or 'No exit', also known as *In Camera*)?

17 Which actor did William Hogarth paint playing the part of Richard III in his 1745 painting — *as Richard III*?

18 In which Tudor comedy, attributed to William Stevenson, do the characters Hodge the servant and Tyb the maid take part in a search for the eponymous item found in the seat of Hodge's breeches?

19 Which play is said to have 'made Gay rich and Rich gay'?

20 Whose thunder was stolen during a performance of *Macbeth* at the Drury Lane Theatre shortly after his own play *Appius and Virginia* was taken off after a handful of performances in 1709?

D is for **Drama**

1 Oberammergau.

2 Polonius, in *Hamlet*. When I asked this question on *Mastermind* in the 1989 series, the contestant replied 'Hamlet'; whereupon I corrected him, adding (for some unfathomable reason), 'No: Polonius, his father'.

3 The Stephen Joseph Theatre, Scarborough. The premieres of all Ayckbourn's plays are held there.

4 *Look Back in Anger*, by John Osborne. The term was given to dramatists whose work attacked the values of the Establishment.

5 Harlequin.

6 Barabas.

7 A play which is intended for reading rather than performing.

8 Oscar Wilde (1854–1900). The play was first performed at the Haymarket theatre in January 1895 and ran for 111 performances, ending on 6 April 1895, the day after Wilde's arrest for homosexuality.

9 Ben Jonson (1572–1637). Jonson only escaped hanging because he had the wit to invoke an obsolete law by which he could claim 'benefit of clergy' (he was the son of a clergyman).

10 Aristophanes (*c* 448–380 BC). The play was *The Birds*. 'Cloud-Cuckoo-Land' was *Nephelokokkygia*, an imaginary city built in the air by birds to separate the gods from mortals.

11 *Playboy of the Western World* (the 'Playboy Riots').

12 The Old Vic. The original name was in honour of Princess Charlotte, only child of George IV, and her husband Prince Leopold of Saxe-Coburg. It opened on a rural site known as 'Cupid's Gardens' in 1818.

13 Sir Herbert Beerbohm Tree (1853–1917).

14 Melpomene.

15 Claque. The groups included *bisseurs*, who cried '*bis*' (encore); *rieurs*, who laughed at the jokes; *commissaires*, who committed the play to memory and pointed out its merits with gusto; *pleureurs*, who held handkerchiefs to their eyes during emotional scenes; and *chatouilleurs* ('ticklers'), who spread good humour by means of quips and general conviviality.

16 Hell.

17 David Garrick (1717–79). The play, which opened in 1741 at Goodman's Fields, was Garrick's first major role.

18 *Gammer Gurton's Needle* (1575). Stevenson created a hilarious drama in which Gammer Gurton searches the ashes in the grate, makes Tyb the maid rake through all the dust she has thrown out and Hodge the servant sift though a pile of flour. Her son Cocke arrives with a gaping hole in his breeches which he displays pantomime-fashion to the delighted audience, saying that he cannot go out like that and chiding his mother for being so careless with her needle.

19 John Gay's *The Beggar's Opera* (1728). It was first presented at Lincoln's Inn Fields by the theatre manager John Rich, and proved to be the most successful play ever presented hitherto.

20 John Dennis (1657–1734). Dennis invented a method of making 'thunder' sound effects by rolling cannon balls down long wooden troughs. During a performance of *Macbeth*, Dennis is reputed to have said, 'Damn them! They will not let my play run, but they steal my thunder.'

General Knowledge   Questions

1 In *A Midsummer Night's Dream*, whose head did Puck turn into that of an ass?
2 Who, in a Beatles' song, 'picks up the rice at the church where a wedding has been'?
3 In which 1993 Steven Spielberg film were extinct animals biologically engineered from fossilised DNA in a secret location on an island off Costa Rica?
4 To which sixteenth-century seafarer and Mayor of Plymouth did Buckland Abbey belong?
5 In *The Flintstones*, what is the name of the company which employs Fred Flintstone?
6 In the version of Vincent van Gogh's painting *The Sunflowers* in the National Gallery, London, where did the artist sign his name?
7 Who, in December 1996, became the first footballer to play in 1,000 League games?
8 The name of which American Civil War battle near San Antonio, Texas, means 'cottonwood' (poplar)?
9 What name, derived from its size and colour, is given to a 'dying' star which has exhausted the supply of hydrogen at its centre, become enlarged to about a hundred times its previous size and begun to burn hydrogen as fuel?
10 The ancient Egyptian sun-god Horus had the head of which bird?
11 In which game are 'squidgers' a piece of equipment and 'squopping' a technique?
12 In 1999, who succeeded Nelson Mandela as leader of the African National Party and went on to become President of South Africa?
13 Of which Far Eastern country are the islands of Luzon, Mindanao, Samar and Negros a part?
14 Which American inventor and manufacturer patented the cylinder lock in 1861?
15 Of which animal is a shoat, or shote, the young?
16 What was the first trade-mark to be registered, in 1875?
17 What is the title of Jean Elliot's poetic lament for the Scots killed at the Battle of Flodden in 1513?
18 Which Member of Parliament was knocked down and killed by a train during the opening of the Liverpool & Manchester Railway in 1830?
19 In Greek legend, which hero was attacked by the monsters Scylla and Charybdis in the Straits of Messina?
20 What was the objective of the sex strike organised by the women of Athens in the *Lysistrata* of Aristophanes?

General Knowledge

1 Bottom, the weaver.

2 Eleanor Rigby.

3 *Jurassic Park*.

4 Sir Francis Drake (*c* 1540–96). Buckland Abbey was built in the thirteenth century as a Cistercian monastery and became the family home of Sir Richard Greville after the Dissolution of the Monasteries. Sir Francis Drake bought it in 1581. It is now owned by the National Trust.

5 The Bedrock Construction Co.

6 On the vase.

7 Peter Shilton (goalkeeper for Leyton Orient). He had also played for Leicester City, Stockport County, Nottingham Forest, Southampton, Derby County, Plymouth Argyle and Bolton Wanderers. Shilton won 125 international caps for England.

8 The Alamo. It was named after a Franciscan mission whose name came from the cottonwood trees which surrounded it.

9 Red giant. Betelgeuse in the constellation of Orion is an example of a red giant.

10 Falcon.

11 Tiddlywinks.

12 Thabo Mbeki (b 1942).

13 The Philippines.

14 Linus Yale (1821–68). He produced an improved cylinder lock in 1865.

15 Pig.

16 The Bass Red Triangle. It appeared in *The Bar at the Folies-Bergère*, painted by Edouard Manet in 1882, now in the Courtauld Institute Galleries, London.

17 *Flow'rs o' the Forest*. Jean Elliot (1727–1805) wrote the poem in Scots. It begins:

> *I've heard of a liltin' at the ewe-milkin',*
> *Lasses a-liltin' before dawn o' day.*
> *Now there's a moanin' on ilka [each] green loanin' [pasture] –*
> *The Flow'rs o' the Forest are a' [all] wede away [carried off].*

18 William Huskisson (1770–1830), MP for Morpeth.

19 Odysseus.

20 To force their soldier husbands to make peace with Sparta.

E is for Exploration

1 Whose 1769 expedition to the South Seas had the task of finding *Terra Australis* and observing the transit of the planet Venus over Tahiti?

2 What is the magnetic stone, containing the mineral magnetite, which sailors once used as a compass?

3 What was the original name of the *Golden Hind*, the ship in which Francis Drake sailed around the world in 1577–80?

4 In the 1969 lunar landing, which of the Apollo 11 astronauts remained in the command module orbiting the Moon while Neil Armstrong and Edwin (Buzz) Aldrin landed the lunar module on the Moon?

5 *Divisament dou Mondi* (nicknamed '*Il Milione*') is an account of the travels of which explorer?

6 In the late tenth century, who founded an Icelandic colony in Greenland and gave the land that name to encourage people to settle there?

7 Which unit of nautical measurement did Richard Norwood devise in 1673?

8 Which Victorian explorer and orientalist, well known for his exploration of Africa, became renowned for his translation of *The Arabian Nights*?

9 What was the mission of NASA's Mars Polar Lander, which was launched in January 1999?

10 The ship of which Arctic explorer was called the *Fram*?

11 In 1796, which Scottish surgeon explored the source of the Nile at the behest of the African Association of London and wrote about his adventures in *Travels in the Interior of Africa*?

12 In October 1869 Henry Morton Stanley received a telegram from James Gordon Bennett, the founder of the newspaper for which he worked, saying 'Find Livingstone'. Which newspaper was it?

13 On 4 January 2000 Fiona Thornewell and Catharine Hartley became the first British women to walk across Antarctica to the South Pole. Which flag did Catharine Hartley plant there?

14 What was the name of the craft made of reeds in which Thor Heyerdahl set off, in 1977, to test the theory that the culture of the ancient Sumerians was spread, using similar sailing crafts, through south-west Asia and the Arabian Peninsula?

15 What name was first given to the Cape of Good Hope by Bartolomeu Dias, who sighted it in 1488?

16 Which French mariner sailed from his home town of St Malo in Brittany to explore the Gulf of St Lawrence in 1534?

17 Which Elizabethan geographer wrote the stories of English navigational feats in *Principal Navigations, Voyages and Discoveries of the English Nation*, first published in 1589?

18 In around 330 BC the Greek explorer and navigator, Pytheas of Marseilles, was commissioned to reconnoitre a new trade route to the tin and amber markets of northern Europe. What name did he give to the land which he found in the far north after sailing past Britain?

19 Which poet, who sailed to the Azores on a voyage led by Walter Raleigh and the Earl of Essex in 1597, wrote *The Storme*?

20 What was the name of the captain who brought Ferdinand Magellan's ship *Victoria* back to Spain to complete the first successful circumnavigation of the world in 1522, after Magellan was killed during the voyage?

E is for Exploration

1 **James Cook** (1728–79).

2 **Lodestone.**

3 The *Pelican*. Drake renamed it in honour of Sir Christopher Hatton (a major shareholder in the expedition, whose crest featured a golden hind) after the execution of Thomas Doughty (Hatton's secretary), the ringleader of a threatened mutiny during the voyage.

4 **Michael Collins.**

5 **Marco Polo** (1254–1324). In 1298, after his travels to China, Marco Polo commanded a Venetian galley at the Battle of Curzola and was taken prisoner by the Genoese, who defeated the Venetian fleet. During his year in captivity he dictated the account of his travels to a fellow-prisoner, a writer of romances named Rusticiano (or Rustichello). The nickname *Il Milione* came about because the account was generally believed to be exaggerated. However, Marco Polo maintained until his dying day that it was all true; the story goes that on his deathbed he was asked to retract the 'fables' and replied, 'I have not told even the half of the things that I have seen.'

6 **Eirík Rauði (the Red).** The Greenland colony was the springboard for the Norse voyagers who discovered and attempted to colonise North America (Vínland) around the year 1000.

7 **Knot** (one nautical mile per hour). The British nautical mile used to be 6,080 feet, but in 1970 the international nautical mile of 1,852 metres was adopted.

8 **Sir Richard Burton** (1821–90).

9 **To search for water on Mars** (its destination was the South Pole of the planet).

10 **Fridtjof Nansen.** Nansen's plan, in 1893, was to allow the ship to become frozen in an ice floe in the Siberian Sea and then drift with a current over the North Pole towards Greenland. He reached a record 86° 4′ N.

11 **Mungo Park** (1771–1806).

12 The *New York Herald*.

13 The *Blue Peter* flag (she is a floor manager for the television programme).

14 *Tigris*. He recorded the voyage in his book *The Tigris Expedition* (1980).

15 **Cape of Storms.**

16 **Jacques Cartier** (1491–1557).

17 **Richard Hakluyt** (1552–1616).

18 **Thule.**

19 **John Donne.** The Islands Voyage of 1597, on which Donne sailed, was designed to intercept the Spanish treasure fleet off the Azores. It failed because of dissension between the two leaders.

20 **Juan Sebastian del Cano.**

General Knowledge Questions

1 After which governor of the Dutch East India Company was Tasmania first named?

2 Which British king was described as 'the wisest fool in Christendom'?

3 What is the literal meaning of the word 'dinosaur'?

4 In which month does the Quarter Day in Scotland known as Martinmas fall?

5 Which museum houses the statue known as the *Venus de Milo*?

6 Where in Edinburgh did Lord Darnley, husband of Mary Queen of Scots, meet his death?

7 If two ships find they are on a head-on collision course, what do the traditional 'rules of the road' at sea require them both to do?

8 At Runnymede there are memorials to commemorate the signing of Magna Carta and the British Commonwealth Airmen of the Second World War. To whom was a third memorial unveiled there in 1965?

9 Which 1974 book opens with the words 'I can see by my watch, without taking my hand from the left grip of the cycle, that it is eight-thirty in the morning'?

10 The symbol of which apostle is a club, the weapon with which he was killed?

11 Alfred Hitchcock's 1963 film *The Birds* was based on a short story of the same title by which author?

12 Which two songwriters wrote the lyrics for the stage musical based on Walt Disney's 1994 film *The Lion King*?

13 What, in addition to potatoes, is the main ingredient of colcannon?

14 What did navigators measure using an astrolabe?

15 What name is given to the wall of a mosque which faces Makkah (Mecca)?

16 What is the common name for *Lunaria annua*, the purple garden flower which produces seeds whose outer coverings are silvery paper-like discs?

17 In the Second World War, what was a 'Moaning Minnie'?

18 Which Hebrew word meaning 'ear of grain', now used in English to mean a phrase or custom which acts as a test of belonging to a social class (or profession), was used in the Old Testament by the Gileadites as a test of pronunciation in order to identify the fleeing Ephraimites?

19 Which sport was featured in the BBC's first television broadcast of a sporting event in 1931?

20 Who was the only survivor of the Burke and Wills expedition which set out from Melbourne in 1860 to cross Australia?

General Knowledge Answers

1 **Anthony van Diemen** (Van Diemen's Land). Its present name comes from the name of the navigator he sent on an exploratory voyage in 1642 – Abel Tasman.

2 **James VI & I** (attributed to Henri IV of France).

3 **Terrible lizard.**

4 **November.** The Feast of St Martin is on 11 November.

5 **The Louvre** (Paris). The statue was carved by a sculptor of Antioch in about 150 BC and was found on the Aegean island of Melos in 1820.

6 **Kirk o' Field.** The bodies of Darnley and his valet, Taylor, were found in the orchard, with no signs of injury caused by the explosion which destroyed the building; they seemed to have been strangled or smothered.

7 **Turn to the right.**

8 **John F. Kennedy** (1917–63).

9 *Zen and the Art of Motorcycle Maintenance*, by Robert M. Pirsig.

10 **St Jude.**

11 **Daphne du Maurier.** *The Birds* was published in 1952 in *The Apple Tree*.

12 **Elton John** and **Tim Rice.** I think of Tim Rice as the 'Masterminder' who got away! In 1973 he applied for *Mastermind* offering 'Pop music' as a specialised subject, but was rejected because pop music was then considered too low-brow. Many years later we asked him to set specialised questions on 'Pop music', which by then had become acceptable. He sent back a very short two-word letter ('No thanks').

13 **Cabbage** (from the Irish *cól ceannon*, meaning 'white-headed cabbage'). Boil 450g potatoes and 450g white cabbage. Mash the potatoes and chop the cabbage finely. Melt 25g butter in a large saucepan and, over a low heat, add the vegetables and mix them well. Season to taste and serve in a piping hot dish. It can also be baked in an ovenproof dish at 200°C/400°F/gas mark 6 until the top is brown.

14 **The altitude of stars** (to determine latitude).

15 **Qibla wall.**

16 **Honesty.**

17 **A German mortar.** 'Moaning' referred to the rising shriek when it was first fired, and 'minnie' was from *Minenwerfer* (literally 'mine-thrower'), meaning 'mortar'.

18 **Shibboleth.**

19 **Horse-racing** (the Derby, which was won that year by Cameronian).

20 **John King.** King, Burke, Wills and Charles Grey reached the tidal marshes of the Flinders River, but on the return journey the others died of starvation.

F is for Football

1 Which football club's recording of *Blue is the Colour* reached Number 5 in the charts in 1972?

2 Which was the first British team to win the European Cup?

3 In 1983–4 who was the first British footballer to win the European Golden Boot?

4 Which was the first country to win the World Cup three times?

5 In 1905 which inside forward and goal-scorer was transferred from Sunderland to Middlesbrough for a record fee of £1,000?

6 Which footballer was the first for whom an English club paid a £1 million transfer fee?

7 Who presided over the report into the crush in which 95 supporters were killed and many others injured at the FA Cup tie between Liverpool and Nottingham Forest at Hillsborough on 15 April 1989?

8 When Alf Ramsey replaced Walter Winterbottom as manager of the England team in 1963, of which League club was he the manager?

9 For which English League football club did 'Dixie' Dean play from 1925–37?

10 What was the name of Huddersfield Town FC former stadium before the McAlpine Stadium opened in 1994?

11 Which footballer famously refused to appear on Eamonn Andrews' *This Is Your Life* programme in February 1961?

12 Which Manchester City goalkeeper, playing in the team which beat Birmingham City 3–1 in the 1956 FA Cup final, completed the game with a broken neck?

13 In 1974 which English president of FIFA did the Brazilian Joao Havelange replace?

14 In 1981 which Football club manager was quoted in *The Sunday Times* saying, 'Football is not a matter of life and death: it's much more important than that'?

15 What is the title of the theme tune of BBC's *Match of the Day*?

16 What was added to football pitches for the 1936–7 season?

17 Who were the 'Famous Five' forwards in the Hibernian team which won the Scottish League in 1948, 1950 and 1951?

18 At which London inn was the Football Association founded on 26 October 1863?

19 Which Arsenal manager persuaded the London Electric Railway to change the name of the Gillespie Road tube station to Arsenal Station?

20 Which Scottish king banned the playing of 'fute ball' (football) in 1424 on pain of a fine of four pennies, in order to encourage archery practice instead?

F is for **Football**

1 **Chelsea.** In 1972 they reached the Final of the League Cup but lost 2–1 to Stoke City.

2 **Celtic.** They beat Inter Milan 1–0 in Lisbon on 25 May 1967 with a goal scored by Archie Gemmell.

3 **Ian Rush.**

4 **Brazil.** This question was asked during the tie-break for first place in a semi-final of the 1994 *Mastermind* series, in which Geoff Thomas and John Wilson had both scored 34. Geoff, a seasoned quizzer, is still kicking himself for giving the answer 'Italy'; he lost the tie-break 3–4.

5 **Alf Common.** The transfer provoked a ruling by the FA which limited transfer fees to £350.

6 **Trevor Francis.** He was transferred from Birmingham City to Nottingham Forest for £1 million in 1979.

7 **Lord Justice Taylor.**

8 **Ipswich Town.**

9 **Everton.** William Ralph Dean (1906–81) began his football career with Tranmere Rovers and transferred to Everton (for £3,000) in 1925. In 1938 he joined Notts County and then, in 1939, Sligo Rovers. In the 1927–8 season he scored a record 60 goals.

10 **Leeds Road.**

11 **Danny Blanchflower** (Robert Dennis Blanchflower, 1926–93).

12 **Bert Trautman.** The extent of his injury was not discovered until three days after the match. He made a good recovery and was back in the team within the year.

13 **Stanley Rous.**

14 **Bill Shankly** (1913–81, manager of Liverpool, 1959–74).

15 *Offside* by Barry Stoller.

16 **An arc was added to the penalty area** to ensure that players could not stand closer than 10 yards to a penalty kick.

17 **Bobby Johnstone, Willy Ormond, Lawrie Reilly, Gordon Smith and Eddie Turnbull.**

18 **The Freemason's Tavern.** Soon afterwards, premises were found in Holborn Viaduct. After several moves its present headquarters were established at 16 Lancaster Gate in London.

19 **Herbert Chapman** (manager of Arsenal, 1925–34).

20 **James I** (1394–1437).

General Knowledge

1 Who was the French lawyer who provided the World Cup trophy in 1930 and after whom it was named in 1946?

2 What was Britain's first winning entry in the Eurovision Song Contest?

3 Which film, released in August 1999, starred Pierce Brosnan and Rene Russo in the roles played by Steve McQueen and Faye Dunaway in the 1968 version?

4 What is the more common name for the brightly coloured climbing plant *Tropaeolum majus*?

5 Which English town is served by Squires Gate Airport?

6 What colourful name was given to the toxin, containing dioxin, which US forces used to defoliate trees during the Vietnamese War (1954–75)?

7 What are abadi, courier and garamond?

8 Which 1954 'play for voices' begins:
> *To begin at the beginning: it is spring, moonless night in the small town, starless and Bible-black. The cobbled streets silent and the hunched courters in Rabbits Wood limping invisible down to the sloe-black, slow, black, crow-black fishing-boat-bobbing sea.*

9 Until 1966, which African capital city had the name of Léopoldville, in honour of Léopold II of Belgium?

10 What kind of garment is a pelerine?

11 Who were the 'Gang of Four' who formed the Social Democratic Party in March 1981?

12 What is measured in oktas (octas)?

13 In Tudor England, which nobleman was rumoured to have arranged the murder of his wife, Amy Robsart, who was found dead at the foot of a staircase at their home?

14 Who was the legendary Greek herald who could shout as loudly as fifty ordinary men and whose name gave rise to a word meaning 'loud-voiced'?

15 Which Dutch physicist invented the first pendulum clock, in 1657?

16 Which creature is sometimes known as a 'pillbug'?

17 What is the more common name for the disease parotitis, which mainly affects children?

18 In English heraldry, which family member is denoted by a rose?

19 For what were the six Burghers of Calais in Auguste Rodin's sculpture commemorated?

20 Which First Division football club tackled hooliganism in the 1986–7 season by banning away supporters from its ground?

General Knowledge

1 **Jules Rimet** (1871–1956). He was president of FIFA (Fédération International de Football Association) from 1921 to 1956.

2 *Puppet on a String*, sung by Sandie Shaw in 1967. The song was written by Bill Martin and Phil Coulter.

3 *The Thomas Crown Affair*. Thomas Crown, a self-made billionaire, can buy anything he wants but is bored. As a challenge, he plans and carries out the theft of a priceless painting from a gallery. Thomas Crown is the last person the New York police suspect, but one person does suspect him – Catherine Banning, the investigator hired to retrieve the painting. She enjoys the chase as much as Thomas Crown does: he meets his match, and finds the challenge he is seeking.

4 **Nasturtium.**

5 **Blackpool.**

6 **Agent Orange.** Afterwards it was found that dioxin harms humans as well as plants.

7 **Word-processing fonts.**

8 *Under Milk Wood* by Dylan Thomas (1914–53). He began writing the play, about a Welsh seaside village, in 1944, under the title *Quite Early One Morning*. It was published the year after his death.

9 **Kinshasa** (capital of the Democratic Republic of Congo, named Zaïre from 1971 to 1997, and before that, Belgian Congo).

10 **A cape,** usually made from a long, narrow piece of material, covered the shoulders. The word comes from the French *pèlerin* (pilgrim).

11 **Roy Jenkins, David Owen, William Rogers** and **Shirley Williams.**

12 **Cloud-cover.** An okta (octa) represents an eighth of the sky visible in any place.

13 **Robert Dudley, Earl of Leicester** (1533–88). Robert Dudley became Master of the Queen's Horse on the accession of Elizabeth of England and she made him a Knight of the Garter in 1559. He had been married to Amy Robsart since 1550 and when she died, in 1560, rumours began to circulate that he had arranged her murder so that he could marry Queen Elizabeth, despite the fact that he had gone to great lengths to ensure that the inquest was held before an impartial jury.

14 **Stentor** ('stentorian'). Stentor (in the *Iliad*) was a warrior in the Trojan War.

15 **Christian Huygens** (1629–93). The pendulum clock was based on Galileo's work on pendulums. Huygens went on to develop Galileo's work on accelerated motion under gravity.

16 **Woodlouse.** Woodlice were once used for medicinal purposes; they were swallowed like pills.

17 **Mumps.**

18 **The seventh son.**

19 **They offered their lives to save the rest of the town during Edward III of England's siege of Calais** (they were spared). The monument was completed in 1895 and stands outside the Hôtel de Ville.

20 **Luton Town.** The ban achieved its aim (the number of arrests dropped from 102 to nil) but it proved problematic, especially for League Cup fixtures for which League regulations stipulated that 25 per cent of tickets had to be made available for away supporters. Luton dropped the ban at the end of the season.

G is for Geography

1 Which is the highest mountain in North America?

2 On which river in Scotland is the city of Dundee situated?

3 Fuerteventura, Gomera and La Palma are in which island group?

4 Which island off the coast of Normandy, now a historic monument, was called Mont Tombe until the eighth century when St Aubert (Bishop of Avranches) built an oratory there, then became a prison after the Revolution and is now a major tourist attraction?

5 On which major waterway are Gatún Lake, the Gaillard (Culebra) Cut and the Miraflores Locks?

6 What is the name of the major seaport which serves Mexico City?

7 Which African country was called Nyasaland until 1964?

8 Which independent state has a birthrate of nil?

9 In which city is Yad Vashem?

10 What was the former name of the Venezuelan town of Ciudad Bolívar, which gave rise to the name of a bitter aromatic tonic which is manufactured there?

11 Which geographical feature is composed of clints and grykes?

12 In which range of mountains in Ireland does the River Liffey rise?

13 Which town in northern France, the birthplace of Robespierre, had a medieval tapestry industry which made its name a synonym for wall-hangings?

14 What is the name of the largest glacier in Europe?

15 What is the name of the waterway, formed by the union of the Tigris and Euphrates rivers, which flows into the Persian Gulf?

16 In which European city is the Tiergarten?

17 In the 1977 film *Close Encounters of the Third Kind*, which dramatically eroded peak in Wyoming in the United States was the location for the landing of an alien spaceship?

18 What is the capital of Mongolia?

19 The Spanish name 'Las Malvinas' for the Falkland Islands came from the French 'Îles Malouine'. How did they get that name?

20 What is the name of the Inuit territory, created on 1 April 1999 from part of Canada, whose name means 'our land'?

G is for Geography   Answers

1 **Mount McKinley** (6,194 metres) in the Denali National Park and Preserve in Alaska. This was a regular rehearsal question on *Mastermind*, and is engraved on my memory as a result!

2 **Tay.**

3 **The Canary Islands.** The main islands are Tenerife, Gran Canaria, Lanzarote and Hierro.

4 **Mont St Michel.**

5 **The Panama Canal.**

6 **Veracruz.**

7 **Malawi.** When Nyasaland gained its independence that year, Lake Nyasa was also renamed Lake Malawi. The lake's original name arose when David Livingstone reached it in 1859 and asked the local people what its name was. There was a mutual misunderstanding: *nyasa* means 'a mass of water', and so the name he gave it meant 'Lake Lake'.

8 **The Vatican City.** However, the population has increased through immigration: in 1985 it was 1,000 and by 1993 it was 1,800.

9 **Jerusalem.** It is a memorial to the Jews who were killed by the Nazis and the name of the Holocaust Martyrs' and Heroes' Remembrance Authority.

10 **Angostura.** The town's full name was San Tomás de la Nueva Guayana de la Angostura. It was changed in 1846 to honour Simon Bolívar.

11 **A limestone pavement.** Clints are large flat blocks of limestone, and grykes are the spaces between them which have become enlarged through erosion.

12 **Wicklow Mountains.**

13 **Arras.**

14 **Vatnajökull** (Lakes Glacier), in Iceland.

15 **Shatt Al-`Arab.**

16 **Berlin.** The park was a deer preserve until the eighteenth century. It was destroyed in the Second World War, but it has now been restored; the restoration includes an 'English garden' donated by Britain, and new zoological gardens.

17 **Devil's Tower** (265 metres or 869 feet).

18 **Ulan Bator.** This question caused us a spot of embarrassment on *Mastermind* in 1973. The contestant replied, quick as a flash, 'Which one, Outer or Inner?' I was flummoxed. I knew the answer was meant to be Ulan Bator, so I asked him what he would say if I asked him the capital of *Outer* Mongolia. 'I'd say, "Pass",' he replied – 'I don't know either.' We should have asked 'What is the capital of the Mongolian People's Republic?'

19 From **St Malo** in Brittany the home of many of the early eighteenth-century French sailors who went to the islands. John Strong, who made the first recorded European landing there in 1690, had given them the English name 'Falkland Islands' in honour of Viscount Falkland, treasurer of the British Navy.

20 **Nunavut.**

General Knowledge

1 In which English county is Legoland?

2 What was M.A.S.H., the title of the 1970 film?

3 Who is the victim in the game of Cluedo?

4 In which of Puccini's operas is a seamstress nicknamed Mimi the heroine?

5 What is the first line of the Christian hymn which contains the following lines:

> *Thou didst tread this earth before us,*
> *Thou didst feel its keenest woe;*

6 A magnum has the capacity of how many standard bottles of wine?

7 What is the common name of *Nigella damascena* which arises from the effect of the many thread-like leaves growing along the whole of its stem?

8 Which maritime hazard is nicknamed a 'growler'?

9 Which cosmetics company was founded in 1886 by David McConnell, a travelling bookseller, who gave a small bottle of perfume free with each book?

10 Which crab, having no hard shell of its own, protects its soft body by taking over the shells of dead molluscs?

11 Which chemical element derives its name from the Greek word for 'colour'?

12 In the constellation Gemini, who are the twins?

13 How many bits, handled as one unit, constitute a byte?

14 Which conductor was associated with the Hallé Orchestra from 1943 to 1968?

15 From which Greek word does the term 'psephology' (the study of elections) derive?

16 In which sport have Sarah Fitz-Gerald and Rodney Eyles of Australia been world champions?

17 For what does the airline acronym QANTAS stand?

18 From which Shakespeare play did William Faulkner take the title of his 1929 novel *The Sound and the Fury*?

19 'Marmorial' is the adjective pertaining to which substance?

20 What was the ancient name of the Dardanelles, the strait between the Sea of Marmara and the Aegean Sea?

General Knowledge Answers

1 **Berkshire** (just outside Windsor).

2 **Mobile Army Surgical Hospital.**

3 **Dr Black.**

4 *La Bohème*.

5 **Lead us, heavenly Father, lead us,** written by George Herbert (1593–1632).

6 **Two.** It contains 'two reputed quarts'.

7 **Love-in-a-mist** (also called 'devil-in-a-mist' and 'love-in-a-puzzle').

8 **A small iceberg.**

9 **Avon.** The company was first called the California Perfume Company. David McConnell renamed it in 1939 after a visit to Stratford-on-Avon.

10 **Hermit crab.**

11 **Chromium** (from Greek *khroma*).

12 **Castor and Pollux,** sons of Zeus and Leda.

13 *Eight* (four binary units of two numbers).

14 **Sir John Barbarolli** (Giovanni Battista, 1889–1970).

15 *Psephos*, a pebble (a pebble was used for casting votes in ancient Greece).

16 **Squash.**

17 **Queensland And Northern Territory Aerial Services.** It is the oldest airline in the English-speaking world, having been founded in 1920.

18 *Macbeth* Act V, Scene v:

> *Life's but a walking shadow, a poor player,*
> *That struts and frets his hour upon the stage,*
> *And then is heard no more; it is a tale*
> *Told by an idiot, full of sound and fury,*
> *Signifying nothing.*

19 **Marble.**

20 **Hellespont.** It means 'Sea of Helle', and was named after Helle (the sister of Phryxus) who drowned there while escaping from her mother-in-law, Ino (Leucothia), on a flying golden ram. The legend is the basis of the story of Hero and Leander.

H is for Human Body Questions

1 What would you be doing, unconsciously, if your soft palate and pharynx were vibrating because of obstruction of the nasal passages?

2 For what were *foreman* (or *towcher*), *longman*, *lecman* and *little man* old names?

3 When bursitis affects the knee, its common name links it to which occupation?

4 Which ancient measurement was taken from the elbow to the tip of the longest finger?

5 What is the common name for the talus bone?

6 For what do the letters HIV stand?

7 Which unit, often used by dieters to calculate their energy intake from food, represents the amount of heat required to raise the temperature of one gram of water by one degree Celsius at normal atmospheric pressure?

8 To which part of the body does the adjective 'buccal' refer?

9 The ancient philosophers believed that good health depended on a balance of the four humours which governed the body: what were they?

10 The psychologist W. H. Sheldon classified three human physical types (somatotypes): round, plump type (endomorphic), muscular type (mesomorphic) and slim, linear type, which he called what?

11 Which sight defect is the opposite of hypermetropia (hyperopia)?

12 The philtrum is a groove on the exterior of the body – where?

13 Which part of the body is affected by cholecystitis?

14 Which disease, spread by a body louse (especially in overcrowded conditions), has been called jail fever, war fever, and camp fever?

15 What name is given to the body's 24-hour cycle of sleeping and waking?

16 Which acid is produced in the muscles during exercise?

17 According to Louis MacNeice, in his poem *Sunday Morning*, which part of man expands to 'tinker with his car'?

18 What kind of representation of the human body is given the name *écorché*?

19 The following mnemonic could help medical students to remember the names and correct order of what: On Old Olympia's Towering Top, A Finn And German Vault And Hop?

20 Who published *De humani corporis fabrica libri septi* (*Seven Books on the Structure of the Human Body*) in 1543, and was given a death sentence (commuted to a pilgrimage to Jerusalem) by the Inquisition for dissecting corpses?

H is for **Human Body**   Answers

1 **Snoring.**

2 **The fingers** (the thumb was known as 'thuma').

3 **Housemaid** (Housemaid's Knee). The bursa is a fluid-filled sac present in parts of the body where there is friction, such as joints like the knee and the elbow ('tennis elbow').

4 **Cubit.** The English cubit was about 46 centimetres, but the Egyptians set theirs at 53 centimetres and the Hebrews at 56 centimetres. The Roman cubit, however, was only 44 centimetres.

5 **Ankle bone.**

6 **Human Immunodeficiency Virus.**

7 **Calorie** (the common name for *kilocalorie*). Nutritionists are now coming into line with other scientists, who use the *joule* to measure energy: one joule is the energy expended in moving one kilogram a distance of one metre by a force of one newton. One kilocalorie = 4.186 kilojoules.

8 **Cheek (also the mouth)**, from the Latin *bucca* (jowl or cheek).

9 **Bile, blood, melancholy and phlegm.** An earlier philosophy related to the influences of the four *elements*: air, earth, fire and water.

10 **Ectomorphic.**

11 **Myopia** (short-sightedness). Hypermetropia (hyperopia) is long-sightedness.

12 **Between the nose and upper lip.**

13 **Gall bladder.**

14 **Typhus.**

15 **Circadian rhythm.**

16 **Lactic acid.**

17 **The heart:**
> *Man's heart expands to tinker with his car,*
> *For this is Sunday morning, Fate's great bazaar.*

from *Sunday Morning* (1935)

18 **One which shows the skin removed so that the muscles can be seen.** *Écorché* means 'scorched'.

19 **The cranial nerves:** Olfactory, Optic, Oculomotor, Trochlear, Trigeminal, Abducens, Facial, Auditory (or acoustic), Glossopharyngeal, Vagus, Accessory (or accessories) and Hypoglossal.

20 **Andreas Vesalius** (1514–64), the Latin name of Andries van Wesel.

General Knowledge   Questions

1 What are characterised by patterns such as loops, whorls and arches?

2 What was the surname of the Dutch painter Rembrandt?

3 Who starred opposite Richard Gere in the 1990 'modern Cinderella' film, *Pretty Woman*?

4 Which eighteenth-century Yorkshire entrepreneur founded the Marylebone Cricket Club?

5 In Shakespeare's *The Merchant of Venice*, how much money did the merchant Antonio borrow from Shylock on behalf of his young friend Bassanio?

6 Which banned alcoholic drink, distilled from wormwood, was known as the 'Green Faerie'?

7 In Tennyson's poem, when 'the mirror crack'd from side to side' who cried 'The curse is come upon me'?

8 What is the third letter of the Hebrew alphabet?

9 What was Andrew Motion's first published poem as Poet Laureate?

10 What was the literary pseudonym of the French writer Amandine Aurore Lucie Dupin, Baronne Dudevant?

11 In 1948 who became the first Prime Minister of Israel?

12 What name was given to the eleven French knights who, in 1119, took monastic vows and bound themselves to protect pilgrims on their way to holy places?

13 With reference to what subject is the phrase 'according to Cocker' used?

14 In 1959 which group created the jazz classic *Take Five*?

15 The French word for 'paper clip' is the same as the English (and French) word for which musical instrument?

16 Which British king's birthday used to be commemorated by Oak Apple Day (29 May)?

17 Who, in the Old Testament, was the husband of Jezebel and harassed the prophets, and whose blood was licked up by dogs when he was killed in battle in Samaria?

18 Which volcano erupted in Washington State in 1980 causing widespread damage?

19 The name of which London borough was a place on the Thames where chalk was landed and whose name is derived from 'chalk landing-place'?

20 The parasitic organism *plasmodium*, carried by an insect, transmits which disease?

General Knowledge

1 Fingerprints.
2 Van Rijn.
3 Julia Roberts.
4 **Thomas Lord** (1755–1832). In 1787 he opened a cricket ground in Dorset Square, London, which became known as the Marylebone County Cricket Club (MCC) and which moved to its present site in St John's Wood in 1814.
5 3,000 ducats.
6 **Absinthe** (from the plant *Artemisia absinthium*).
7 **The Lady of Shalott**, published in *Poems* (1842).
8 **Gimmel** (ג).
9 **An Epithalamium** (for the marriage of Prince Edward and Sophie Rhys-Jones).
10 **George Sand** (1804–76).
11 **David Ben Gurion**, originally David Gruen (1886–1973), who was born in Poland and emigrated to Palestine in 1906.
12 **Templars.** The name came from their headquarters at the site of the old Temple of Solomon in Jerusalem. The first house of the Templars in England was near Holborn Bars in London.
13 **Mathematics.** Edward Cocker (1631–75) wrote *Arithmetick*. The phrase was popularised by Arthur Murphy in his farce *The Apprentice* (1756). It has come to mean 'reliably' or 'correctly'.
14 **The Dave Brubeck Quartet.**
15 **Trombone.**
16 **Charles II** (1630–85). It was also the date on which Charles entered London at the Restoration in 1660. The 'oak apple' commemorates the Boscobel Oak near Shifnal, Shropshire, in which he hid after the Battle of Worcester in 1651. Oak Apple Day was a public holiday until 1859, and is still celebrated by the Chelsea Pensioners as their 'Founder's Day'.
17 **Ahab** (1 Kings 22:38).
18 **Mount St Helens.** Mount St Helens had been dormant since 1857. On 18 May 1980 there was an earthquake with a magnitude of 5.1 on the Richter scale, which caused a huge landslide on the northern slope of the mountain. An explosion of ash, gas and rocks came from the 2,950-metre-high volcanic cone, which was completely blasted away, leaving a horseshoe-shaped crater with a rim whose highest elevations reached about 2,400 metres.
19 **Chelsea**, from the Old English *cealc* (chalk) and *hyth* (landing-place). The latter part of the word has been distorted to 'sea'.
20 **Malaria.** *Plasmodium* is carried by anopheline mosquitoes.

I is for Inventions

1 Which Derbyshire-born aeronautical engineer designed the R100 airship, the bouncing bomb and the first swing-wing aircraft?

2 Hans Lippershey (1608), Galileo (1610), Isaac Newton (1668) and William Herschel (c 1780) designed different types of what?

3 In 1712 who was the first engineer to introduce steam to an engine with a piston?

4 Who invented the aqualung in 1943 while fighting with the French Resistance during the Second World War?

5 Between 1642 and 1644 which French mathematician designed the first digital calculator to help his father (a local administrator) in his tax computations?

6 The French artist Louis Daguerre is often credited with the invention of photography, but who was his partner, whose invention he refined?

7 Which invention of Whitcomb Judson of Chicago, in 1891, was originally called the 'clasp locker and unlocker for shoes'?

8 What is added to rubber when it is vulcanised?

9 What did the chemist John Walker of Stockton-on-Tees invent in 1827, which he called 'Congreves'?

10 Which English entrepreneur produced the first synthetic dye?

11 What did William Hunt invent in 1849 to hold things together?

12 What is the trade-name of the strong, woven synthetic material used for hulls and sails, radial tyres and bullet-proof vests?

13 What did the German chemist Christian Schöenbein find that he had invented in 1845, when he used his wife's apron to mop up spilled chemicals and hung it above the stove to dry, whereupon it burst into flames and burned so quickly that it seemed to disappear?

14 In 1881 what did Alexander Graham Bell devise to help the doctors caring for President James Garfield after he was shot?

15 Which Swiss scientist and engineer invented the cling-fastening principle of Velcro in 1951 after studying the burrs which his spaniel, Inky, had collected on its ears during a country walk?

16 Which American blacksmith invented the steel plough in 1837?

17 In 1870 John Wesley Hyatt invented the first synthetic plastic (later called celluloid) in response to a $10,000 reward offered by a New York firm for a satisfactory substitute for ivory in the manufacture of what?

18 Between 1620 and 1624 Cornelis Drebbel (or Cornelius van Drebel), a Dutch inventor, built and tested (on the River Thames) the first what?

19 What was stored in the Leyden (Leiden) Jar?

20 Percival Everitt of the United States is credited with inventing this (now ubiquitous) sales device in 1883, but Heron of Alexandria had invented one in the first century BC and described it in his book *Pneumatica*. What is it?

I is for Inventions

1 **Sir Barnes Neville Wallis** (1887–1979).

2 **Telescope.**

3 **Thomas Newcomen** (1663–1729).

4 **Jacques Cousteau** (1910–97).

5 **Blaise Pascal** (1623–62).

6 **Joseph Niepce.** Niepce produced a photograph in 1822, but the long exposure time (about eight hours) made it impractical. He became bankrupt and went into partnership with Daguerre in 1829.

7 **Zip-fastener.** Judson died in 1909, before the onomatopoeic term 'zipper' was coined by B. F. Goodrich, whose company started marketing galoshes with zippers in 1923. Judson's invention had not been a commercial success during his lifetime.

8 **Sulphur.** In 1844 Charles Goodyear had been adding sulphur to rubber in his attempts to stabilise its texture; it became stiff and hard in cold conditions and soft and sticky in warm ones. When he accidentally spilled some of the mixture on to his stove, he discovered that after the mixture had been heated it became become dry and flexible when both hot and cold.

9 **Friction matches.** He named the matches after William Congreve's rocket (1808), which was first used in the Napoleonic Wars, and marketed them as 'Walker's Friction Lighters'.

10 **William Perkin** (1838–1907). In 1856 the eighteen-year-old schoolboy was trying to produce synthetic quinine; he failed, but he noticed a purple tint (later named 'mauvine') in the mess he had made. He promptly left school and opened a dye factory, which made him a millionaire.

11 **The safety pin.** In the seventh century BC the Etruscans had also used a form of safety pin made of gold.

12 **Kevlar** (polyparaphenylene terephthalamide). It was invented in 1971 by Stephanie Kwolek, Herbert Blades, and Paul W. Morgan of DuPont.

13 **Nitrocellulose** (guncotton).

14 **A metal-detector.** The doctors could not find the bullet lodged in the president's body, but they ignored Bell's instructions to remove all metals from the vicinity of the patient, leaving him on a mattress containing metal springs. Bell was denounced as a charlatan when his device failed to help.

15 **Georges de Mestral** (he opened his first Velcro factory in 1957 at Aubonne).

16 **John Deere** (1804–86). He was often asked to repair broken cast-iron ploughs which could not cope with the dense soil of the prairies.

17 **Billiard balls.**

18 **Submarine.** It had an outer hull made of greased leather over a wooden frame. It was propelled by oars through the sides and sealed with close-fitting leather flaps. Drebbel successfully manoeuvred the submarine at depths of four to five metres below the surface.

19 **Electrical charge or static electricity.** It was the predecessor of the capacitor. It was invented by the Dutch physicist and mathematician Pieter van Musschenbroek at the University of Leiden in 1746 and, independently, by the German inventor Ewald Georg von Kleist in 1745.

20 **Coin-operated vending machine.** In Heron's machine, a cup of fluid would be dispensed when a five-drachma coin was inserted in a slot at the top. There was no coin-return system and it did not give change.

General Knowledge

1 Which American company, originally a manufacturer of explosives, first produced nylon in 1938?

2 After which type of establishment was Lloyd's of London named?

3 By what name is the sixteenth-century Italian painter Jacopo Robusti better known?

4 As what is pyrites (sulphide of iron) commonly known?

5 The 1971 film *The Music Lovers* was about which composer?

6 In south-west France, which two rivers unite to form the Gironde estuary?

7 Anzac Day is a public holiday in Australia and New Zealand: what event does it commemorate?

8 What is the name of the female figure who personifies France, the equivalent of Britain's Britannia?

9 As what is Karim Al-Hussain better known?

10 After which Prince Edward was Prince Edward Island in Canada named?

11 Which English composer wrote the orchestral tone-poem *Egdon Heath* in 1927?

12 From which source did Aldous Huxley take the title of his 1936 novel *Eyeless in Gaza*?

13 By what name are the followers of Zoroaster (commonly named 'Zoroastrians') properly known?

14 Who was the sculptor of the statue of Peter Pan in Kensington Gardens, London?

15 In which British city are the parliamentary constituencies of Wavertree, Garston and Riverside?

16 To which animals does the adjective 'viverrine' apply?

17 Which London theatre did Bernard Miles found in 1951 and name after a historic tavern which was destroyed in the Great Fire of London in 1666?

18 Which Russian chemist first successfully tabulated the elements in ascending order of their atomic weight in his 'Periodic Table'?

19 Which unit is the measure of the fineness of yarns?

20 For which method of photographically reproducing three-dimensional images did the Hungarian-born British physicist Dennis Gabor win the Nobel Prize for physics in 1971?

General Knowledge

1 **DuPont** (founded by French immigrant Éleuthère Irénée du Pont in Delaware in 1802).
2 **Coffee house.** Edward Lloyd (d *c* 1730), who owned the coffee house in Lombard Street, London, from 1688 to 1726, started *Lloyd's News* (later *Lloyd's List*) for the merchants and ship-owners for whom his coffee house became a popular haunt.
3 **Tintoretto** (1518–94), the son of a silk-dyer (*tintore*).
4 **Fool's gold.**
5 **Pyotr Ilyich Tchaikovsky** (1840–93).
6 **Dordogne** and **Garonne.**
7 **The landing at Gallipolli on 25 April 1915** of the Australia and New Zealand Army Corps.
8 **Marianne.** The bare-breasted, bonneted Marianne was the standard-bearer of the revolutionary forces of 1789 and has been a symbol of the republic ever since. In 1999 France chose a new model for Marianne: the 21-year-old actress Laetitia Casta.
9 **Aga Khan.** Born in 1937, he is the fourth Aga Khan. This hereditary title, meaning 'master ruler', is given to the imam (spiritual leader) of the Nizari Ismaili sect of Shi'ite Muslims. The first (Aga Khan I) was Hasan Ali Shah (1800–81).
10 **Edward, Duke of Kent** (1767–1820), the father of Queen Victoria.
11 **Gustav Holst** (1874–1934).
12 *Samson Agonistes* by Milton: 'Eyeless in Gaza, at the mill with slaves.'
13 **Parsees.**
14 **George Frampton** (1860–1928).
15 **Liverpool.**
16 **Ferrets and mongooses** (family *Viverridae*).
17 **The *Mermaid.*** The Mermaid Tavern in Bread Street had been the meeting-place of the Mermaid Club, founded by Sir Walter Raleigh, whose members included Francis Beaumont, John Fletcher and Ben Jonson.
18 **Dmitri Mendeleyev** (1834–1907).
19 **Denier**, from a small coin worth one twelfth of a sou (Latin: *denarius*).
20 **Holography.**

J is for Jewellery

1 The birthstone for which month is opal?

2 Which Russian jeweller exhibited his Imperial Easter eggs at the Paris Exhibition of 1900?

3 On a hallmark, which precious metal is indicated in England by a lion passant and in Scotland by a lion rampant?

4 Which king introduced the statute which instituted hallmarking in England?

5 What name is given to a gem made from two stones arranged in differently coloured layers, with figures carved in the top layer, which is set in relief against the other?

6 Which precious stone, formed from corundum (an oxide of aluminium), is second only to diamond in hardness?

7 What was the name of the largest diamond ever found, which was presented to Edward VII in 1907 by the South African government and cut into smaller stones which are now set in the English Crown Jewels?

8 Which Imperial unit, for use in transactions in precious metals, was one of the seven units authorised for retention in specialist use when other Imperial units were phased out in Britain in December 1999?

9 What is the 'Welcome Stranger', found in 1869?

10 After how many years of marriage is an emerald wedding anniversary celebrated?

11 Which jeweller established the term 'sterling' as the standard for silver in the United States in 1851?

12 On which scale is the hardness of minerals measured?

13 What name is given to the way in which stones such as diamonds are cut so as to have facets which reflect light in different directions?

14 What did a pouncet usually contain?

15 Which precious stone did Ben Jonson describe in the following lines from *The Alchemist* in 1610:

> He that has once the flower of the sun,
> The perfect — which we call elixir . . .
> Can confer honour, love, respect, long life,
> Give safety, valour, yea, and victory,
> To whom he will.

16 Of which precious stone is aquamarine a variety?

17 'Carat' is the internationally standardised unit of weight for precious stones: what is its equivalent in grams?

18 What name is given to the setting of gems into stone, for example on the marble walls of the Taj Mahal?

19 Which violet-blue variety of quartz was used by the ancient Greeks for making cups and goblets because it was regarded as a charm against inebriety?

20 A piece of which opaque variety of quartz, found in most parts of Scotland (especially in the Campsie Fells), was set into the gold and silver baton presented to the Queen to commemorate the 1986 Commonwealth Games in Edinburgh?

J is for Jewellery

1 October.
2 Carl Fabergé (1846–1920).
3 Sterling silver.
4 Edward I (1272–1307).
5 Cameo.
6 Sapphire.
7 **Cullinan Diamond** (named after Sir Thomas Major Cullinan, chairman of the Premier Diamond Mine, Johannesburg, where it was found in 1905). The two largest stones cut from it are the Star of Africa (in the sceptre) and Cullinan II (in the Imperial State Crown).
8 **Troy ounce** ($\frac{12}{175}$ pound). The other six were: inch, foot, yard and mile (for use on road traffic signs, distance and speed measurement), pint (for use as a measure of milk in returnable containers and for dispensing draught cider or beer) and acre (for land registration).
9 **The largest gold nugget ever found.** It weighed 71,440 grams, and was found in Victoria, Australia, by John Deason and Richard Oates.
10 Fifty-five.
11 **Tiffany** (founded in 1837 in New York by Charles Lewis Tiffany and John B. Young), when it adopted the standards of English silver.
12 **The Mohs scale** (devised by Friedrich Mohs in 1812).
13 **Brilliant** (adjective). In a perfect brilliant (noun) there are 58 facets.
14 **A sponge soaked in pungent vinegar** (to ward off diseases and offensive odours). It was a silver box whose sides were 'pounced' (pierced with holes). Pouncets were popular among English gentlemen of the mid-sixteenth to early seventeenth century.
15 **Ruby.** The Perfect Ruby was another name given by alchemists to the Elixir of Life.
16 Beryl.
17 **0.2 grams.** The word 'carat' comes from the Greek *keration* (little horn).
18 *Pietra dura.* Cavities are cut into the stone and the gems (cut to fit exactly) are set into them. The name, but not necessarily the technique, originated in Florence, where the technique was popular in the sixteenth century.
19 **Amethyst.** Its name comes from the Greek *a* (not) and *methuein* (to intoxicate).
20 Jasper.

General Knowledge

1 For which 1949 musical (and 1953 film) was the song *Diamonds are a Girl's Best Friend* written?
2 Which painting by Sir Edwin Landseer is owned by John Dewar & Sons and featured on the labels of their whisky bottles?
3 In which of Charles Dickens' novels does the midwife Sarah Gamp appear?
4 About which dance did the nineteenth-century writer and entertainer George Grossmith sing the following lines?
   You should see me dance the —
   You should see me cover the ground,
   You should see my coat-tails flying
   As I jump my partner round . . .
5 At which battle in Ireland in 1690 did the army of William of Orange decisively defeat that of James VII & II?
6 What is buckram?
7 In the 1957–61 ITV series *The Army Game*, who was excused from wearing boots?
8 What is the name of the arm of the North Sea which separates Norway and Denmark?
9 Which Roman road runs between Lincoln and Axmouth, on the coast of Devon?
10 What is the word for an underground creeping stem which sends out shoots?
11 In 1909 what did David Lloyd George call 'Balfour's poodle'?
12 Who was the original lead singer with the 1960s pop group, the Tremeloes?
13 How many Noble Truths are there in Buddhism?
14 What is the distinguishing feature of an animal classed as an ungulate?
15 Thomas Arne wrote the music in 1740, but who wrote the words of *Rule Britannia*?
16 The name of which element derives from the Greek word for 'violet-coloured'?
17 The title of which of Alan Bennett's plays is also the title of one of the Harrow School songs?
18 On the signs of public houses called 'The Five Alls', a king is depicted ('I rule all'), together with members of which four occupations?
19 Which employee of the Arthur Wilkinson pottery became well known in the 1930s for her 'Bizarre' ware?
20 What is the name of the large diamond acquired by the British on the annexation of the Punjab in 1849 and placed among the crown jewels of Queen Victoria?

General Knowledge   Answers

1 *Gentlemen Prefer Blondes*, written by Jule Styne and Leo Robin.

2 *The Monarch of the Glen* (1851). The painting had had several owners before it was bought for 5,000 guineas in 1916 by Thomas Dewar from Mr Barratt of Pears' Soap.

3 **Martin Chuzzlewit**. Sarah Gamp always carried a faded, cotton umbrella – hence the nickname 'gamp' for umbrella.

4 **Polka**.

5 **Battle of the Boyne**. After his flight from England at the end of 1689, King James tried to recover his kingdoms by an invasion of Ireland, from which he hoped to invade England and Scotland. After initial successes, he was routed by William of Orange (William III) at the River Boyne on 11 July 1690.

6 **A strong, coarse linen cloth**, stiffened with gum or paste, which originated in Bukhara in Uzbekistan.

7 **Private 'Bootsie' Bisley** (played by Alfie Bass), who was allowed to wear plimsolls instead of regulation army boots because of problems with his feet.

8 **Skaggerak**.

9 **Fosse Way**, named after the ditch (Latin *fossa*) on each side of it.

10 **Rhizome**.

11 **The House of Lords**: 'The House of Lords is not the watchdog of the constitution. It is Mr Balfour's poodle.' It is quoted in Roy Jenkins' book, *Mr Balfour's Poodle* (1954).

12 **Brian Poole**.

13 **Four**: 1) Human life is full of suffering; 2) People themselves create this suffering; 3) People can make this suffering cease; 4) The Noble Eightfold Path is a guide for life.

14 **It has hooves**.

15 **James Thomson** (1700–48). It was part of Arne's masque *Alfred*, which was written at the command of Frederick, Prince of Wales, and first performed before him at Cliveden House, near Maidenhead, Berkshire.

16 **Iodine** (from *iodes*).

17 *Forty Years On* (Bennett's first play, performed in 1968). The song was written in 1872 by the music master John Farmer and the English master Edward Bowen.

18 **Priest** ('I pray for all'), **soldier** ('I fight for all'), **farmer** ('I pay for all') and **lawyer** ('I plead for all'). The Four Alls are the first four.

19 **Clarice Cliff** (1899–1972).

20 **Koh-i-Noor**. The diamond was set in the centre of the Queen's State Crown fashioned for use by Queen Elizabeth the Queen Mother at her coronation in 1937. It has been worn by queens, but not kings, because it is reputed to bring good luck to women who wear it but bad luck to men.

K is for Kings

1 Who was King of Spain at the time of the attempted invasion of England by the Armada in 1588?

2 Which king of a Middle Eastern country died on 7 February 1999?

3 What was the family name of George V before he changed it to Windsor during the First World War?

4 Who was the first husband of Mary Queen of Scots?

5 Who was the last King of Italy?

6 Which king of England, buried in Winchester Cathedral, was also king of Denmark and of Norway?

7 Phumiphon Adunyadet (also known as Bhumibol Adulyadej) is the leader of which constitutional monarchy?

8 Which Scottish king was killed when his horse fell from a cliff at Kinghorn in Fife?

9 The statue of which ninth-century king in England stands in his birthplace of Wantage in Oxfordshire?

10 Where in Scotland did Macbeth meet his death in 1057?

11 Who was the queen of George IV, whom he forcibly excluded from his coronation in 1821?

12 Who proclaimed himself King of Albania in 1928, but left the country in 1939 when it was annexed by Italy?

13 Which order of knighthood was founded in 1818 by the prince regent, later King George IV, to commemorate the British protectorate over the Ionian Islands and Malta?

14 When Egbert (Ecgberht) became King of England in 829, of which of the Seven Kingdoms (the Heptarchy) was he the ruler?

15 What was the name of the Frenchman who became King Karl XIV Johan of Sweden in 1818?

16 Which Persian king was defeated by the Greeks at the Battle of Marathon in 490 BC?

17 Who was King of the Iceni tribe (who ruled the area which is now mainly Norfolk and Suffolk) and husband of Boudica?

18 During the Napoleonic Wars, which country did a Danish adventurer named Jörgen Jörgensen take over (with British help) for two months in the summer of 1809, thereby earning himself the nickname of 'The Dog-Days King'?

19 Whose was the first of the 59 signatures on Charles I's death warrant in 1649?

20 What was the name of the horse of Gustav II Adolf of Sweden (the 'Lion of the North') which rode away into the mist after the king was killed during the battle at Lützen (near Leipzig), in 1632?

K is for Kings

1 **Philip II** (1527–98), who had been married to Queen Mary Tudor of England (half-sister of Elizabeth, with whom he was now at war).

2 **King Hussein of Jordan**, who had ruled the country since 1952.

3 **Saxe-Coburg-Gotha.** Lord Stamfordham, the king's Private Secretary, thought up the new, more English-sounding name, and George V declared by royal proclamation (1917) that descendants of Queen Victoria in the male line who were also British subjects should adopt it.

4 **François II of France.** They married in 1588 when François was the Dauphin; he died in 1560, a year after he became King of France.

5 **Umberto II** (1904–83). He succeeded his father, Victor Emmanuel III, who abdicated in 1946, but in a referendum later that year the Italians voted in favour of a republic and Umberto was forced to leave Italy.

6 **Canute** (Knut) (1016–35).

7 **Thailand.**

8 **Alexander III.** When he died his only heir was his granddaughter, Margaret ('The Maid of Norway'), the child of his daughter Margaret (who had died) and Erik II of Norway. Alexander, who was still only in his forties, married again, but he died five months later while riding from Edinburgh to spend the night with his new wife at Kinghorn.

9 **Alfred the Great** (King of Wessex, 871–99).

10 **Lumphanan** (near Aberdeen); not, as Shakespeare's play has it, at Dunsinane in Perthshire.

11 **Caroline of Brunswick** (1786–1821). Ten years before his marriage to Caroline, George IV had secretly gone through a ceremony of marriage with Maria Fitzherbert (a Catholic), but this marriage was not recognised by Parliament. The king tried to divorce Caroline, and then to bribe her to renounce the title of Queen and live abroad. Caroline refused, and she was turned away from the coronation ceremony a few days before she died.

12 **King Zog**, originally Ahmed Bey Zogu (1895–1961).

13 **The Order of St Michael and St George.**

14 **Wessex.**

15 **Jean Bernadotte** (1763–1844), a lawyer from Pau in south-west France, who was promoted to marshal in Napoleon's army.

16 **Darius I** (548–486 BC) of the Achaemenian dynasty.

17 **Prasutagus** (d AD 60).

18 **Iceland** Jörgen Jörgensen (1780–1841) was serving in the Royal Navy (and as an agent for a London soap-producer on the side). Iceland was a Danish colony then, and Denmark was at war with Britain. In June 1809 he sailed on a British frigate which was going to Iceland to protect a trade mission; with the help of some shipmates, Jörgensen arrested the Danish Governor and proclaimed himself 'Protector of all Iceland and Chief Commander on Land and Sea'. In August a British man-of-war arrived; Jörgensen was arrested and taken back to England.

19 **John Bradshaw** (1602–59), the president of the court at Charles I's trial in 1649.

20 **Streiff.** The horse has been stuffed and is displayed in the Palace Armoury in Stockholm. The theme of a horse disappearing into the mist after a battle was used in the screenplay (by John Steinbeck) of the 1952 film *Viva Zapata.*

General Knowledge

1 Which British king convened the Hampton Court conference in 1604 which led to the Authorised Version of the Bible?

2 What do white blood cells produce to fight antigens?

3 In which country is the volcano Krakatoa?

4 What is the common name for the poisonous plant *Atropa belladonna*, featured in L. P. Hartley's novel *The Go-Between*?

5 In which 1998 film does the lead character initially write a play entitled *Romeo and Ethel, the Pirate's Daughter*?

6 How many gold medals did the black American sprinter Jesse Owens win at the 1936 Berlin Olympics?

7 Which Eurovision Song Contest winning song was originally written for the Samaritans?

8 What is the popular name for decompression sickness?

9 What was the name of the Swedish Prime Minister who was assassinated in 1986?

10 In which series of adventure stories and films are John Clayton and Jane Porter the leading characters?

11 Which post-Impressionist French artist, renowned for his paintings of Tahiti, was the subject of Somerset Maugham's 1919 novel *The Moon and Sixpence*?

12 In the Old Testament, who interpreted the troubled dreams of Nebuchadnezzar?

13 Which English playwright and actor wrote the play *Blithe Spirit* in 1941?

14 The name of which United States city means in Spanish 'The Meadows'?

15 What are the names of the four Inns of Court in London?

16 What is the name of the Derbyshire village which isolated itself in order to contain the Great Plague which had reached the village in 1665?

17 By what name is the pioneering Swiss architect Charles Jeanneret better known?

18 What kind of animal is an alan (or alant)?

19 In Greek mythology which goddess was the avenger of crime and dispenser of justice?

20 In titles of royalty in Anglo-Saxon times, such as Edgar the Ætheling, what is the meaning of 'Ætheling'?

General Knowledge

1 **James VI & I** (1566–1625, King of Scotland from 1567 and of England from 1603).
2 **Antibodies.**
3 **Indonesia.** Its eruption in 1883 was one of the most catastrophic ever recorded. It began on 20 May and continued until 27 August. Another eruption began in 1927, when a new island, Anak Krakatoa ('Child of Krakatoa'), was created; by 1973 the island had risen to more than 186 metres above sea level.
4 **Deadly nightshade.**
5 *Shakespeare in Love.*
6 **Four** (100 metres, 200 metres, long jump and 4 × 100 metres relay).
7 *Love Shine a Light* (1997), sung by Katrina and the Waves.
8 **The bends.**
9 **Olof Palme** (1927–86).
10 *Tarzan* (by Edgar Rice Burroughs).
11 **Paul Gauguin** (1848–1903).
12 **Daniel** (Daniel 2–5).
13 **Noël Coward** (1899–1973).
14 **Las Vegas.** The name was given to it in 1855 by its first settlers, the Mormons from Utah. They were attracted by the artesian springs in the arid valley along the Old Spanish Trail after which they named it. The Mormons abandoned the site in 1857 and the US Army built Fort Baker there in 1864.
15 **Gray's Inn, Inner Temple, Lincoln's Inn and Middle Temple.** They are four voluntary societies which have the exclusive right of calling to the English Bar.
16 **Eyam.**
17 **Le Corbusier** (1887–1965).
18 **Dog.** These hunting dogs are thought to have been introduced to Britain in the early fifth century from Spain by the Alani, a barbarian tribe.
19 **Nemesis.**
20 **A person of noble birth.** It was usually restricted to members of a royal family; in the *Anglo-Saxon Chronicle* it is used almost exclusively for members of the royal house of Wessex. 'Æthel' (noble) was an element in the name of several Anglo-Saxon kings, such as Æthelbert, Æthelwulf, Æthelred.

L is for **London**

1 What does the Monument in London commemorate?

2 Which company of architects designed the Millennium Dome?

3 Which equestrian track in Hyde Park, whose name is said to be a corruption of the French *route du roi*, leads from St James's Palace to Kensington Palace?

4 What was the name of the 22-storey Canning Town tower block which partially collapsed in 1968?

5 To whom is the Cross at Charing Cross Station a memorial?

6 What is the address of the Sherlock Holmes Museum in London?

7 Which district of London is bounded by Oxford Street, Charing Cross Road, Coventry Street and Regent Street?

8 Who led the army of Britons who razed London (Londinium) to the ground in AD 60–61?

9 Who wrote the following lines?

> *Unreal City,*
> *Under the brown fog of a winter dawn,*
> *A crowd flowed over London Bridge, so many,*
> *I had not thought death had undone so many.*
> *Sighs, short and infrequent, were exhaled,*
> *And each man fixed his eyes before his feet,*
> *Flowed up the hill and down King William Street,*
> *To where Saint Mary Woolnoth kept the hours*
> *With a dead sound on the final stroke of nine.*

10 About which London politician was it said in March 2000: 'The ego has landed'?

11 In which London hospital is the Florence Nightingale Museum?

12 Of which London palace is Banqueting House the only surviving part?

13 Where were the first parking meters installed in London?

14 Which textile manufacturer built a house in the grounds of the medieval Eltham Palace in 1936 and donated it to the nation before his death in 1947?

15 What are the names of the seven regiments which form the Royal Guard?

16 Where in London was the Scottish leader William Wallace hanged, drawn and quartered in 1305?

17 Which street was thought of as a *cordon sanitaire* to separate the East End from the West End, a division which was still in evidence in the nineteenth century?

18 Who founded the London Zoo in Regent's Park?

19 Which neo-classical villa in Hampstead, bequeathed to the nation by Edward Guinness (1st Earl of Iveagh) at his death in 1927, houses a collection of paintings which includes Vermeer's *Girl with a Guitar* and works by Rembrandt and Gainsborough?

20 Which London Underground line was the last to use steam passenger trains in 1961?

1 **The Great Fire of London** (1666). The Monument stands near the north end of London Bridge. Its height of 61.5 metres is the exact distance from its base to the baker's shop in Pudding Lane where the Fire began. The Monument was designed by Christopher Wren.

2 **Richard Rogers Partnership**. The consulting engineers were Buro Happold, Laing and McAlpine.

3 **Rotten Row**. It was originally given the name '*route du roi*' because it formed part of the old royal route of the Plantagenets from Westminster to the royal forests.

4 **Ronan Point**.

5 **Eleanor of Castile** (wife of Edward I). It is a replica (erected by Edward Middleton Barry in 1865) of the original which Edward I put up in 1290 in the ancient village of Charing – one of the twelve crosses at the places where Eleanor's funeral cortège stopped on its way south from Harby, Nottinghamshire, to Westminster.

6 **221b Baker Street (W1)**, the address at which Holmes lived from 1881 to 1904 in the Conan Doyle stories. In reality it was a lodging-house from 1860 to 1934, and the maids who worked there were related to a Mr Holmes (although there are no records of the lodgers themselves). A Dr Watson (registered as an 'artificial teeth manufacturer') lived next door to it in the 1890s.

7 **Soho**. The name came from an old hunting cry; the area once consisted of fields on which hares were hunted.

8 **Boudica**. She led an army from the Iceni and Trinovantes tribes from south-eastern England; they sacked Colchester, St Albans and then London before they were defeated by the Roman general Suetonius Paullinus somewhere along Watling Street between London and the Midlands.

9 **T. S. Eliot**, in 'The Burial of the Dead', from *The Waste Land* (1922).

10 **Ken Livingstone** (by Frank Dobson) after he had announced his intention to stand as an independent in the election for Lord Mayor of London.

11 **St Thomas's**.

12 **The Palace of Whitehall**.

13 **Mayfair**, in 1958. Carlton Magree (editor of a newspaper in Oklahoma City) thought up the idea of parking meters when he was chairman of a committee working on the control of parking. The first parking meters were introduced in Oklahoma City in 1935.

14 **Samuel Courtauld** (1871–1947), the nephew of Samuel Courtauld (1793–1881) who founded the silk and rayon business in 1816.

15 **Lifeguards and the Blues and Royals** (which together make up the Household Cavalry), **Grenadier, Coldstream, Scots, Irish and Welsh Guards** (these five are infantry).

16 **Smithfield**. He was tried in Westminster Hall and found guilty of treason.

17 **Regent Street**.

18 **Sir Stamford Raffles** (in 1828). The animals which had been kept in the Royal Menagerie were transferred there.

19 **Kenwood House**. It was built in 1704; Lord Mansfield bought it in 1754 and commissioned Robert Adam to make extensive alterations to it. Guinness bought it in 1925 and filled it with his collection of paintings.

20 **The Metropolitan Line**.

General Knowledge

1 The last remaining tea clipper in the world, which was launched in 1869, is kept at Greenwich; what is its name?

2 Which Australian was the only golfer to win the Open three times in succession during the twentieth century?

3 The title of which 1961 book (and 1970 film) has come to mean a 'no-win' situation?

4 In which television puppet series did Spotty the Dog appear?

5 In which British rock band, formed in 1965, was the singer and guitarist Syd Barrett replaced by David Gilmour?

6 What kind of animal is a Dandie Dinmont?

7 In Greek mythology, whose head was so hideous that anyone looking at it was turned to stone?

8 What is the name of the group of about 1,300 islands (formed from coral on the tops of ancient volcanic mountains) in the North Indian Ocean, none of which has a greater area than five square miles?

9 In the Old Testament, from what kind of wood was the Ark of the Covenant made?

10 Which fantasy novel, published in 1937, has an alternative title *There and Back Again*?

11 For what purpose did the phrase 'Queen Anne's dead' come to be used?

12 Which Derbyshire town has a church with a twisted spire?

13 Which map, drawn in about 1290 and showing Jerusalem at the centre of a flat world, is kept in Hereford Cathedral?

14 Which British artist featured a cemetery in his home town in his 1923–27 painting *The Resurrection: Cookham*?

15 In Arthurian romances, what was the 'Siege Perilous'?

16 The presence of which organic substance is revealed by Benedict's Test?

17 What is familiarly known as the 'Sillitoe' tartan?

18 Which measure of length, used in land surveying, was named after the mathematician Edmund Gunter (1581–1626)?

19 In which British town is there a Museum of the Mousetrap?

20 Since 1514, which of the twelve Livery Companies of London has taken precedence over the others?

General Knowledge

1 *Cutty Sark*, originally built in 1869 at Dumbarton for Captain John Willis. The name comes from the 'cutty sark' (short shift) worn by a witch in *Tam O'Shanter* (1791) by Robert Burns.

2 **Peter Thomson** (1954, 1955 and 1956).

3 *Catch-22*, by Joseph Heller (1923–99). 'Catch-22' was a rule or 'catch' applied to a bombing squadron whose only aim was to avoid being killed. The pilots had to have a rational mind to be allowed to fly. It was rational to have concern for one's own safety; one pilot was deranged, and so could be grounded, but if he asked to be grounded, he must be of a sound mind, and so would have to fly more missions.

4 *The Woodentops*, which was shown during *Watch with Mother* (BBC). It ran from 1955 to 1958 and the same programmes were repeated until 1973.

5 **Pink Floyd.** Syd Barrett joined Roger Waters, Nick Mason and Richard Wright, who played under the name of Architectural Abdabs, and renamed them Pink Floyd Sound.

6 **Dog** (a Scottish hunting terrier). It was also the name of a tough little Border farmer in *Guy Mannering* by Sir Walter Scott (1815).

7 **Medusa**, the leader of the Gorgons, who had snakes instead of hair. Perseus, the hero, cut off her head.

8 **The Maldives.**

9 **Acacia.** Christ's crown of thorns was also made from acacia, an almost incorruptible wood.

10 *The Hobbit* by J. R. R. Tolkien (1892–1973).

11 **To slight the bearer of stale news.** It arose when the news of Queen Anne's death was kept secret for several weeks because she had no living legitimate heir, and the government feared a Jacobite rising in support of her half-brother, James Edward Stuart, the Catholic son of James VII & II.

12 **Chesterfield.** The spire of the fourteenth-century Church of Our Lady and All Saints was built when there was a shortage of skilled woodworkers because of the Black Death. The wood for the spire was not seasoned properly, and the weight of the lead covering warped the wooden frame.

13 **Mappa Mundi.** It is thought to have been produced by monks working under the direction of Richard of Hadlingham, whose name is inscribed on the map.

14 **Stanley Spencer** (1891–1959).

15 **The empty chair which awaited the perfect knight in search of the Holy Grail.**

16 **Glucose.**

17 **The black and white diced cap-band worn by police officers in Scotland** (and in many parts of England). The 'tartan' was named after Percy Sillitoe (1888–1962). He earned a national reputation as the tough Chief Constable of Glasgow City Police from 1931 to 1943. He pioneered the wearing of caps (rather than helmets) for police officers in cars in Glasgow.

18 **The chain (Gunter's chain).** It is 20.1 metres (22 yards) long and marked in 100 links.

19 **Newport**, Gwent. Its treasures include a 5,000-year-old Egyptian trap and a French one in the shape of a guillotine.

20 **Mercers.**

M is for Mountains

1 Which capital city in the Americas is overlooked by the volcano Popocatépetl?

2 What is the name of the highest point on the Isle of Man?

3 According to the Bible, to which mountain (from which an order of mendicant friars took its name in the twelfth century) did Elijah summon Ahab to choose between God and Baal?

4 Which Swiss ski resort, whose name means 'in the meadow', lies at the foot of the Matterhorn at an elevation of 1,616 metres?

5 In 1897 Matthias Zurbriggen was the first climber to reach the summit of the highest peak in South America; what is its name?

6 Through which mountain range in the United States does the Blue Ridge Parkway run?

7 Which mountain was called Peak XV until 1865, when it was renamed in honour of a British geologist?

8 In which English county is Helvellyn?

9 What is the name of the mountain near Rio de Janeiro from whose peak the giant statue of Christ the Redeemer overlooks the city?

10 Which group of people is traditionally banned from Mount Athos in Greece?

11 Which resort in the French Alps, situated on the River Arve at an elevation of 1,037 metres, is the starting point for the ascent of Mont Blanc by cable car?

12 In which European country is Mount Esja?

13 In which country is Mount Kościuszko (2,228 metres) the highest peak?

14 Which mountain is considered to be the Earth's largest volcano?

15 Mount Olympus, the home of Zeus in Greek mythology, is on the border of which two regions of Greece?

16 The eighteenth-century artist Richard Wilson is known chiefly for his paintings of which mountain in the United Kingdom?

17 In which group of islands is the volcanic island Stromboli?

18 Which is the second highest mountain in Japan?

19 On which mountain near Troy did the Judgement of Paris, in Greek legend, take place?

20 According to Hindu mythology, which legendary mountain in the centre of the world was the abode of Indra, the god of the sky?

M is for **Mountains** Answers

1 **Mexico City**. The perpetually snowcapped mountain rises to 5,465 metres above sea level. After lying dormant for more than 50 years, Popocatépetl erupted in December 1994, scattering ash over the city of Puebla.

2 **Snaefell** (617 metres).

3 **Mount Carmel** (1 Kings, 18:19). Its name in Hebrew (*karmel*) means 'garden'. The mendicant friars are the Carmelites (White Friars).

4 **Zermatt**.

5 **Aconcagua** (Argentina), which rises to 6,960 metres above sea level.

6 **Appalachians**. The road, which is 755 kilometres long, links the Shenandoah National Park at its northern end with the Great Smoky Mountains National Park at its southern end, running along mountain crests with elevations of up to 1,800 metres.

7 **Mount Everest**. The geologist was Sir George Everest (1790–1866), who was Surveyor-General of India from 1830.

8 **Cumbria**.

9 **Corcovado** (704 metres), in the Carioca Range. Its name means 'Hunchback'.

10 **Women**. The 2,033-metre-high mountain is the holy mountain of the Eastern Orthodox church and is dedicated to the Virgin Mary. A semi-autonomous republic of monks lives in monasteries there.

11 **Chamonix**. The resort is connected by the highest cable-car system in the world, almost to the summit of Mount Midi (3,842 metres).

12 **Iceland**. It overlooks the capital, Reykjavík.

13 **Australia**. It is in the Snowy Mountains of the Australian Alps, in New South Wales. It was named in 1840 by the explorer Paul Strzelecki in honour of the Polish patriot and statesman Tadeusz Kościuszko (1746–1817).

14 **Mauna Loa** in the Hawaii Volcanoes National Park, which was designated a World Heritage site in 1987. The volcano extends upward about five kilometres from the ocean bed to sea-level, and then rises an additional 4,169 metres. It covers about half the island of Hawaii.

15 **Macedonia and Thesaly**.

16 **Snowdon** (*Y Wyddfa*), painted in 1774. One of his best known paintings is *Snowdon from Llyn Nantlle* (now in the Walker Art Gallery, Liverpool).

17 **Lipari Islands** (also known as the Eolie Islands), in the Tyrrhenian Sea to the north-east of Sicily. The last serious eruption was in 1921, but the volcano is still active: lava flows continuously from its crater to the sea. Lipari is the source of the name for a fine-grained granite (rhyolite) known as 'liparite'.

18 **Mount Ontake** (3,063 metres). The highest is Mount Fuji (3,776 metres).

19 **Mount Ida** in north-western Asia Minor (now Turkey).

20 **Mount Meru**. The roof which covers the shrine in a Hindu temple represents Mount Meru.

General Knowledge

1 Which is the highest mountain in Canada?
2 When Edward Jenner first developed a vaccination for smallpox in 1796, from which disease of animals did he produce the vaccine?
3 For which English county did Basil D'Oliveira play first-class cricket?
4 What does a wainwright make?
5 What is the name of the only legal private army in Britain?
6 The name of which Soviet espionage organisation, made familiar by the James Bond films, comes from its motto meaning 'Death to spies'?
7 Which book opens with the words 'The primroses were over'?
8 In the Old Testament, which wife of Ahasuerus (Xerxes) of Persia risked her life to save her people (the Jews) from Haman's plot to have them killed?
9 From which opera does the aria O Fortuna come?
10 What was the name of the demarcation line, proposed in 1919, which formed the basis for the Soviet–Polish border after the Second World War?
11 In 1969, which singer recorded a best-selling album during a television documentary at San Quentin prison, California?
12 Which Hungarian international footballer defected to the West during the 1956 Soviet invasion of Hungary, later joining Real Madrid and eventually becoming manager of the Greek team Panathinaikos?
13 How did Tracey Emin shock the art world in 1999?
14 The name of which Caribbean island means 'land of many springs'?
15 Calamine, used to treat stings and burns, is a carbonate of which element?
16 What type of creature is a colobus?
17 Which physicist was in charge of the Manhattan Project at Los Alamos in New Mexico to develop the atomic bomb and afterwards worked on US atomic energy policy, promoting peaceful uses of atomic energy and opposing the development of the hydrogen bomb?
18 What was Coronation Street originally going to be named, until a canteen worker at Granada pointed out that it sounded like a lavatory cleaner?
19 Which Scottish chemist and physicist invented the vacuum flask in 1898?
20 Before he made the huge sculptures of the heads of Presidents George Washington, Thomas Jefferson, Abraham Lincoln and Theodore Roosevelt on Mount Rushmore in South Dakota, the sculptor Gutzon Borglum had been asked to carve the heads of which three men on Stone Mountain in Georgia?

General Knowledge Answers

1 **Mount Logan** (5,951 metres) in the Kluane National Park and Reserve in Yukon. This was another of the rehearsal questions we used for years on *Mastermind* – and it's just about the only one I really knew by heart!

2 **Cowpox** ('vaccination' comes from the Latin *vacca*, meaning cow). Jenner had noticed milkmaids' immunity to smallpox and deduced that this came from their exposure to cowpox; his first vaccination was carried out using cowpox matter from the hands of a milkmaid, Sarah Nelmes.

3 **Worcestershire.** He was born in Cape Town, South Africa, but emigrated to England and qualified to play for Worcestershire and England by residence. He first played for Worcestershire in 1965 and England in 1966.

4 **Wagons or carts.**

5 **The Atholl Highlanders,** whose headquarters are at Blair Castle in Perthshire. They are descended from the regiment raised in 1777 during the American War of Independence (the regiment never reached America and was disbanded in 1783). The corps is now about 50 strong.

6 **SMERSH** (from '*smert sh*pionam'). Its mission was to maintain security in the armed forces and to look for potential traitors within the military and intelligence services; one of its famous victims was Leon Trotsky (murdered in 1940 by Pavel Sudoplatov).

7 *Watership Down* by Richard Adams (1972).

8 **Esther.** Ahasuerus had a law that no one must enter his inner court without being summoned and that if they *were* summoned they must obey. He married Esther after dismissing his previous queen for breaking that law. To save the Jews, Esther had to go before the king to plead for them. She survived, and Jews commemorate her bravery and their deliverance with the joyful festival of Purim.

9 *Carmina Burana* by Carl Orff (1937). *O Fortuna* was the music used in the Old Spice 'surfer' television advertisement.

10 **Curzon Line,** named after Lord Curzon (1859–1925). He was Foreign Secretary when the demarcation line was proposed.

11 **Johnny Cash** (*Johnny Cash at San Quentin*).

12 **Ferenc Puskas** (b 1927).

13 **With her three-dimensional work *My Bed*** (1998), which was exhibited at the Tate Gallery in 1999. It consisted of a soiled, untidy bed, surrounded with litter such as used condoms and cigarette packets.

14 **Jamaica.** The name comes from *Xaymaca* (from the language of the Arawaks, the indigenous people of Jamaica).

15 **Zinc.**

16 **Monkey** (found in Africa). Its name comes from the Greek *kolobos* (docked); it has short thumbs.

17 **Robert Oppenheimer** (1904–67).

18 *Florizel Street.*

19 **James Dewar** (1842–1923). He also discovered cordite (with Frederick Abel).

20 **The Confederate generals Robert E. Lee and Stonewall Jackson and President Jefferson Davis.** Borglum began work on Stone Mountain in 1916, and the head of Lee was unveiled in 1924 but he abandoned the project after disputes with his patrons, and others completed it. He began work on Mount Rushmore in 1927 and completed it in 1941.

N is for Norse Mythology Questions

1 Who was the 'All-Father' of the Norse pantheon, whose sayings were enshrined in the *Hávamál*, the 'Words of the High One'?

2 Frey was the Norse god of fertility. What was the name of his twin sister and fertility goddess?

3 Which thirteenth-century Icelandic saga-historian wrote the *Prose Edda*, a compendium of Norse mythology for students?

4 Which of the Norse gods was the god of mischief?

5 What was the name of Óðin's eight-legged grey horse?

6 What was the name of the World Tree which held the Norse cosmos together?

7 According to a poem in the *Edda*, who was the god's emissary when Frey fell in love with the Giant maiden Gerð?

8 What is the literal meaning of *bifröst*, the rainbow which connected Middle Earth and Ásgarð, the home of the gods?

9 Which of the gods had such keen hearing that he could hear grass sprouting and sheep's wool growing?

10 What were the names of the two main families of gods in Norse mythology?

11 What was the name of Frey's magic ship, which always had a fair wind in its sails and which he could fold up like a handkerchief and carry in his pocket?

12 What was the purpose of the magic fetter, Gleipnir, which the dwarves made for the gods?

13 Which of the gods lost his arm in Fenrir's jaws when the Wolf was being fettered?

14 Who was killed by the dwarves so that his blood could be mixed with honey to produce the mead of wisdom?

15 What was the name of Thór's mighty hammer, which was stolen by the Giants and which he retrieved after dressing up as a bride for Thrym, the King of the Giants?

16 With what did the blind god Höður kill his brother, the shining White God, Baldur, as a result of the trickery of Loki?

17 What was the special property of Draupnir ('the Dripper'), the magic gold arm-ring owned by Óðin?

18 At the Norse equivalent of Armageddon the 'ship of the dead' (Naglfar), crewed by the Giants, slipped its moorings and put to sea to fight the gods. Of what was the ship made?

19 Who was the keeper of the Apples of Immortality, whom Loki rescued when she had been abducted by the Giants?

20 What happened to the toe of the giant Aurvandill, after it got frostbite when Thór was carrying him across a river?

N is for Norse Mythology Answers

1 Óðin.

2 Freyja.

3 Snorri Sturluson.

4 Loki.

5 Sleipnir.

6 Yggdrasill.

7 Skírnir (in *Skírnismál*). The poem has been interpreted as an echo of a sacred fertility rite: Frey was the god of fertility, and 'Gerð', in Icelandic, means 'field of barley'.

8 Quivering Bridge.

9 Heimdall. He was the son of nine mothers; he was the watchman of the gods, and stood on perpetual guard against the Giants.

10 Æsir and Vanir.

11 Skíðblaðnir.

12 To chain the Wolf, Fenrir. It looked as frail as silk, but was woven from five invisible ingredients: the sound of a cat, the spittle of a bird, the beard of a woman, the breath of a fish, and the roots of a mountain.

13 Týr, the ancient Germanic god of the sky. Tuesday is named after him.

14 Kvasir. He was said to be the wisest man in the world, and had been made from the spittle of all the gods.

15 Mjöllnir. Thór had three magic possessions – his hammer, his strength-increasing belt (*Megingjör*), and his iron gauntlets (*Járngreipr*) for wielding the hammer.

16 With a branch of mistletoe. The gods had collected pledges from everything in the world not to harm Baldur, but the mistletoe was not asked for a pledge because it was not considered dangerous. The gods were convinced that Baldur was now impervious to any harm, and would amuse themselves by shooting and throwing things at him. Höður, being blind, could not take part, until Loki gave him a branch of mistletoe fashioned into a javelin and directed Höður's aim at Baldur, who was pierced to the heart.

17 It dripped eight gold arm-rings every ninth night.

18 The nails of dead people.

19 Iðunn, the wife of Bragi, the god of poetry. Loki changed himself into a falcon, and Iðunn into a nut, and flew off with her in his talons.

20 It became a star – 'Aurvandill's Toe'. Thór broke off the afflicted toe and hurled it into the firmament. The Old English equivalent of 'Aurvandill' was 'Earendel', a name for the morning star.

General Knowledge Questions

1 Which day of the week is named after the Norse god of thunder?

2 Which horse won the Grand National for the third time in 1977?

3 Which 1942 animated film by Walt Disney was based on a children's story written in 1929 by the Austrian novelist Felix Salten?

4 Which 1972 record by Chuck Berry was his only single to reach Number 1 in the UK charts?

5 What name, meaning 'Enlightened One', was given to the religious leader Prince Gotama Siddattha who lived in north-east India from about 563 to 483 BCE?

6 What name was given to the one-off tax (introduced by the Labour government in 1997) on the excess profits earned by 33 public utilities by public flotation since 1983?

7 What are the names of the four Quarter Days in England?

8 The site of the Long-Range Weapons Establishment rocket-testing centre in South Australia was built near which small town whose name is an old Aboriginal word for a throwing stick?

9 Which substance, found in many fruits, makes jam 'set'?

10 Which fictional resident of Nutwood did Mary Tourtel create in 1920?

11 Men who held which public office were given the soubriquet 'Jack Ketch'?

12 In 1865 which British mountaineer was the first to climb the Matterhorn in an expedition in which four of his party fell to their deaths?

13 What name was given to the free schools for poor children which John Pounds, a shoemaker, began in 1818 in Portsmouth?

14 In medieval times which magic word was written in the form of an inverted triangle and used as an amulet to ward off diseases and cure fever?

15 Finn, Soling and Star are categories in which sport?

16 Which English crime novelist had his first success with *The Four Just Men* in 1905?

17 What kind of living thing is an earthstar?

18 In 1650 which Irish prelate calculated that the Earth had been created in October 4004 BC?

19 What are classified using the Munsell system, devised by Albert H. Munsell in 1913?

20 What was the Old Norse word for the 'Doom of the Gods', when the world would come to an end?

General Knowledge Answers

1 **Thursday** (from Thór).
2 **Red Rum**, ridden by Tommy Stack and trained by Don (Ginger) McCain.
3 *Bambi*.
4 *My Ding-a-Ling*. It was deemed obscene and banned by the BBC.
5 **The Buddha**.
6 **Windfall tax**. The companies affected were BAA, British Energy, British Gas, British Telecom, National Power, Powergen and the regional electricity companies, privatised water and sewerage companies and Railtrack. The tax was calculated at 23 per cent of the difference between the value of the company at the time of flotation and the value as determined by reference to average annual profits over a period of up to four years following privatisation.
7 **Lady Day (25 March), Midsummer Day (24 June), Michaelmas (29 September) and Christmas Day (25 December)**.
8 **Woomera**.
9 **Pectin**. To make jam from fruits which contain little pectin, such as strawberries, commercially prepared pectin is added.
10 **Rupert Bear**. Mary Tourtel (1874–1948) wrote the *Rupert the Bear* cartoon strip for the *Daily Express* from 1920 to 1938, after which the illustrator Alfred Bestall continued it until 1965.
11 **Public hangman**. Jack Ketch was a notoriously incompetent hangman who died in 1686. He executed James, Duke of Monmouth, bastard son of Charles II, in 1685 for his attempt to overthrow his half-brother, King James VII & II.
12 **Edward Whymper** (1840–1911). He was an illustrator and wood-engraver by trade, but became better known for his mountaineering feats.
13 **Ragged Schools**.
14 **Abracadabra**. Various derivations for 'abracadabra' have been suggested, including the Hebrew *abreg ad hābra* ('strike dead with thy lightning') or *Ab* (Father), *Ben* (Son), *Ruach Acadosch* (Holy Spirit) and the Greek *Abraxas* (a word based on a mathematical formula and used to personify a deity).
15 **Yachting**. A Finn is a type of dinghy, and solings and stars are keelboats.
16 **Edgar Wallace** (1889–1981). The book was made into a film in 1939 (in the USA it was given the title *The Secret Four*) and a television series was based on it. The book was published with the final chapter missing, and readers were invited to solve the mystery and win a prize.
17 **Fungus**. Earthstars belong to the same genus as puffballs; the name refers to the star-like base which is revealed when the outer coat peels back. They are usually found among dead leaves in the summer or autumn.
18 **Archbishop James Ussher of Armagh** (1581–1656). He worked it out by going through the genealogies of the biblical patriarchs listed in the Old Testament, about which he wrote in his *Annales Veteris et Novi Testamenti* (1650–54).
19 **Colours**. Colours are measured on scales of hue, value, and chroma, which correspond respectively to dominant wavelength, brightness, and strength or purity. The system is used internationally to specify opaque colours of dyed or pigmented surfaces.
20 **Ragnarök**.

O is for **Olympics**   Questions

1 In which year did Mark Spitz win seven gold medals in swimming events?
2 What are the colours of the five rings on the Olympic flag?
3 What was the prize for winners of events in the ancient Olympic Games?
4 How many times did the American sprinter Carl Lewis win the Olympic gold medal for the long jump?
5 Whose long jump record of 29 feet 2½ inches (8.9 metres) at the 1968 Mexico Olympics was not beaten until 1991 (by Mike Powell)?
6 After visiting the excavations of the ancient Olympic site in Greece in 1894, who was inspired to revive the Olympic Games?
7 For which runner's fall in the 3,000 metres in the 1984 Olympics was Zola Budd blamed?
8 Which East German skater, a gold-medallist for figure skating at the 1984 and 1988 Olympics, won an Emmy in 1990 for her performance in the film *Carmen on Ice*?
9 Which American runner won the gold medal for the marathon in 1908 in London after the leader, Dorando Pietri of Italy, reached the stadium well ahead of the field but, with only one lap of the stadium circuit to go, collapsed?
10 Which football team won the gold medal in the 1996 Olympics?
11 Which gymnast was awarded a perfect score of 10 – the first in Olympic history – in 1976 at Montreal?
12 Which British swimmer won the gold medal for the 100 metres women's backstroke in 1956?
13 A statue of which Finnish track star, who won nine Olympic gold medals between 1920 and 1932, stands outside the Olympic Stadium in Helsinki?
14 What was the name of the dog mascot of the 1992 Olympics in Barcelona?
15 In which Olympics did Princess Anne take part as a member of the British three-day event team?
16 Which event was discontinued after the 1924 Paris Olympics, when officials and Red Cross workers were still searching for missing competitors hours after the race had finished?
17 Which American Olympic gold medal sprinter was nicknamed the 'Milwaukee Meteor'?
18 Why were the 1908 Olympic Games, originally scheduled for Rome, moved to London?
19 Who won the first event (the hop, step and jump, now known as the triple jump) of the first modern Olympics in 1896 in Athens?
20 Which Roman emperor banned the ancient Olympic Games in AD 393?

O is for **Olympics**

1 **1972** (Munich). The gold medals were for the 100 and 200 metres freestyle and butterfly, 4 × 100 and 4 × 200 metres freestyle relays and the 4 × 100 metres medley relay.

2 **Blue, yellow, black, green, and red.** The blue ring is on the left next to the pole. The rings represent the unity of the five continents taking part.

3 **An olive garland.**

4 **Four** (1984, 1988, 1992 and 1996).

5 **Bob Beamon.** Mike Powell's jump in 1991 was 8.95 metres.

6 **Pierre de Coubertin** (1863–1937).

7 **Mary Decker** (USA).

8 **Katarina Witt.**

9 **John Hayes.** Pietri had fallen and got to his feet several times, waving away the officials who tried to help him. In the end, unable to crawl, let alone run, he was carried over the finishing line, and was disqualified. He spent two days in hospital after the race, and was presented with a special gold cup by Queen Alexandra.

10 **Nigeria.** They beat Argentina 3–2 in the final to become the first African team to win a major international football tournament.

11 **Nadia Comaneci** of the Soviet Union.

12 **Judy Grinham.** It was Britain's first Olympic swimming victory for women since Lucy Morton won the 200 metres breaststroke in 1924.

13 **Paavo Nurmi** (1897–1973), nicknamed 'The Flying Finn'.

14 **Cobi.**

15 **1976** (Montreal).

16 **Men's cross-country running.**

17 **Archie Hahn.** He won gold medals for the 100 metres in 1904 and 1906 (the 1906 event was one of the 'intercalary' games held in Athens).

18 **Mount Vesuvius had erupted in 1906** causing widespread devastation.

19 **James Connolly,** with a jump of 44 feet 11¾ inches (13.63 metres). His jump was three feet clear of his nearest rival.

20 **Theodosius I.** He was a Christian, and it is thought that he banned the games because of their pagan associations.

General Knowledge

1 Which 1981 film, directed by David Putnam, tells the story of the 100 metres sprinters Eric Liddell and Harold Abrahams at the 1924 Olympics?

2 In 1963 which group recorded *You'll Never Walk Alone*, which was adopted as the anthem of Liverpool Football Club?

3 Three rivers in England, three in Scotland and two in Wales have the same name – what name?

4 At sea, when are the 'dog watches'?

5 The design of which item of decorative pottery, originally made by the Staffordshire potter Ralph Wood in 1761, came from a print depicting a man named Philpot?

6 In the ancient world what collective term was given to the five regular solid figures?

7 The word 'chatelaine' for a female keeper of a castle came to be used for a functional item of jewellery. Where was it worn?

8 Which large-leaved houseplant features in the title of a 1936 novel by George Orwell?

9 Annibale Carracci (1560–1602) is generally regarded as the originator of which art form in which people's features are exaggerated?

10 Which are the only two mammals to lay eggs?

11 In heraldry, what colour is 'murrey'?

12 Frances Stuart, Duchess of Richmond and Lennox, the original model for the figure of Britannia, was the mistress of which British king?

13 Which metal is the densest element?

14 Which is the ninth month of the Muslim year?

15 Which three languages are featured on the Rosetta Stone?

16 By what name is valerian sometimes known because of its curative properties?

17 Which English actor wrote the pantomime *Harlequin's Invasion* (1759), which included the song *Heart of Oak*?

18 According to the book of Genesis, how old was Methuselah (the oldest person mentioned in the Bible) when he died?

19 What was the 'old grey whistle test' after which the 1971 BBC2 television programme was named?

20 Who was the Native American truck-driver who won the pentathlon and the first-ever decathlon gold medals at the Stockholm Olympics in 1912, but was later disqualified as a professional because he earned $25 a week for playing in a baseball team?

General Knowledge   Answers

1 *Chariots of Fire*. Harold Abrahams won the gold medal for the 100 metres. Eric Liddell, the Scottish sprinter, had refused to run in the 100 metres because his heat was on a Sunday, and won the 400 metres instead.

2 Gerry and the Pacemakers. The song came from the musical *Carousel*.

3 Avon. It means 'river'! It comes from the Celtic word *abonā*.

4 4–6 pm and 6–8 pm. These two-hour (instead of the usual four-hour) watches enable seafarers to vary their daily rota.

5 A Toby jug. The poem *Toby Philpot* was adapted from the Latin by Francis Fawkes (1720–77) and illustrated in a print sold to Ralph Wood by London print-seller Carrington Bowles. 'Toby Fillpot' was also the nickname of Harry Elwes (d 1761), a Staffordshire man, famed for the prodigious quantities of ale which he drank. There are now hundreds of varieties of Toby jugs, depicting various people, including one called the 'Magnum', featuring my own 'fillpot features'; it is the prize awarded for the annual in-house quiz of the Mastermind Club.

6 Platonic solids: tetrahedron, hexahedron, octahedron, dodecahedron, and icosahedron. The planes of each of them are equal and regular.

7 Around the waist. It was an ornamental chain (popular in the eighteenth century) on to which hooks were fastened to hold keys, seals, purses and other items needed by a human chatelaine.

8 Aspidistra (*Keep the Aspidistra Flying*).

9 Caricature.

10 Echidna (spiny anteater) and duck-billed platypus.

11 Purple/red (mulberry).

12 Charles II.

13 Osmium (Os).

14 Ramadan. A Muslim year has either 354 or 355 days, and so the date of Ramadan is eleven or ten days earlier each year on the Gregorian calendar.

15 Greek, Egyptian hieroglyphic and 'demotic'. The Rosetta Stone (now in the British Museum) was discovered near Alexandria in 1799, and in 1822 the young French scholar Jean François Champollion used it to decipher hieroglyphic symbols.

16 Allheal.

17 David Garrick (1717–79). The music was written by William Boyce.

18 969 years: 'Thus all the days of Methuselah were nine hundred and sixty-nine years; and he died.' (Genesis 5:27).

19 It derives from 'old greys'. They were elderly doorkeepers and other employees of music publishers to whom songwriters used to play their compositions. If the 'old greys' were still whistling the tunes after a week or more, then the songs were deemed worthy of publishing.

20 Jim Thorpe. His medals were taken from him, but in 1983 the International Olympics Committee reinstated him as co-winner and returned the medals to his children during a special ceremony. In 1950 American sports writers and broadcasters chose Thorpe as the greatest American athlete and football player of the first half of the twentieth century, and in 1954 a town in Pennsylvania was named after him.

P is for Perfume

1 What is the name of Calvin Klein's 'unisex' perfume, produced in 1994?

2 Marilyn Monroe once said, 'The only thing I wear in bed is . . .' – what?

3 Which perfume product, based on neroli, lemon and lavender, was first produced by Jean Farina of Cologne in the early nineteenth century?

4 Which perfume, created in 1935, was marketed as 'the costliest perfume in the world'?

5 The bottle of which perfume was modelled on a female torso wearing a corset which was a replica of one designed for Madonna (and which she wore as an outer garment)?

6 Which German author wrote the gripping 1985 novel *Perfume* about a French perfumer who was also a murderer?

7 Which modern perfume is based on one produced in 1768 as the result of a challenge issued by Count Orloff of Russia to Bayleys, the English Court perfumers, to produce a perfume with the aroma of leather, which was fashionable among the Russian nobility?

8 Which town in Provence has been the centre of the French perfume industry since the sixteenth century?

9 What is the name of the fragrance for babies which Annick Goutal produced in 1989?

10 Which astronaut featured in the launch of the men's fragrance π (*Pi*) by Givenchy in 1999?

11 Whose is *Mon Parfum*, launched in 1984?

12 French perfumers of the sixteenth to eighteenth centuries were usually manufacturers and perfumers of which article of clothing?

13 Which perfume and cosmetics company was founded by Florence Graham in 1910 in New York?

14 Myrurgia of Spain launched a perfume named *Only* in 1990 in association with which singer?

15 A television advertisement for which fragrance by Chanel featured people opening and closing shutters on the windows of a building to the music of *Dance of the Knights* from Prokofiev's *Romeo and Juliet*?

16 A perfume house in Grasse, France, founded by Eugene Fuchs after the First World War, was named after which eighteenth-century French painter known for his genre paintings of contemporary life?

17 Which perfume ingredient, mainly used as a fixative, is produced in the intestine of the sperm whale and is found floating on the sea?

18 From which plant does the perfume ingredient orris come?

19 How did *Chanel No 19*, created by Henri Robert, get its name?

20 Farnesol is a synthetic perfume ingredient with the fragrance of which flower?

P is for **Perfume**

1 *CK One*.
2 *Chanel No 5* (according to an answer she gave to a journalist who asked her what she wore in bed).
3 **Eau de Cologne**. The original formula is the basis of *Eau-de-Cologne* produced by the 4711 Mullhens Company of Cologne.
4 *Joy* (by Jean Patou). To produce just 28 grams of perfume takes 10,600 jasmine flowers and about 48 dozen roses. At first Jean Patou thought that the perfume was too expensive to market but his publicity agent, Elsa Maxwell, turned this disadvantage into a positive slogan.
5 *Jean-Paul Gaultier* (1992). Gaultier has re-released the perfume with its bottle 'dressed' in different ways, including a corset made to look like brass, a flesh-coloured cloth corset and, in 1998, a limited edition dressed in a black velvet strapless gown.
6 **Patrick Süskind** (b 1949).
7 *Imperial Leather*, originally named *Eau de Cologne Imperiale Russe* and changed, when Cussons took over Bayleys early in the twentieth century, to *Imperial Russian Leather* (they dropped 'Russian' from its name in 1939).
8 **Grasse**. The climate there is particularly suitable for growing crops of flowers used in perfumery such as bitter orange blossom, jasmine, jonquil, lavender, rose and violet.
9 *Eau de Bonpoint*.
10 **Edwin (Buzz) Aldrin**, the astronaut who accompanied Neil Armstrong and Michael Collins in the Apollo 11 flight in 1969 and walked on the Moon with Armstrong.
11 **Paloma Picasso**, the jewellery-designer daughter of the artist Pablo Picasso. The perfume was produced by l'Oréal.
12 **Gloves**, which were perfumed to disguise the smell of the tanning process which remained on the leather of the gloves.
13 **Elizabeth Arden**. The name came from an adaptation of the title of a book, *Elizabeth and her German Garden* (1898) by Elizabeth von Arnim (1886–1941). The company's first perfume was *Blue Grass* (1936).
14 **Julio Iglesias**.
15 *L'Égoïste* (1990). It was the relaunch of a perfume previously named *Bois Noir*, which was first created in 1987 but which had not been popular.
16 **Jean-Honoré Fragonard** (1732–1806), who lived in Grasse and whose father was a glover and haberdasher.
17 **Ambergris**. Ambergris is thought to protect the whale's intestine from irritation by the indigestible parts of the squid and cuttlefish on which it feeds. Fresh ambergris is soft and black and has an unpleasant smell, but after exposure to sun, air and sea water it hardens, its colour fades to a light grey or yellow, and it develops a pleasant fragrance. In perfumery it is ground and dissolved in alcohol.
18 **Iris**. The rhizomes of the plant are stored for two years or more and then powdered before orris is steam-distilled from them.
19 **In honour of Gabrielle (Coco) Chanel (1883–1971)**. Her birthday was on 19 August.
20 **Lily of the valley**.

General Knowledge

1 The name of which type of perfume means 'rotten pot'?

2 By what name was the early film comedian Arthur Stanley Jefferson better known?

3 In which book by Charles Dickens do Nathaniel Winkle and Augustus Snodgrass appear?

4 In the 1940s where did 'Bevin Boys' work?

5 Which early-twentieth-century artist is known chiefly for his humorous drawings of complicated mechanical contraptions, as in *How to Dispense with Servants in the Dining Room*?

6 In Roman mythology, what was the collective name of the three merciless goddesses of vengeance who punished earthly sinners?

7 From what is the Mexican drink tequila made?

8 Which popular nineteenth-century novelist was nicknamed 'the Great Unknown' by his publisher and 'the Wizard of the North' by readers of his day?

9 What new title did Beethoven give to his symphony 'The Bonaparte' when Napoleon declared himself Emperor?

10 Which architect, who designed the Liverpool Anglican Cathedral, also created the 1924 and 1935 versions of the Post Office telephone kiosk?

11 Which parts of a flowering plant produce the pollen?

12 In which country is Mount Ararat on whose peak, according to the Old Testament, Noah's Ark came to rest?

13 Of which English independent school for girls was Dorothea Beale the headteacher from 1858 to 1906?

14 In 1853 which ex-mayor of Bradford began building an industrial community which he called Saltaire at a beauty spot on the banks of the River Aire?

15 Which British explorer commanded expeditions in the ships *Nimrod*, *Endurance* and *Quest*?

16 What is the shape of an ankh?

17 The title of which BBC1 children's series in the 1960s was the home of Windy Miller, the farmer Jonathan Bell and PC McGarry?

18 In 1741–43 who first introduced rules and 'mufflers' (the forerunners of boxing gloves) for boxing?

19 In heraldry what is an animal doing if it is 'urinant'?

20 The bottle of which 1988 perfume was modelled on the body of Olive Oyl from the Popeye cartoons?

General Knowledge

1 *Potpourri*. It refers to the use of dried flowers (rather than their smell) for perfuming rooms.

2 **Stan Laurel** (1890–1965), who was born in Ulverston, Lancashire. He had toured with a British company as a comedian and moved to the USA in 1910, where he formed a duo with the American Oliver Hardy in 1926.

3 *The Pickwick Papers*, published in 1837. They were both members of the Pickwick Club.

4 **In coal mines.** Under the Emergency Powers (Defence) Act 1940 (when Ernest Bevin was Minister of Labour and National Service), one in ten men between the ages of 18 and 25 who were called up for National Service were directed to work in the mines.

5 **(William) Heath Robinson** (1872–1944), who also illustrated books such as *The Arabian Nights* and *The Water Babies*.

6 **The Furies** (Greek *Erinyes*): Tisiphone (the Avenger of Blood), Alecto (the Implacable) and Megaera (the Jealous One).

7 **The juice of the agave cactus** (*Agave tequilana*). Tequila contains 40–50 per cent alcohol and is named after the town of Tequila, where it is produced.

8 **Sir Walter Scott** (1771–1832). He published *Waverley* anonymously in 1814, after which the other novels were published as being 'by the author of *Waverley*'; he did not acknowledge his authorship until 1827.

9 *The Eroica* (*Symphony No 3*).

10 **Sir Giles Gilbert Scott** (1880–1960).

11 **Anthers** (small pouches at the tips of the stamens).

12 **Turkey.** Mount Ararat (Agr), at 5,137 metres, is the highest mountain in Turkey.

13 **Cheltenham Ladies' College.** Dorothea Beale (1831–1906) also founded St Hilda's College, Oxford. She was immortalised in an anonymous verse with a fellow suffragette, Frances Mary Buss (Principal of North London Collegiate School):

> *Miss Buss and Miss Beale,*
> *Cupid's darts do not feel.*
> *How different from us,*
> *Are Miss Beale and Miss Buss.*

14 **Titus Salt** (1803–76). It took twenty years to build Saltaire. At its centre was Salt's textile mill, in which he used the latest technology to reduce noise, clean the factory floor and prevent air pollution.

15 **Ernest Shackleton** (1874–1922) on his voyages to the Antarctic. Shackleton died on board the *Quest*.

16 **A looped cross.** It was an ancient Egyptian symbol of eternal life, often used with symbols of opposites, such as Sun and Moon, life and death.

17 *Camberwick Green*, created by Gordon Murray.

18 **Jack Broughton** (1755–1825). His rules were superseded by those of the Marquis of Queensberry in 1867.

19 **Diving** (usually a fish with its head pointing downwards and its tail erect). The word comes from the Latin *urinare* (to dive).

20 *Cheap and Chic* by Moschino. Advertisements for the perfume showed a female model wearing a sailor's hat and neckerchief (and apparently nothing else) with a bottle of the perfume poised on her bicep, and the legend 'Spinach for women'.

Q is for Quizzes

1 Which member of the Royal Family took part in a television quiz programme in 1987?

2 Who, according to Greek legend, answered correctly the first recorded quiz question in antiquity – the riddle of the Sphinx?

3 What is the name of the *Mastermind* theme tune?

4 Who is 'Mycroft', the question-setter and adjudicator in the radio quiz series *Brain of Britain*?

5 What is a 'quizzing-glass'?

6 In which ITV game show did Leslie Crowther invite contestants to 'Come on down'?

7 Which 1966–71 television quiz, presented by David Vine, was a general knowledge contest between two football clubs with teams of three players and a celebrity guest?

8 What choice was offered to contestants in the 1955–68 ITV quiz programme *Take Your Pick* if they survived the 'Yes/No Interlude' and had chosen their golden key?

9 Which ITV quiz programme, which ran from 1971 to 1983, was announced each week with the opening words 'From Norwich . . .'?

10 Who was the first *Mastermind* champion, in 1972?

11 According to the proverb, who 'ask questions which wise men cannot answer'?

12 Who were the original team leaders of *Call My Bluff* in 1965?

13 Which television quiz presenter was the producer of *Bless This House* and *Father, Dear Father*?

14 During the Christmas period which British school publishes its annual general knowledge test in the *Guardian*?

15 Which 1994 film, directed by Robert Redford, was about a scandal of the 1950s in which the brilliant Charles Van Doren, from a distinguished academic family, was found to have colluded in a 'fixed' television quiz which his opponent had been bribed to lose?

16 Who was the quizmaster of the American radio (and later television) show *You Bet Your Life*?

17 Who is said to have invented the word 'quiz'?

18 On which American quiz show was *University Challenge* based?

19 To what was John Thorpe referring, in Jane Austen's *Northanger Abbey*, when he said to his mother, 'Where did you get that quiz of a —, it makes you look like an old witch?'

20 What was the name given to the inquisitor of the 1930s radio quiz show (also the name of the programme) who questioned the studio audience and rewarded them with silver dollars for correct answers?

Q is for Quizzes

1 **The Princess Royal** took part in *A Question of Sport* in January 1987. A total of 18 million viewers watched Princess Anne playfully threaten her team captain, Liverpool footballer Emlyn Hughes, with her handbag and tell him that he couldn't spell 'yachting'.

2 **Oedipus**. When Oedipus arrived at Thebes he met the Sphinx, who asked riddles of passers-by and ate those who could not answer them. The riddle was: 'Which creature walks sometimes on two legs, sometimes on three and sometimes on four – and is at its weakest when it uses the most legs?' Oedipus answered, 'Man' (as a baby, he walks on four legs, then on two, and ends up using a stick to help him to walk).

3 *Approaching Menace* (by Neil Richardson). Bill Wright, the programme's creator, had asked the BBC Gramophone Library for a selection of music which would engender a feeling of foreboding and expectation, and *Approaching Menace* was the first one he listened to.

4 **Ian Gillies**, who had taken part as a contestant in 1964, won *Brain of Brains* in 1965 and then *Top Brain* in 1971. The nickname comes from Mycroft, the 'even cleverer' elder brother of Sherlock Holmes, who said of him, 'All other men are specialists, but his specialism is omniscience.'

5 **A monocle**.

6 *The Price is Right* (1984–88). The contestants had to estimate the retail price of the prize; the one whose estimate was the closest won it.

7 *Quizball*.

8 'Open the box' or 'Take the money'.

9 *Sale of the Century* (presented by Nicholas Parsons).

10 **Nancy Wilkinson** (1919–99). I treasure Nancy's memory as the polymath champion who set the standard for the 24 winners who followed her. After a brilliant career at Oxford she was recruited into the 'Enigma' code-breaking team at Bletchley Park, and then lectured in literature, Latin, biology, commerce and music. She had a wonderful intellectual curiosity about everything – the essence of a true Masterminder.

11 **Fools**.

12 **Frank Muir and Robert Morley** (with Robin Ray presiding).

13 **William G. Stewart**, the presenter of *Fifteen to One*.

14 **King William's College** in Castletown, Isle of Man. Pupils aged 14 and over take the test unseen on the last day of the autumn term. It is a fiendishly difficult quiz, and is published during the Christmas holiday to drive parents (and others) to their wits' end.

15 *Quiz Show*, which featured the NBC game show *Twenty One*.

16 **Groucho Marx**. The humorous quiz show began on the radio in 1947, moved to television in 1950 and continued until 1961.

17 **Mr Daly of Dublin**. The story goes that, in about 1780, theatre manager Daly made a bet that he could introduce a new word into the English language within 24 hours. He wrote the word 'quiz' on walls and other surfaces around the city, and within 24 hours people were heard enquiring what it meant.

18 *College Bowl*.

19 **Hat**.

20 **Doctor IQ**.

General Knowledge

1 The first programme ever broadcast on Channel 4, on 2 November 1982, was a 'quizzical' programme named what?

2 Which retail chain began in 1884 as the 'Penny Bazaar' in a market in Leeds?

3 Which 1960s model was nicknamed 'The Shrimp'?

4 Which 'blithe spirit', a member of the family *Alaudidae*, did Shelley celebrate in a poem?

5 What is scouse, from which the term 'Scouser' (someone from Liverpool) comes?

6 What does the Jewish festival Rosh Hashana celebrate?

7 Where in its body are the reproductive organs of a snail?

8 Which Scotsman founded the Bank of England in 1694?

9 Who wrote the following lines in 1902:
  I keep six honest serving-men
  (They taught me all I knew);
  Their names are What and Why and When
  And How and Where and Who.

10 In 1954, not long after he had beaten the four-minute mile barrier, Roger Bannister ran in another race in which he and another runner completed a mile in less than four minutes; who was the other runner?

11 What is the name of the subatomic particle first postulated by Murray Gell-Mann in 1964, whose name he took from a phrase in James Joyce's *Finnegans Wake*?

12 Which of Verdi's operas, based on a poem by Byron, opens on the shore of an island in the Aegean sea?

13 Which king of Romania was deposed in 1947?

14 Which printing press did William Morris set up in 1891?

15 In the painting *The Baptism of Christ* by Piero della Francesca, in the National Gallery, London, from what is John the Baptist pouring water over Christ's head?

16 What nickname was given to the Rev Geoffrey Studdert Kennedy (Chaplain to the Forces) because of his habit of giving cigarettes to soldiers in the trenches during the First World War?

17 Between which two stations did the London Underground run when it first opened in 1863?

18 Which Devon village holds an annual festival named 'The Rolling of the Tar Barrels' on 5 November?

19 What is a cembalo?

20 Which company produced the *Mastermind* trophy of an engraved crystal bowl each year for the entire 25 years of the series?

General Knowledge   Answers

1 **Countdown**. Channel 4 began broadcasting at 4.45 pm on that date. *Countdown*, with Richard Whiteley has been running ever since.

2 **Marks and Spencer**. When workhouse worker Tom Spencer (1851–1905) and salesman Michael Marks (1859–1907) set up the stall their advertising slogan was 'Don't ask the price. It's a penny.'

3 **Jean Shrimpton**, who shocked race-goers at the Melbourne Gold Cup in 1965 by wearing a white shift dress whose hem was at least 10 centimetres above her knees, with no hat, no gloves and no stockings.

4 **Skylark** (1820). The lark was also hymned by William Wordsworth.

5 **Stew** ('lobscouse' in full). It was originally made from left-over meat, potatoes and other vegetables; 'blind scouse' contained no meat and was likely to be served just before payday.

6 **New Year**. It is celebrated on the first and second days of the month of Tishri, which coincides with September/October in the Gregorian calendar. The Jewish Era in use today is dated from the year of creation in Jewish chronology (*anno mundi* or AM, Latin for 'in the year of the world'), whose equivalent is 3761 BCE.

7 **On the side of its head** – snails are hermaphrodites.

8 **William Paterson** (1658–1719). He resigned as Director of the bank in 1695 and went to Edinburgh to promote a new scheme for establishing a Scottish colony in Darien on the Isthmus of Panama. The scheme failed, and Paterson returned with some of the survivors in 1699.

9 **Rudyard Kipling** (1865–1936), in *Just So Stories*.

10 **John Landy**. Bannister's time was 3 minutes 58.8 seconds and Landy's was 3 minutes 59.6 seconds.

11 **Quark** ('Three quarks for Muster Mark').

12 **Il Corsaro** (1848), based on *The Corsair* (1813), and first performed in Trieste.

13 **King Michael** (b 1921). In 1944 he played an important part in the overthrow of the dictator Ion Antonescu, but the rise of Communism in Romania forced him to abdicate.

14 **The Kelmscott Press**. Morris designed three type styles for his press, based on those of the fifteenth century; one of his most lavishly illustrated books was *The Works of Geoffrey Chaucer*, published in the 1890s.

15 **A scallop shell**. The painting (*c* 1440–45) was originally intended for the Priory of John the Baptist in San Sepolchro at Borgo in Italy.

16 **Woodbine Willie**.

17 **Paddington** (then Bishop's Road) and **Farringdon** (then Farringdon Street).

18 **Ottery St Mary**. The insides of about eight or nine barrels are coated with bitumen and set alight. Strong young men, their heads and shoulders protected by sacking soaked with water, carry the barrels towards the village square, passing them one to another when they can no longer stand the heat. The barrels are rolled into the centre of the square, to the cheering of the assembled crowd. The custom is said to have begun as a celebration of the landing of William of Orange at Torbay on 5 November 1688.

19 **A musical instrument**; it is short for clavicembalo, an accompanying harpsichord, usually played by the conductor in classical orchestral music.

20 **Caithness Glass**. Dennis Mann designed and engraved each one. It always featured the nine Greek Muses.

R is for Railways

1 What name is given to the fast trains which run on the Tokaido line between Tokyo and Osaka in Japan?

2 Which early railway company in Britain was known by the initials LMS?

3 What is the name of the world's fastest steam locomotive, which was withdrawn from service in 1963?

4 What kind of train is represented by the initials APT?

5 Who wrote the poem *From a Railway Carriage*, which includes the following lines?

> *All of the sights of the hill and the plain*
> *Fly as thick as driving rain;*
> *And ever again, in the wink of an eye,*
> *Painted stations whistle by.*

6 Who constructed the world's first steam railway locomotive, in 1804, at the Penydaren Ironworks in South Wales?

7 Which city has a rail transport network named DART?

8 Which 1945 David Lean film immortalised the clock at Carnforth station in Lancashire?

9 What kind of train rides on an air cushion created by electromagnetic reaction between an on-board device and another embedded in the track?

10 In Turner's 1844 painting *Rain, Steam and Speed*, what kind of animal is running alongside the train?

11 In 1813 which British engineer built *Puffing Billy*, which is now in the Science Museum's transport collection at Wroughton in Wiltshire?

12 For what type of rail transport did Irishman Louis Brennan obtain a patent in 1903?

13 Over which stretch of water in Britain is the Britannia Railway Bridge, built in 1849 by Robert Stephenson?

14 By what name did the railway between Haywards Heath and Horsted Keynes in Sussex come to be known?

15 Platforms 1 and 2 of which station in Britain cut through the castle in whose great hall Edward I of England nominated John Balliol as King of Scotland in 1292?

16 In 1884 the London Underground station Eastcheap was given which name, by which it is still known?

17 What was the name of the last broad-gauge passenger train to run in Britain, on 21 May 1892?

18 Which early British railway runs through the Olive Mount cutting and across Chat Moss?

19 Which musician composed *Different Trains* (1988), which incorporates tape-recordings of people travelling by train with the sounds of a string quartet?

20 Where are the terminals of the 9,441-kilometre-long Trans-Siberian railway?

R is for **Railways** Answers

1 **Bullet Trains (Shinkansen)**, which run at speeds up to 130 miles per hour.

2 **London, Midland and Scotland**.

3 *Mallard* (designed by Sir Nigel Gresley), which was recorded travelling at 126 miles per hour on the London and North Eastern Railway on 3 July 1938. *Mallard* is on display at the National Railway Museum in York.

4 **Advanced Passenger Train**, developed in Britain in 1981. Its automatic tilting suspension is designed to enable it to take corners at high speed.

5 **Robert Louis Stevenson** (1850–94).

6 **Richard Trevithick** (1771–1833). The engine won a wager for the ironworks' owner, Samuel Homfray, by hauling a load of 10 tons of iron and 70 men along 10 miles of track.

7 **Dublin** (Dublin Area Rapid Transport).

8 *Brief Encounter*.

9 **Maglev** (from 'magnetic levitation'). The first maglev system in Britain began in 1991, on the shuttle between Birmingham International Airport and Birmingham International Railway Station.

10 **A hare**.

11 **William Hedley** (1779–1843). *Puffing Billy* pulled coal trucks along about five miles of track from a mine at Wylam, Northumberland, to the dockside at Lemington on the Tyne.

12 **Monorail**. The German August Scherl was also developing a monorail, and the world's first true monorail systems were demonstrated on the same day (10 November 1909). A previous 'monorail' built by the French engineering company Lartigue relied on extra wheels to keep the vehicles upright, but those built by Brenann and Scherl had gyroscopes for balance.

13 **Menai Strait**. Beside it is Thomas Telford's suspension road bridge (1827).

14 **The Bluebell Line**. The story goes that the driver used to stop the train for the passengers to pick the bluebells which grew in profusion along its route. The track (part of the route from East Grinstead to Lewes) was closed by British Railways in 1960 and later became the first standard-gauge railway to be reopened by enthusiasts.

15 **Berwick-upon-Tweed**. The remains of the main buildings of the castle were demolished to make way for the station, which was opened in 1846.

16 **Monument**.

17 **The *Cornishman***. On its last journey (on the seven-foot gauge Great Western Railway) it ran from London Paddington to Penzance and back. The next morning work began to convert this last-remaining wide-gauge track to the standard 4 feet 8½ inches and was completed within 30 hours, allowing the Sunday night mail train to run on time.

18 **The Liverpool and Manchester Railway** (opened in 1830), built by George Stephenson. Stephenson's plan was to make the railway as short as possible, by keeping it as straight as possible; there were no detours around obstacles such as Olive Mount and Chat Moss. The cutting, through solid sandstone at Olive Mount in Liverpool, is 20 metres deep in places. To cross Chat Moss, Stephenson gave up trying to fill in the seemingly bottomless bog and, having noticed tough, coarse plants floating on the bog, he created a floating raft from heather and brushwood to support the railway.

19 **Steve Reich** (b 1936).

20 **Moscow** and **Nakhodka** (the port station for **Vladivostok**).

General Knowledge

1 Whose abode, in a radio (and, later, BBC television) series, was 23 Railway Cuttings?

2 In the children's poem *An Elegy on the Death and Burial of Cock Robin*, who killed Cock Robin?

3 Which 1988 Olympic 100 metres, 200 metres and 400 metres relay gold medallist was nicknamed 'Flo Jo'?

4 What name is given to the larva of the cranefly ('daddy longlegs')?

5 Which three islands in the Inner Hebrides are familiarly known as 'the Cocktail Islands'?

6 Which Surrealist artist's name was given to a perfume whose bottle has the shape of a pair of lips?

7 Which fifteenth-century English earl was known as 'The Kingmaker'?

8 What is the religion of Falashas?

9 Which scale (on which pure water has a value of 7) measures acidity and alkalinity?

10 In the 1790s which Geneva jeweller set up a carbonated drinks company which is now an multi-national company?

11 Which US novelist became known as 'King of the Beat Generation' with his 1957 novel, *On the Road*?

12 Which opera by Ravel is the tale of a naughty child whose misdeeds include putting out his tongue at his mother, tearing up his books and slashing the curtains?

13 At which sea-battle were Mark Antony and Cleopatra defeated by Octavian's fleet in 31 BC?

14 Who were awarded the Nobel Prize for physiology or medicine in 1923 for their discovery in 1921 of the hormone insulin, an imbalance of which causes diabetes?

15 Which British rock band, formed in 1977, took as its name the Nazi slang term for a military brothel?

16 Which Austrian philosopher, who taught the subject at Cambridge University, expressed the axiom (in his *Tractatus Logico-Philosophicus*, 1921) that all philosophy is a critique of language?

17 If a fungus is coprophilous, on what does it live?

18 Which Botticelli masterpiece was bought by the National Galleries of Scotland for £10.25 million in 1999?

19 Which figure of speech means: the use of the same verb or adjective in different senses with two or more nouns, to one of which it is strictly applicable; for example, 'He seized his chance and my handbag'?

20 Which celebrated Scottish 'poet and tragedian' wrote a poem on the Tay Railway Bridge disaster of 1879, which begins with the following lines? –
Beautiful Railway Bridge of the Silvery Tay!
Alas, I am very sorry to say
That ninety lives have been taken away
On that last Sabbath day of 1879,
Which will be remember'd for a very long time.

General Knowledge   Answers

1 **Tony Hancock**, in *Hancock's Half-Hour*, which was first broadcast on radio in November 1954 and on television in September 1956.

2 **The sparrow**:
   '*I,' said the sparrow,*
   '*With my bow and arrow.'*

3 **Florence Griffith Joyner** of the USA.

4 **Leatherjacket** (so named because of its tough brown skin).

5 **Rum, Eigg** and **Muck**.

6 **Salvador Dali** (1904–89). Dali had become interested in perfumes while working on the painting *L'Aphrodite de Cnide*, whose face is shown on the package of the perfumes in the range (including *Salvador Dali*, *Eau de Dali* and *Dali Pour Homme*), launched by Parfums Salvador Dali in 1993.

7 **Richard Neville, Earl of Warwick** (1428–71), who first supported Henry VI and then joined the Yorkist cause to depose Henry and establish Edward IV as king. He was killed at the Battle of Barnet having joined the Lancastrians to reinstate Henry VI after Edward had forced him into exile in France.

8 **Judaism**. They are Ethiopians who are recognised as Jews by Israel, because it is believed that they may be descended from the 'ten lost tribes' of Israel. When Joshua led the twelve tribes of Israel into Canaan, ten tribes formed the independent Kingdom of Israel in the north and two others set up the Kingdom of Judah in the south. After the conquest of the northern kingdom by the Assyrians in 721 BCE, the ten tribes were gradually assimilated with other peoples and disappeared from history.

9 **pH**. It is a logarithmic index for the concentration of hydrogen ions in an aqueous solution. A pH value below 7 indicates acidity, and above it alkalinity.

10 **Jacob Schweppe**. He soon moved to London, and Schweppe's soda waters became a popular 'over-the-counter' remedy for various ailments.

11 **Jack Kerouac** (1922–69). He coined the term 'Beat Generation' in that novel, about the youthful discontent of the 'Beat Generation' of the 1950s.

12 *L'Enfant et les Sortilèges*.

13 **Actium**, off the west coast of Greece.

14 **Frederick Banting** and **Charles Best**.

15 **Joy Division**. Ian Curtis, Bernard Dicken, Peter Hook and Steven Morris from the Greater Manchester area first called themselves 'Warsaw'.

16 **Ludwig Wittgenstein** (1889–1951). He attempted to create a language system which was as precise and logical as mathematics.

17 **Dung**.

18 *The Virgin Adoring the Sleeping Christ*, also known as *Madonna and Child*, painted in 1480–85. It had been in the collection of the Earl of Wemyss and March at his family home, Gosford House in East Lothian.

19 **Zeugma**.

20 **William McGonagall** (1825–1902), who has earned the title of 'the world's worst poet' for the pathos, irrelevance, confused scansion and wayward rhymes of his verses. The original Tay Railway Bridge (designed by Sir Thomas Bouch) opened in 1878. During a storm on the night of 28 December 1879, the central section collapsed under a train: 75 people were killed.

S is for **Saints**

1 Which saint saw a vision of the Virgin Mary at Massabielle on the River Gave in 1858?

2 Which symbol is associated with St Peter?

3 Which play by T. S. Eliot was about the martyrdom of St Thomas à Becket in 1170?

4 Who was described in the Bible as 'a man full of faith and power' and is venerated as the first Christian Martyr?

5 In the third century AD a Roman soldier became the first Christian martyr in Britain; who was he?

6 The High Kirk of Edinburgh is named after which eighth-century anchorite who built a hermitage in France and became the patron saint of beggars, lepers and cripples?

7 Which Suffolk town was named after a martyr who had succeeded Offa as King of Mercia and, according to tradition, was killed by invading vikings when he refused to give up his Christian faith?

8 According to tradition, which early saint and martyr was tortured on a spiked wheel?

9 Behind the altar of which English cathedral are the remains of St Cuthbert entombed?

10 The former name of which city in Scotland came from the dedication of its first church to St John?

11 Which saints were the parents of the Virgin Mary?

12 Which of the London churches whose bells are commemorated in the nursery rhyme *Oranges and Lemons* also has, after its saint's name, a reference to the Danish settlers buried there?

13 The 1957 film *St Joan* was based on a play written in 1924 by whom?

14 With which English cathedral is St Swithin particularly associated?

15 In 1212 which saint founded the Poor Clares, a religious order for women?

16 To which saint did women once pray if they wanted to get rid of their husbands?

17 Pope John Paul canonised Teresa Benedicta of the Cross (1891–1942) in October 1998; by what name was she known before she became a Carmelite nun?

18 Which sainted Norse Earl of Orkney built St Magnus Cathedral, in Kirkwall, in the twelfth century, in honour of his uncle?

19 Which sixteenth-century Venetian saint, canonised in 1767, was declared the patron of orphans and abandoned children in 1928?

20 Jan Mostaert's *Portrait of a Young Man* (c 1520) depicts in its background the legend of which saint who used to forego mass so that he could go hunting, but reformed when he saw a vision of the Crucifixion between the horns of a stag?

S is for **Saints**

1 **Saint Bernadette of Lourdes** (Bernadette Soubirous, 1844–79).
2 **A key** (the key of heaven).
3 *Murder in the Cathedral* (1935).
4 **St Stephen,** one of the 'seven men of honest report full of the Holy Ghost and wisdom' chosen by the Apostles to serve in the temple in Jerusalem. He was accused of blasphemy and stoned to death.
5 **St Alban,** for whom the name of the Hertfordshire town was changed from the Roman Verulamium. The present cathedral of St Albans was built on the site of his execution (for harbouring a Christian priest).
6 **St Giles.** A Frankish king was so impressed with the holiness of Aegidius (as he was then named) that he built a monastery on the site of the hermitage.
7 **Bury St Edmunds,** named after St Edmund (841–870).
8 **St Catherine of Alexandria** (d 307), one of the patron saints of teachers; the Catherine Wheel firework is derived from this story.
9 **Durham.** St Cuthbert was first buried in 687 on the island of Lindisfarne, where he had been a monk at the priory. The monks exhumed his body in 875 (to keep it safe from invading vikings) and kept moving it until 995, when they arrived at the uninhabited area where Durham is now.
10 **Perth** (formerly St Johnstone).
11 **St Anne** and **St Joachim.**
12 **St Clement's** (St Clement Dane) in the Strand. The novelist Winifred Ashton took her pen name, Clemence Dane, from it.
13 **George Bernard Shaw.** The screenplay was by Graham Greene and the cast included the unknown Jean Seaberg as Joan of Arc.
14 **Winchester.** St Swithin, Bishop of Winchester, died in 862 and asked to be buried in the churchyard of the minster so that the 'sweet rain of heaven might fall' upon his grave. When plans were made to take his body inside the cathedral on 15 July 971, it rained solidly for forty days; hence the tradition that rain on St Swithin's Day brings rain for the next forty days too.
15 **St Francis of Assisi.** The order was named after its first abbess, Clare of Assisi.
16 **St Uncumber** (**St Wilgefortis**). According to legend, St Wilgefortis was a beautiful Portuguese princess who wanted to stay single but was plagued with suitors; she prayed that she might grow a beard to deter them. Her prayer was granted, but one enraged would-be suitor had her crucified. Sir Thomas More wrote that she was named 'Uncumber' because women 'reken that for a pecke of oats she will not fail to uncumber them of their husbondys'.
17 **Edith Stein.** She is the first saint of Jewish origin – a Jew who converted to Roman Catholicism and joined the Carmelite order in Cologne. After she took refuge from the Nazis in the Netherlands, she was taken to Auschwitz concentration camp, where she was killed.
18 **St Rögnvald.** I was allowed to choose the location for the last final of *Mastermind* in 1997 – and it had to be St Magnus Cathedral.
19 **St Jerome Emiliani.**
20 **St Hubert,** a patron saint of hunters, who became Bishop of Liège and died in 727. The painting is now in the Walker Art Gallery, Liverpool.

General Knowledge

1 Which saint is regarded as the patron saint of hopeless causes?

2 Which sport is linked with the surnames Butt and Fletcher?

3 In what are The Juggler, The Female Pope and The Empress numbers 1, 2 and 3 respectively?

4 The first chapter of which 1997 children's book is entitled 'The Boy who Lived'?

5 Which two races, one on the flat and one National Hunt, comprise the 'Spring Double'?

6 What is the meaning of the Sanskrit word 'Mahatma', the name given to Mohandas Gandhi?

7 Who had hits in the 1960s with *Little Bitty Tear* and *On Top of Old Smokey*?

8 Which Scottish novelist wrote the 1993 novel *Trainspotting* on which the 1996 film, starring Ewan McGregor, was based?

9 What was the name of the television character who, in moments of anger, turned into 'The Incredible Hulk'?

10 Which gas is produced by the Haber-Bosch process?

11 Who, in Greek mythology, was the goddess of Hearth and Family?

12 From which opera by Delibes does the *Flower Duet* come?

13 Which Russian-born aeronautical engineer built the first successful helicopter, the VS-300, in 1939–41?

14 What name did Sir Walter Scott give to the house he built near Melrose, in the Borders region of Scotland?

15 What is the trade name of the film colour process using three separate negatives of blue, green and red images, invented in 1922 by Daniel F. Cormstock and Herbert T. Kalmus?

16 'Hibernation' of animals means being dormant during the winter; what is the term used for being dormant during the summer?

17 What were the names of the 'Four Maries', the companions of Mary Queen of Scots in her youth?

18 Which Russian-born French artist designed the stained glass mosaics for the Knesset in Jerusalem during the 1960s and for the ceiling of the Paris Opera House in 1964?

19 Which Bishop of Brecknock and archdeacon of St David's wrote *Itinerarium Cambriae* and *Cambriae descripto* in 1191 and 1194 respectively after touring Wales with the future King John to raise soldiers for Henry II of England's Third Crusade?

20 Which rocky island group to the west of Scotland has the name of a saint who never existed?

General Knowledge Answers

1 **St Jude** (one of the twelve Apostles, whose day, 28 October, is shared with St Simon, with whom he was martyred in Persia).

2 **Archery**. One meaning of 'butt' is a target for archery, and a fletcher made arrows.

3 **The Tarot pack**. The other tarots of the Major Arcana are The Emperor, The Pope, The Lovers, The Chariot, Justice, The Hermit, The Wheel of Fortune, Strength (or Fortitude), The Hanged Man, Death, Temperance, The Devil, The Lightning-Struck Tower, The Star, The Moon, The Sun, The Last Judgement, The World (or Universe) and the Fool.

4 *Harry Potter and the Philosopher's Stone* by J. K. Rowling.

5 The **Lincoln** and the **Grand National**.

6 **Great soul**.

7 **Burl Ives** (1909–95).

8 **Irvine Welsh** (b 1958). Although the film was set in Edinburgh it was shot almost entirely in Glasgow.

9 **Dr Bruce Banner**. The ITV series (1978–82) was based on a children's comic character created by Stan Lee.

10 **Ammonia**. Fritz Haber (1868–1934) worked on the process of synthesising ammonia from nitrogen and hydrogen, for which he was awarded the Nobel Prize for chemistry in 1918. The process was developed at an industrial level by his brother-in-law Carl Bosch (1874–1940), who shared the 1931 Nobel Prize with Friedrich Bergius for work on high-pressure methods in chemistry.

11 **Hestia**. The equivalent Roman goddess was Vesta, after whom wax matches (and, later, 'Swan Vestas') were named.

12 *Lakmé* (1883). It was used in many advertisements for British Airways.

13 **Igor Sikorsky** (1889–1972).

14 **Abbotsford**. Scott purchased the land in 1811 and created a Gothic-style mansion. It is still the home of Scott's direct descendants, and remains virtually unchanged; it contains his library, family portraits, armoury and an extensive collection of historical memorabilia (his 'gabions').

15 **Technicolor**.

16 **Aestivation**. Snails aestivate when conditions become too hot and dry; they retreat into their shell and seal the opening by covering it with a secretion ('slime') which hardens.

17 **Mary Beaton, Mary Fleming, Mary Livingstone** and **Mary Seaton**.

18 **Marc Chagall** (1887–1985).

19 **Giraldus Cambrensis** (*c* 1146–*c* 1223), also known as Gerald of Wales and Girald de Barri.

20 **St Kilda**. The Old Norse name of the island, Skildir, was misread on charts and an errant full stop was inserted after the 's'. The Norse word means 'shields', and was perhaps a description of the shape of the islands in the group as seen from sea level.

T is for Time

1 Which clocks are named after lions' teeth?

2 What name is given to the study of time and clocks?

3 Who wrote the 1895 novel *The Time Machine*, in which humans of the future evolve into two species, Morlocks (who are practical) and Eloi (who are not)?

4 How many degrees of longitude represent an hour's difference in time?

5 Whose chronometer, tested in 1761–62, proved to be accurate enough to enable navigators to find the longitude to within 30 miles during a sea voyage and thereby won the British government's prize of £20,000?

6 What does a clepsydra use for measuring the passage of time?

7 Which calendar has an extra month (Adar) in a leap year?

8 On 1 January 2000, it was the 25th day of the 11th month of a Chinese year represented by which animal?

9 On what kind of device is a gnomon used for indicating the time?

10 How far does light travel in one nanosecond?

11 Which pope's edict *Inter gravissimas* caused the calendar to be adjusted by removing ten days from October 1582 and fixed the rule for leap years, producing the calendar which is still in use?

12 In the calendar of which people are there months named Siqinnaarut (Sun is possible), Saggaruut (caribou hair sheds) and Tauvigjuaq (great darkness)?

13 What name is given to a pendulum clock designed for highly accurate time-keeping?

14 In which 1986 film did John Cleese appear as a headteacher who was obsessed by time-keeping?

15 What name was given to large clocks in inns, because of legislation in Britain in 1797 which introduced a tax on all clocks?

16 Who, in a poem by T. S. Eliot, had: 'time yet for a hundred indecisions,/And for a hundred visions and revisions'?

17 Which planet's year consists of 668.6 solar days (sols)?

18 Who was the first director of the magnificent Paris Observatory, who discovered the division of Saturn's rings which still bears his name?

19 Which 1931 painting by Salvador Dali shows soft watches and clocks draped over rocks and the branch of an olive tree?

20 In the Regent Arcade shopping mall of which English town is the Wishing Fish clock, designed by Kit Williams and unveiled in 1987?

T is for Time   Answers

1 **Dandelion clocks** (from the French *dents de lion*, a name given to the plant because of its jagged leaves).

2 **Horology**.

3 **H. G. Wells** (1866–1946).

4 **Fifteen**. There are 24 meridians of longitude, 15 degrees apart, numbered both eastwards and westwards from 0° (Greenwich Meridian) to 180°.

5 **John Harrison** (1693–1776), the subject of Dava Sobel's book *Longitude*.

6 **Water**. The clepsydras used in ancient Greece and Egypt consisted of a stone vessel shaped like a truncated cone with a small hole in the bottom through which water dripped. Markings on the inside of the vessel showed how much water had escaped and thus how many hours had passed.

7 **The Jewish calendar**. The calendar is based on lunar months of 29 or 30 days. It includes the following types of year: Minimal Common (353 days), Regular Common (354 days), Full Common (355 days) and, to keep pace with the solar calendar, Regular Leap years (384 days) and Full Leap years (385 days) in which this extra month is added after the fifth month (Shebat).

8 **Rabbit**. The Year of the Dragon began on 5 February 2000.

9 **Sundial**. The gnomon is the pointer; the angle of inclination of the gnomon should equal that of the latitude of the place in which it is used so that, when the sundial is aligned in a north–south direction (pointing to the nearest Pole), the gnomon is parallel with the Earth's axis.

10 **One foot**. A nanosecond is one thousand millionth of a second.

11 **Gregory XIII** (after whom the Gregorian calendar was named). A miscalculation in the Julian calendar had meant that, because the year is slightly shorter than 364¼ days, it accumulated three extra days in 400 years.

12 **Inuit**. The traditional Inuit year has thirteen lunar months whose names describe the weather and the habits of the animals which were hunted.

13 **Regulator**.

14 *Clockwise*.

15 **Act of Parliament clocks**. These large clocks had become common in the 1720s but, after the tax was introduced, many people did without a clock in their homes and, instead, relied on clocks in inns. For some it might have been a good excuse to escape to the inn 'just to find out the time'!

16 **J. Alfred Prufrock**, in *The Love Song of J. Alfred Prufrock* (1917).

17 **Mars**. It orbits the Sun once in 687 Earth days and spins on its axis once every 24 hours and 37 minutes.

18 **Giovanni Domenico Cassini** (1625–1712). In 1672 Cassini proposed that the Prime Meridian (0°) should run through Paris.

19 *The Persistence of Memory*. Dali later wrote that his inspiration came from his favourite landscape at Port Lligat in Catalonia and a very ripe Camembert cheese.

20 **Cheltenham**. A duck at the top of the clock lays a stream of golden eggs, which pass into the rim of a large rotating wheel and then into the cabinet of the clock. Each egg sets off the mechanism to release a mouse from one of the many trapdoors in the cabinet. The large 'Wishing Fish' (suspended below the cabinet), from which the clock gets its name, blows a stream of bubbles into the mall every half hour; if you catch a bubble you can make a wish!

General Knowledge

1 When it was introduced in 1936, what did telephone-callers dial to hear the 'speaking clock'?

2 What is the most southerly point on mainland Britain?

3 What was the name of the bumbling monk of Mountacres Priory played by Derek Nimmo in the 1968–70 television series *Oh Brother!* ?

4 What was the name of the small, three-wheeled vehicle invented in 1985 by Sir Clive Sinclair?

5 Whom did Gene Tunney beat to become world heavyweight boxing champion in 1926?

6 On a lever, what is the word for the pivot around which movement takes place?

7 Which 1936 musical featured the Cole Porter song *I've Got You Under My Skin*?

8 The name of which of the Balearic Islands means 'island of perfumes'?

9 Which French composer is renowned for his use of birdsong?

10 Who played the part of Oskar Schindler in Steven Spielberg's 1993 film *Schindler's List*?

11 The Lion Gate was the entrance to the citadel of which Bronze Age Greek city?

12 What is a 'mermaid's purse'?

13 Which Italian artist painted portraits of Queen Elizabeth in 1955 and President Kennedy in 1961?

14 Jean-Henri Dunant of Switzerland, who was awarded the Nobel Peace Prize in 1901, inspired the foundation of which international organisation?

15 Which liberal-minded tutor to the young Princess (later Queen) Elizabeth of England wrote *Toxophilus* (a treatise on archery) and *The Scholemaster* (in which he denounced the use of force in education)?

16 Which French word is used on menus to describe the thick cut taken from the middle of fish such as cod, salmon or turbot weighing 900 kilograms or more?

17 Whose invasion of Austria and Hungary sparked the War of the Austrian Succession (1740–48)?

18 Which Chancellor of the Exchequer introduced Premium Bonds in 1956?

19 As what was the church of Santa Maria Rotunda in Rome known before 610, when Pope Boniface IV converted it to a church dedicated to all martyrs?

20 Who made the clock in the Clock Tower (St Stephen's Tower) at Westminster for which Big Ben chimes?

General Knowledge Answers

1 **TIM** (in numbers, 846). The listener would hear the time every ten seconds from a recorded voice, which began, 'At the third stroke it will be . . .'

2 **Lizard Point** in Cornwall. Its name comes not from the local wildlife but from the Cornish words *lys* (court) and *ardh* (high); the court is thought to have been at the village of Lizard.

3 **Brother Dominic.**

4 **C5.** It was driven by a washing machine motor and powered by rechargeable batteries.

5 **Jack Dempsey** (the 'Manassa Mauler'). The pair met again in 1927 in a fight which came to be known as the 'the battle of the long count'. Dempsey lost his chance of a seventh-round knockout by standing over Tunney instead of going to a neutral corner of the ring. The count could not begin until he had done so; Tunney got up on the count of nine and continued until the tenth round, when he won on points.

6 **Fulcrum.**

7 *Born to Dance.*

8 **Ibiza.** The name is of Punic origin: *ī* (island) and *busim* (perfumes).

9 **Olivier Messiaen** (1908–92), who notated the songs of numerous birds in France and classified them by region.

10 **Liam Neeson.** The film, directed by Steven Spielberg, was based on the 1982 novel *Schindler's Ark* (republished in 1993 as *Schindler's List*), by Thomas Kenneally.

11 **Mycenae** (the capital of Agamemnon) in the Peloponnese. The gate's name comes from the relief (*c* 1250 BC) above it which depicts two lions facing one another.

12 **The horny egg-case of fish** such as the dogfish, ray, skate and shark.

13 **Pietro Annigoni** (1910–88).

14 **The Red Cross.** Jean-Henri Dunant (1828–1910) distinguished himself in 1859 at Solferino, the last battle of the second War of Italian Independence, by treating the wounded from both the Austrian and the French/Italian armies. He worked with the Geneva Society for Public Welfare, which helped to found the International Committee for the Relief of the Wounded. In 1875 this organisation became the International Committee of the Red Cross.

15 **Roger Ascham** (*c* 1515–68). *Toxophilus* was published in 1545, and Roger Ascham's widow published *The Scholemaster* after his death, in 1570.

16 **Darne.**

17 **Frederick II (the Great) of Prussia** (1712–86). He invaded Silesia soon after the accession of the 23-year-old Empress Maria Theresa. France and Spain joined the Prussian side and Britain supported Austria.

18 **Harold Macmillan** (1894–1986).

19 **The Pantheon.** It was built in about AD 120 by Hadrian, who also built the Pantheon in Athens.

20 **Edward John Dent** (1790–1853). It was completed after his death by his stepson, **Frederick Dent.**

U is for **Universe**

1 After the Sun, which is the closest star to the Earth?

2 What name is given to a cosmic body of extremely intense gravity from which nothing, not even light, can escape?

3 Which 1988 best-seller about cosmology is subtitled *From the Big Bang to Black Holes*?

4 What was the name of the spacecraft in which John Glenn orbited the Earth in 1952?

5 Which planet has a moon named Charon, after the old man in Greek mythology who ferried the spirits of the dead across the Rivers Styx and Acheron?

6 Which star, in the constellation Canis Major, looks the brightest from the Earth?

7 What term is used for the shape of the Moon between 'half' and 'full'?

8 Which planet takes 164.8 Earth years to orbit the Sun, and has not completed an orbit since it was discovered in 1846?

9 In 1985–6 what did the European space probe *Giotto* observe?

10 Contrary to the beliefs of others of his time (and even until as late as the fifteenth century), which ancient Greek philosopher argued that the Earth is a sphere which rotates on its axis and orbits the Sun?

11 In Holst's *Planets* suite (composed in 1914–16), which planet is 'the Magician'?

12 For what is 'quasar' an abbreviation?

13 Where is the European Space Agency's launch centre?

14 Which American astronomer provided the first evidence of the expansion of the universe and is considered to be the founder of extragalactic astronomy?

15 Which constellation is named after the mother of Andromeda in Greek mythology?

16 Which Astronomer Royal was quoted in 1956 as saying that the idea of space travel was 'utter bilge'?

17 Which is the brightest star in the constellation Taurus (the Bull)?

18 The most abundant annual shower of meteors falls between 27 July and 17 August; what is its name?

19 In 1605 which German astronomer discovered that planetary orbits were elliptical, and not circular?

20 What name is given to the limit which defines the minimum distance to which a large satellite can approach its primary body without being torn apart by tidal forces caused by the pull of gravity?

U is for **Universe**

1 **Proxima Centauri**, which is 4.3 light-years away.

2 **A black hole**. A black hole can be formed by the death of a massive star.

3 *A Brief History of Time* by Stephen Hawking (b 1942).

4 *Friendship*, which was launched from Cape Canaveral, Florida. Glenn made three orbits, whose altitude ranged from approximately 159 to 261 kilometres, and landed in the Atlantic Ocean near the Bahamas.

5 **Pluto**.

6 **Sirius**. The second brightest star is Arcturus, in Boötes constellation.

7 **Gibbous**. The word means, literally, 'hunch-backed'.

8 **Neptune**, discovered by Johann Gottfried Galle.

9 **Halley's Comet**. Two Soviet spacecraft, *Vega 1* and *Vega 2*, also observed it.

10 **Aristarchos of Samos** (*c* 215–143 BC).

11 **Uranus**. The others are Mars (the Bringer of War), Venus (the Bringer of Peace), Mercury (the Winged Messenger), Jupiter (the Bringer of Jollity), Saturn (the Bringer of Old Age) and Neptune (the Mystic).

12 **Quasi-Stellar Object** (QSO), a distant object which looks like a star but is thought to be the nucleus of a galaxy.

13 **Kourou** (in French Guyana).

14 **Edwin Hubble** (1889–1953). The Hubble Space Telescope (put into orbit by the crew of the space shuttle *Discovery* in 1990) was named after him.

15 **Cassiopeia**. Cassiopeia of Ethiopia boasted that she was more beautiful than the sea nymphs (Nereids). For this, Poseidon punished Ethiopia by flooding it and sending the sea-monster from which Perseus rescued Andromeda.

16 **Richard van der Riet Woolley**. He was interviewed by the *Daily Telegraph* in January 1956, immediately after he took up his appointment. *Apollo 11* landed on the Moon in 1969. The Astronomer Royal retired in 1972.

17 **Aldebaran**, the 'red eye' of the Bull. Aldebaran is easy to spot because it is lined up with Orion's 'belt', to which it looks fairly close.

18 **Perseids**, named after the descendants of Perseus in Greek mythology.

19 **Johannes Kepler** (1571–1630). His work relied on the accurate observations of the movements of the planets made by the Dutch astronomer Tycho Brahe.

20 **The Roche limit**, first calculated by the French astronomer Édouard Roche (1820–83). The Roche limit is equivalent to 2.44 times the radius of the larger of two bodies in space. The Moon is 60 radii away from the Earth and, although artificial satellites are closer than this, they are too small to develop substantial tidal stresses. The rings of Saturn are thought to be the debris of a moon which was demolished when it moved within the Roche limit.

General Knowledge

1 Which UK and USA number one hit by the Tornadoes in 1962 was the name of the first commercial telecommunication satellite?

2 Which designer created the 'New Look' in 1947?

3 Who was the original narrator, in 1984, of the ITV children's series *Thomas the Tank Engine and Friends*?

4 The Strait of Bonifacio separates which two Mediterranean islands, one French and one Italian?

5 What kind of animals belong to the group known as annelids?

6 Which French word, meaning 'hunter', is used for a sauce or garnish made with mushrooms?

7 Which 1986 musical by Andrew Lloyd Webber was based on a novel written in 1911 by the French writer Gaston Leroux?

8 As what is the blue or white garden plant *Muscari botryoides*, which grows from small bulbs, better known?

9 The *Pali Canon* contains the teachings of which religious leader?

10 Which Scottish world boxing champion was inducted into the International Boxing Hall of Fame in June 2000?

11 Which two parts have been played in films of the same book in 1939, 1971 and 1992 by Merle Oberon and Laurence Olivier, Anna Calder-Marshall and Timothy Dalton, and Juliette Binoche and Ralph Fiennes?

12 What were the names of the two poets who were Oliver Cromwell's Latin secretary and the assistant to the Latin secretary?

13 Which South African Prime Minister was assassinated in 1966?

14 In a poem published in 1983, which Liverpool poet complained that he did not want the Universe heaped on his plate?

15 A fisherman's bend, a bowline, a sheepshank and a cat's paw are all types of what?

16 In Voltaire's picaresque novel *Candide* (1759), who was the optimist who kept saying that all was for the best in the best of all possible worlds?

17 Between 1911 and 1913 which London group of painters, led by Walter Sickert, introduced post-Impressionism to Britain?

18 What is a 'tussie-mussie'?

19 Which Irish philosopher put forward a theory (to prove the existence of God) that no material objects existed unless they were perceived by the senses, claiming that objects ceased to exist when they were not being observed by people?

20 Which British mathematician and astronomer is best known as the proponent of the steady-state theory of the universe?

General Knowledge

1 *Telstar*, written by Joe Meek.
2 **Christian Dior.** The 'New Look' was a complete change from the Second World War fashion of padded shoulders and short skirts; it featured natural shoulders, a natural waistline and a much longer, voluminous skirt.
3 **Ringo Starr.**
4 **Corsica** (French) and **Sardinia** (Italian). The strait is named after the town of Bonifacio in Corsica; although Bonifacio is on French territory, it is traditionally Genoese and has retained the Genoese dialect.
5 **Segmented worms,** such as earthworms, bristleworms and leeches.
6 *Chasseur.*
7 *The Phantom of the Opera* (based on *Le Fantôme de l'Opéra*).
8 **Grape hyacinth.**
9 **The Buddha.** The *Pali Canon* is also referred to as *Pali Tipitaka*, which is Sanskrit for 'Three Baskets'. Originally, the scriptures were written on palm leaves and placed in baskets. The *Tipitaka* are: *Vinaya* (rules for monastic life), *Sutta* (the discourses of the Buddha) and *Abhidhamma* (scholastic writings on ethics, psychology, and epistemology).
10 **Ken Buchanan** (world lightweight champion 1970–72).
11 **Catherine and Heathcliff** in Emily Brontë's *Wuthering Heights* (1847).
12 **John Milton** (Latin secretary) and **Andrew Marvell** (assistant).
13 **Hendrik Verwoerd** (1901–66), the leader of the Nationalist Party who promoted a strict apartheid policy.
14 **Roger McGough**, in *Sky in the Pie!*
15 **Knot.**
16 **Dr Pangloss**, whose name means 'all tongues'.
17 **Camden Town Group.**
18 **A nosegay.** Tussie-mussies, popular in Elizabethan times, were made up of fragrant flowers or herbs, chosen for their symbolic meanings to convey a message or sentiment: for example, daisy for faithfulness and rose for love.
19 **Bishop George Berkeley** (1685–1753), after whom Berkeley in California is named. His theory was lampooned by the English theologian Ronald Knox (1888–1957):

> There was a young man who said, 'God
> Must think it exceedingly odd
> If he finds that this tree
> Continues to be
> When there's no one about in the Quad.'

Back came the anonymous reply:

> Dear Sir,
> Your astonishment's odd:
> I am always about in the Quad.
> And that's why the tree
> Will continue to be,
> Since observed by
> Yours faithfully,
> God.

20 **Sir Fred Hoyle** (b 1915). The theory holds that the universe is expanding and that matter is being continuously created to keep the mean density of matter in space constant.

V is for **Variety**

1 In which pantomime does Dandini appear?

2 Which music-hall singer sang *I'm One of the Ruins that Cromwell Knocked About a Bit* and *Oh, Mr Porter*?

3 Who produced the first operettas by Gilbert and Sullivan and built the Savoy Theatre in London (1881), after which the 'Savoy Operas' were named?

4 The song *The Daring Young Man on the Flying Trapeze* immortalised which French music-hall performer, after whom the close-fitting garment he wore was named?

5 What name was given to the floating theatres of North American rivers such as the Mississippi and Ohio, which provided entertainment for the pioneer settlements from about 1817 until the American Civil War drove them off the rivers in 1861?

6 What name was given to the form of entertainment pioneered by Tony Pastor in the late nineteenth century in the USA to replace variety, which had lost its respectability?

7 By what name was the vaudeville singer Sonia Kalish better known?

8 As what kind of character did Grock (1880–1959) perform?

9 In whose honour were all clowns nicknamed 'Joey'?

10 Which Liverpool-born actor and playwright wrote the farce *Charley's Aunt* (1892)?

11 Who was the first music-hall singer to be knighted – a Scot who made his début singing Irish songs but found that audiences preferred the Scottish songs to which he resorted when short of material for encores, such as *Roamin' in the Gloamin'* and *I Love a Lassie*?

12 Which was the first purpose-built music-hall to open in London?

13 By what name was 43 King Street, Covent Garden, known which became famous for 'blue' entertainment?

14 In a music-hall song written by Fred Albert, who were 'too proud to beg, too honest to steal'?

15 Which singer, who died in 1942, made his name singing songs about food, such as *Boiled Beef and Carrots* and *Hot Tripe and Onions*, as well as *I'm 'Enery the Eighth I am*?

16 To which song, popularised by Mark Sheridan, did the troops march out to the First World War?

17 In 1928 which composer, married to the cabaret singer Lotte Lenya, wrote the music for Bertolt Brecht's *Die Dreigroschenoper* (*The Threepenny Opera*)?

18 What was the name of the doll with which Fred Russell first performed his act in 1896?

19 Which American-born French singer and dancer introduced her *dance sauvage* to Paris in 1925 with *La Revue Nègre*?

20 What was the stage name of the French music-hall entertainer Joseph Pujol whose speciality was producing a prodigious range of noises – orchestral music, artillery barrages and so on – by farting?

V is for Variety

1 *Cinderella*.

2 **Marie Lloyd** (Matilda Alice Victoria Wood, 1870–1922).

3 **Richard D'Oyly Carte** (1844–1901).

4 **Jules Léotard** (1830–70).

5 **Showboats**.

6 **Vaudeville**. Tony Pastor presented the first vaudeville show in 1881 in New York. It included acrobatics, comedy, dancing and singing.

7 **Sophie Tucker** (1884–1966).

8 **Clown**. His real name was Charles Adrien Wettach.

9 **Joseph Grimaldi** (1778–1837), the creator of the English clown, who introduced the costume of baggy trousers, a livery coat with red patches, a wig and a white face with eye patches.

10 **Brandon Thomas** (1849/56–1914).

11 **Sir Harry Lauder** (Hugh MacLennan, 1870–1950).

12 *The Canterbury*, which Charles Morton ('the Father of the Halls') opened in 1852, following the success of his 'musical evenings' at the Canterbury Arms, of which he was the landlord from 1849. A bomb destroyed the building during the Second World War.

13 **Evans Music-and-Supper Rooms**. It was named after a former owner, W. C. Evans, who encouraged his patrons to outdo one another in singing bawdy songs. John Greenmore ('Paddy Green') took it over in 1844 and added a hall with a stage. The performers were all male and so were most of the patrons; women were admitted only if they had a male escort and gave their names and addresses, and even then they had to watch the performance from behind a grille!

14 **The shabby genteel**, popularised by Victor Liston (1838–1913).

15 **Harry Champion** (1866–1942).

16 *Here We Are, Here We Are, Here We Are Again*. One of Mark Sheridan's other popular songs was *Oh, I Do Like to be Beside the Seaside*.

17 **Kurt Weill** (1900–50). Bertolt Brecht had based the operetta on John Gay's play *The Beggar's Opera*.

18 **Coster Joe**.

19 **Josephine Baker** (1906–75).

20 **Le Pétomane**. In 1892 Joseph Pujol (1857–1945) topped the bill at the Moulin Rouge in Paris with his unusual act, and in 1895 he opened his own theatre, the *Pompadour*. Three years later he sued the *Moulin Rouge* for presenting a female 'Pétomane', but before the case came to court she was shown to be a fraud who had concealed whistles and bellows under her skirt. Pujol retired from the stage in 1914 when the outbreak of the First World War made his *tour de force* of mock artillery barrages seem inappropriate. I put this into the 1990 edition of *Chambers Biographical Dictionary*, which I edited, as a 'wild card' entry – mainly because of the memorable television documentary in which Joseph Pujol was portrayed by Leonard Rossiter.

General Knowledge

1 By what nickname was the vaudeville star Jimmy Durante known?

2 In July 1965 the song *Everyone's Gone to the Moon*, recorded by an under-graduate of Trinity College, Cambridge, reached Number 4 in the UK charts. He went on to become a television presenter – who is he?

3 Who was the first footballer in the world to win 100 caps for his country?

4 Which Jane Austen novel opens with the words, 'The family of Dashwood had been long settled in Sussex'?

5 What kind of animals are Ramshorn, Wandering, Marsh and Dwarf?

6 Which Scottish town is served by Dalcross Airport?

7 Which English author wrote *Barrack Room Ballads* in 1892?

8 Which sport is governed by the Fédération Internationale d'Escrime?

9 What is the English name of the Welsh city Abertawe?

10 What was the pseudonym of the American painter and photographer Emanuel Rabinovitch who made the Surrealist films *Anemic Cinema* (1924) and *L'Étoile de Mer* (1928)?

11 What name is given to the storms of the pampas of South America caused by the cold south wind meeting warm air moving in from the tropical north?

12 What was the full name of the Italian map-maker after whom America was named?

13 The title of Sir Walter Scott's novel *The Heart of Midlothian* refers to which historic building, demolished in 1817 and commemorated by the design of a heart set into the cobblestones in front of the entrance to St Giles' High Kirk in Edinburgh?

14 By what name is *Guaiacum officinale*, the wood from which crown green bowls are made, more commonly known?

15 Which needlewoman from Philadelphia made the flags for the navy of Pennsylvania and, according to legend, made the first 'Stars and Stripes' flag, which was adopted as the national flag of the United States of America?

16 Which starchy thickening agent, used in cooking, comes from the tubers of *Maranta arundinacea*, a herbaceous perennial cultivated in the West Indies, South-east Asia, Australia, and South Africa?

17 Which Irish scientist published *The Skeptical Chemist* in 1661, in which he defined for the first time the idea of an element as a substance which cannot be broken down into simpler ones?

18 Which Paris perfume and fashion house produced the perfume *Shocking* in 1937?

19 What kind of clock tells the time according to the positions of 'fixed' stars, rather than by the apparent motion of the Sun?

20 Which French author, who wrote *L'Envers du music-hall* (*Music-Hall Sidelights*) in 1913, was a music-hall performer for a time?

General Knowledge

Answers

1 **Schnozzle**, from his big nose. Jimmy Durante's showbusiness career spanned 50 years, from New York bars in the 1920s to Broadway in the 1930s and then to Hollywood.

2 **Jonathan King** (b 1944).

3 **Billy Wright.** William Ambrose Wright (1924–94) gained his 100th cap on 11 April 1959, when England beat Scotland 1–0 at Wembley. He had joined Wolverhampton Wanderers at the age of 14 and continued to play for them until 1959.

4 *Sense and Sensibility*, which was originally written as *Elinor and Marianne* in 1795–6, given a new title and much altered before it was published in 1811.

5 **Freshwater snails.**

6 **Inverness.**

7 **Rudyard Kipling** (1865–1936).

8 **Fencing.** It was set up in 1913 to agree a set of international rules for the sport.

9 **Swansea.** The Welsh name means 'city at the mouth (*aber*) of the River Tawe'.

10 **Man Ray** (1890–1976). He also produced 'rayographs' (photographs made by exposing light-sensitive paper, but without the use of a camera).

11 **Pamperos.**

12 **Amerigo Vespucci** (1454–1512), who sailed to the New World in 1499. In 1508 he was appointed as Pilot-Major for Spain and had the responsibility of examining pilots' and ships' masters' licences for voyages, and making the official map of the newly discovered lands and of the routes to them. The German cartographer Martin Waldseemüller was the first to give Vespucci's name to the continent of America, on the basis of exaggerated accounts of his travels.

13 **The Tolbooth prison.**

14 **Lignum vitae.** It is so dense that, unlike most woods, it does not float in water.

15 **Betsy Ross** (1752–1836). The story goes that in June 1776, Betsy Ross's late husband's uncle, George Ross, visited her with George Washington, who gave her a sketch of his ideas for the flag, which she stitched soon afterwards.

16 **Arrowroot.**

17 **Robert Boyle** (1627–91).

18 **Schiaparelli.** Elsa Schiaparelli (1890–1973) brought it out to accompany her 'shocking pink' fashion collection that year.

19 **Sidereal clock.** Astronomers rely on sidereal clocks because any given star will cross the same meridian at the same sidereal time throughout the year. The sidereal day is almost 4 minutes shorter than the mean solar day of 24 of the hours shown by ordinary timepieces.

20 **Colette** (Sidonie-Gabrielle Colette, 1873–1954).

W is for **Words**

1 From which everyday commodity does the word 'salary' come?

2 What is the collective noun for a group of crows?

3 Malapropism (the incorrect use of a word containing similar sounds to the correct one) was named after Mrs Malaprop, in which of Sheridan's plays?

4 For what does the acronym UNCLE (as in *The Man from UNCLE*) stand?

5 From which industry does the expression 'on tenterhooks' come?

6 Which element, discovered in 1817 by the Swedish chemist Jöns Jacob Berzelius, is named after the Greek goddess of the Moon?

7 In the reign of Charles II, which five ministers formed a government 'cabal' (an acronym of their initials) which governed from 1667 to 1673?

8 For which Latin word is *viz* an abbreviation?

9 Who, in Shakespeare, said the following words, and in which play?
   Taffeta phrases, silken terms precise,
   Three-pil'd hyperboles, spruce affectation,
   Figures pedantical; these summer flies
   Have blown me full of maggot ostentation:
   I do forswear them.

10 In the shortened form of Cockney rhyming slang, what are 'ampsteads (sometimes shortened even more, to 'amps)?

11 Which word for a catchphrase used to be the war cry of the Scottish Highland clans?

12 In 1931 who first developed the game he named 'Lexico' and later 'Criss Cross', which was marketed by James Brunot as 'Scrabble' in 1948?

13 What is the source of the phrase 'to pipe down'?

14 Which Russian author popularised the term 'nihilism', and in which novel?

15 Which term is used to denote the smallest unit of sound in a word?

16 Which term refers to an ironical understatement in which an affirmative is expressed by the negative of its opposite: for example, 'no laughing matter', 'I shan't be sorry'?

17 Who defined oats as 'a grain, which in England is generally given to horses, but in Scotland supports the people'?

18 Taphephobia is an irrational fear of what?

19 The name of which unit of currency comes from St Joachimsthal in the Erzgebrige (Ore Mountains) in Czechoslovakia?

20 In 1911, which American author and journalist produced a volume of cynical definitions now known as *The Devil's Dictionary*?

1 **Salt**, from the Latin *salarium* (payment to soldiers in salt, or money paid to soldiers so that they could buy salt).
2 **Murder**.
3 *The Rivals* (1775): 'Illiterate him, I say, quite from your memory' and 'He is the very pineapple of politeness'. A celebrated reply by Liverpool Football Club manager Bill Shankly to the malapropism, 'Pass the dromedary sugar, please' was 'Certainly – one hump or two?'
4 **United Nations Command for Law and Enforcement**.
5 **Textiles**. Tenterhooks were the hooks with which damp fabric was attached to the tenter (wooden frame) on which it was stretched. Otterburn Mill in Northumberland claims to have the last remaining tenters in Britain.
6 **Selenium** (after Selene). Jöns Jacob Berzelius (1779–1848) discovered an ore of exceptionally high selenium content just a few days before he presented his findings on selenium, and named it eucairite ('just in time')!
7 **Clifford, Ashley, Buckingham, Arlington** and **Lauderdale**. This derivation of the word is coincidental. The real derivation comes from the Hebrew *cabbala* or *kabbalah*, which at root signifies 'tradition', in the strict Latin sense of 'That which is received, or passed on'. Originally *kabbalah* indicated any religious tradition, but the word came to be used especially of mystical tradition.
8 *Videlicit* (namely).
9 **Biron** (to Rosaline) in *Love's Labour's Lost*: Act V, Scene ii.
10 **Teeth** (Hampstead Heath).
11 **Slogan**, from the Gaelic *sluaghghairm*: *sluagh* (army or host) and *gairm* (cry or shout).
12 **Alfred M. Butts** (1899–1993), an architect from Poughkeepsie, New York State. *Scrabble* was first sold in Great Britain in 1954. J. W. Spear & Sons, a subsidiary of Mattel, now have the rights throughout the world (excluding Canada and the USA). The story goes that Jack Strauss, the chairman of Macy's store in New York, came across *Scrabble* while on holiday in 1952. He asked the games department to send him a couple of sets, and was astounded to discover that Macy's didn't stock it. They soon did!
13 In the Navy, **'Pipe down'** was the call on a boatswain's pipe to signal 'Lights out'.
14 **Ivan Turgenev** (1818–83) in *Fathers and Sons* (1862). The term (for negative systems of philosophy) was not new, but it became confused with a type of revolutionary anarchism.
15 **Phoneme**.
16 **Litotes**.
17 **Samuel Johnson** (1709–84) in his *Dictionary*. He also defines a pension as 'an allowance made to anyone without an equivalent. In England it is generally understood to mean pay given to a state hireling for treason to his country.' He was later lampooned when he received a pension himself!
18 **Being buried alive** (from Greek *taphos*, a grave).
19 **Dollar**. The mint at St Joachimsthal produced silver coins named *joachimsthalers*, later shortened to '*thalers*'; 'dollar' is a corruption of this word.
20 **Ambrose Bierce** (1842–*c* 1914). *The Devil's Dictionary* was first published in 1906 as the *Cynic's Word Book*.

General Knowledge

1 After which French town is denim named?

2 According to the New Testament, on which hill was Jesus praying and meditating when Judas Iscariot identified him to the authorities?

3 The rock garden plant, kidney vetch (*Anthyllis vulneraria*), is known familiarly as 'ladies' fingers'; which vegetable is also known by that name?

4 At the age of 18 years and 59 days, Michael Owen became the youngest international footballer to play for England in the twentieth century; who was the previous record-holder?

5 In which London Square are there statues of William Shakespeare and Charlie Chaplin?

6 Which English town, where mineral springs were discovered in about 1618, gave its name to the more familiar term for hydrated magnesium sulphate?

7 Which 1985–7 BBC television quiz programme was presented by Angela Rippon?

8 Which pioneer of Futurism shocked society with his painting *Nude Descending a Staircase* in 1912?

9 Which ancient Phoenician city was captured and destroyed by the Romans in 146 BC at the end of the Third Punic War?

10 What was the name of the dog featured on record labels listening to 'His Master's Voice'?

11 What is a calumet?

12 Which detective-story writer created the amateur detective Albert Campion?

13 The title of which 1966 film, directed by François Truffaut, based on a 1953 novel of the same title by Ray Bradbury, is the temperature at which books are reduced to ashes?

14 What was the name of the London coffee house where the speculators and dealers who eventually formed the Stock Exchange used to meet?

15 Which British sporting journalist published *Boxiana; or Sketches of Ancient and Modern Pugilism* in 1812–13?

16 In which Spanish city is the Great Mosque known as La Mezquita, which was begun in the eighth century and is now a Christian cathedral?

17 What is the word for a short melodic phrase repeated throughout a musical composition?

18 In warfare, for what does the acronym THAAD stand?

19 Graves' disease is caused by excessive production of what?

20 In a poem entitled *These Words*, who described words as 'the radium of thought,/The close-packed atoms of our human story'?

General Knowledge Answers

1 **Nîmes**. The fabric was originally named *serge de Nîmes*.

2 **The Mount of Olives (Olivet)**, a limestone ridge (834 metres) to the east of Jerusalem. Its name comes from the grove of olive trees which used to grow on its western flank. On the three summits of the ridge are the Hebrew University of Jerusalem, the village at-Tur (previously Olivet) and a small mosque.

3 **Okra** (*Hibiscus esculentus*).

4 **Duncan Edwards**, who died in the Munich air crash in 1958 along with seven other Manchester United players. He first played for England against Scotland at Wembley in 1955 at the age of 18 years and 183 days (England won 7–2). Michael Owen's international debut was in a match which England lost 2–0 to Chile at Wembley in February 1998.

5 **Leicester Square**.

6 **Epsom** (Epsom salts). The town became a popular spa, and Thomas Shadwell wrote a comedy, *Epsom Wells* (1672), which portrayed the licentious goings-on there.

7 *Masterteam*.

8 **Marcel Duchamp** (1887–1968).

9 **Carthage** (now in Tunisia).

10 **Nipper** (1884–95). When the owner of Nipper, Mark Barraud, died, his brother Francis, a painter, took the dog home to Liverpool. There Nipper discovered the Phonograph, a cylinder recording and playing machine, and Francis Barraud painted a picture of Nipper looking into the trumpet in a puzzled way (*Dog looking at and listening to a Phonograph*). He eventually sold it, renamed *His Master's Voice*, in 1899, to The Gramophone Company, which adopted the name His Master's Voice. The company has since been taken over by EMI and the original painting is at its headquarters in London.

11 **A pipe smoked by Native North Americans** (the 'pipe of peace'). The stem is made from a reed about 76 centimetres long and the bowl from red marble.

12 **Margery Allingham** (1904–66).

13 *Fahrenheit 451*, about a futuristic society where books are outlawed.

14 **Jonathan's** in Change Alley. In 1773 the brokers who used to meet there acquired premises in Sweeting's Alley which came to be known as the Stock Exchange coffee house. The Stock Exchange in Capel Court was opened in 1802, financed by money they raised.

15 **Pierce Egan** (1772–1849).

16 **Cordoba**. The original mosque was built by the first Umayyad ruler of Spain, `Abd ar-Rahman I (731–88). It was converted to a cathedral in 1236.

17 *Ostinato* (obstinate). A single-pitch ostinato can be heard in the 'Scarbo' movement in Ravel's piano work *Gaspard de la nuit* (1908).

18 **Theatre High Altitude Area Defence** (Missile).

19 **Thyroid hormone**. It is a common form of hyperthyroidism (thyrotoxicosis), named after the Irish physician Robert James Graves (1796–1853), who was among the first to describe it.

20 **Richard Church** (1893–1972).

X is for **Xmas**

1 Which two pop musicians wrote *Do They know It's Christmas?* in 1984?

2 What is the birthstone of anyone born in December?

3 Which Irving Berlin musical featured a dream of a white Christmas?

4 According to legend, Joseph of Arimathea thrust his staff into the earth on Weary-All Hill, where it took root and grew into a tree (*Crataegus oxyacantha*) which blossoms at Christmas time. What is its popular name?

5 Who wrote the 1954 short story *A Child's Christmas in Wales* (a reminiscence of all his childhood Christmases)?

6 Which eleven-year-old chorister from St Paul's Cathedral Choir School recorded the 1996 album *The Choirboy's Christmas*?

7 What are used as candle-holders at Christingle services?

8 Where did the domesticated turkey, traditionally eaten at Christmas, originate?

9 Who wrote the words of the Christmas carol whose first line is 'In the bleak midwinter'?

10 Which biblical event is commemorated by Twelfth Night?

11 How many gifts did 'My True Love send to me' during the Twelve Days of Christmas?

12 In the much-parodied long narrative *In the Workhouse: Christmas Day*, written in 1879 by George R. Sims, what are the two lines which come after these:

> *It is Christmas Day in the Workhouse,*
> *And the cold bare walls are bright*
> *With garlands of green and holly,*
> *And the place is a pleasant sight;*
> *For with clean-washed hands and faces,*
> *In a long and hungry line,*

13 By which familiar names are olibanum and opopanax known?

14 Which saint, whose feast-day is 13 December, is honoured in Sweden as 'Queen of the Light'?

15 Which playwright, who used the pen-name Roland Allen, wrote the 1962 play *Christmas v. Mastermind* – the first to be published under his own name?

16 According to Louisa May Alcott, Christmas wouldn't be Christmas without – what?

17 Which old English carol was sung before Prince Henry at St John's College, Oxford, at Christmas in 1607?

18 Which comedian said, 'Santa Claus had the right idea – visit people only once a year'?

19 Why is Parliament sometimes referred to as 'St Stephen's'?

20 Who were the publishers of the first commercial Christmas card in Britain, in 1846?

1 **Bob Geldof** and **Midge Ure**. Many pop stars performed on the recording, and recording, printing and distribution companies provided their services free of charge.

2 **Turquoise** or **zircon**.

3 **Holiday Inn** (*I'm Dreaming of a White Christmas*, 1942).

4 **The Glastonbury Thorn**.

5 **Dylan Thomas** (1914–53).

6 **Anthony Way**. He made his name in the 1994 BBC television series *The Choir*, based on the 1988 novel of the same title by Joanna Trollope.

7 **Oranges**. Each part of the 'Christingle' is a symbol: orange (the world), candle (Christ, the 'light of the world'), four cocktail sticks pushed into the orange and holding raisins (God's love from the four corners of the world) and a red ribbon tied round the orange (the death and resurrection of Christ).

8 **The United States**. The name 'turkey' is a misnomer; it was originally given to an African guinea-fowl imported to Europe through Turkey, because it was thought to have come from Turkey.

9 **Christina Rossetti** (1875). It was originally a poem entitled *Mid-Winter*.

10 **The visit of the three Magi to the infant Jesus**. Twelfth Night is the eve of the twelfth day after Christmas, Epiphany.

11 **364**. On the first of the twelve days one gift was sent (a partridge in a pear tree); on the second day two of another gift were sent (turtle doves) *plus* the gift from the previous day; on the third day three of another gift (French hens) were sent *plus* the gifts from the previous days and so on.

12 *The paupers sit at the tables,*
  For this is the hour they dine.

13 **Frankincense and myrrh**.

14 **St Lucia** or **Lucy**, a virgin martyr who died at Syracuse in the Diocletian persecutions in 304.

15 **Alan Ayckbourn** (b 1939). *Christmas v. Mastermind* was a play for children, first performed at the Victoria Theatre, Stoke-on-Trent, of which Alan Ayckbourn became a founding member and Associate Director.

16 **Presents**, in *Little Women* (1868), chapter 1.

17 **Boar's Head Carol**. The boar's head was carried in, accompanied by a fanfare of trumpets and the singing of the carol, which begins:
  The boar is dead
  So, here is his head;
  What man could have done more
  Than his head off to strike,
  Meleager like
  And bring it as I do before?

18 **Victor Borge** (b 1909).

19 **The House of Commons used to sit in the Chapel of St Stephen** in the Palace of Westminster from about 1550 until a fire in 1834 destroyed the palace except for Westminster Hall, the Jewel Tower, the cloisters, and the crypt of St Stephen's Chapel. The chapel is commemorated by St Stephen's Tower which houses Big Ben in the new Houses of Parliament.

20 **Sir Henry Cole & J. C. Horsley**. Temperance supporters condemned it because it showed a family group cheerfully drinking wine.

General Knowledge

1 Christmas Island was 'discovered' in 1615 by a member of the British East India Company, and named on Christmas Day, 1643. To which country's administration does it belong?

2 For which congenital disability was 'spastic' the common name?

3 In the 1982 children's book *The BFG* by Roald Dahl, for what does 'BFG' stand?

4 In which sport is the Thomas Cup contested?

5 What is the common name for the evergreen plant *Ilex aquifolium*?

6 Which motorway is described by the Highway Authority of England and Wales as 'the St Albans spur'?

7 In classical mythology, who was the Muse of History?

8 Who designed the Marble Arch in London?

9 Of which novel is this the opening sentence: 'It is a truth universally acknowledged, that a single man in possession of a good fortune must be in want of a wife'?

10 In March 1876, which American inventor did Alexander Graham Bell beat in the race to patent the telephone (or 'autograph telegraph')?

11 What collective term, derived from the Latin word for 'swaddling clothes', describes books printed before 1500?

12 Which Jamaican-born 'doctress' and herbalist set up the 'British Hotel' near Sebastopol during the Crimean War?

13 Who won the marathon in the first modern Olympic Games in 1896?

14 The name of which son of Zeus and a nymph has been given to a locking case for bottles of spirits?

15 Some of the survivors from which ship were rescued by Grace Darling and her father in September 1838?

16 What is the name of the first woman in the world to be elected a Head of State in 1980?

17 In the P. G. Wodehouse novels, what was Jeeves's Christian name?

18 Whose portrait is on the reverse side of current (2000) Bank of England £50 notes?

19 Whose garter is alleged to have inspired the foundation of the Most Noble Order of the Garter in 1348?

20 Which Renaissance artist painted *Mystic Nativity* (1500) which is now in the National Gallery, London?

General Knowledge　　　　　　　　　Answers

1 Australia.
2 Cerebral palsy.
3 'Big Friendly Giant'.
4 Badminton.
5 English holly.
6 M10.
7 **Clio**. The Nine Muses were the daughters of Zeus and Mnemosyne (the personification of Memory). The other Muses are Calliope (heroic or epic poetry), Erato (lyric and love poetry), Euterpe (music), Melpomene (tragedy), Polyhymnia (sacred poetry or mime), Terpsichore (dancing and choral song), Thalia (comedy) and Urania (astronomy).
8 **John Nash** (1752–1835).
9 *Pride and Prejudice* by Jane Austen (1813).
10 **Elisha Gray** (1835–1901). He filed a caveat on Bell's patent on the same day (7 March) but lost the patent rights after a long legal battle in the US Supreme Court. He later formed the Western Electric Company.
11 **Incunabula**.
12 **Mary Seacole** (1805–1881).
13 **Spyridon Louis**.
14 **Tantalus**. He offended the gods and, as punishment, was plunged up to the chin in a river of Hades. There was a tree whose clusters of fruit hung just out of reach, and the waters of the river receded whenever he tried to drink. A tantalus displays bottles of spirits which cannot be opened without the key.
15 **The *Forfarshire***. The *Forfarshire* was one of the first British paddle steamers, and sailed from Hull to Dundee. It was wrecked on the Big Harcar Rock, in the Farne Islands, on the morning of 8 September.
16 **Vigdís Finnbogadóttir** (b 1930). She was elected President of Iceland in 1980, and retired in 1996. The *second* woman to be elected a Head of State was Mary Robinson, who was President of Ireland from 1990 to 1997.
17 **Reginald**. When this question was used on *Mastermind* in the 1977 series, in a specialised set on the 'Life and Works of P. G. Wodehouse', I was accused of blasphemy by an outraged viewer who thought I had asked 'What was *Jesus'* Christian name?'!
18 **Sir John Houblon** (1632–1712), a London merchant, and the first Governor of the Bank of England, from 1694 to 1697.
19 **The Countess of Salisbury**. After watching a grand tournament at Windsor, King Edward III was inspired to form his own Round Table of knights. The story has it that at a celebration ball after the Siege of Calais, the Countess of Salisbury dropped her blue garter. The king picked it up and bound it below his left knee, which gave rise to much sniggering from his knowing courtiers; whereupon the king rebuked them with the immortal words: *Honi soit qui mal y pense* – 'Shame on whoever thinks evil of this'.
20 **Sandro Botticelli** (Alessandro Filipepi, 1445–1510). The painting depicts angels and men embracing, olive branches and seven devils fleeing underground. A Greek inscription on it explains the imagery by reference to the predictions of the New Testament Book of Revelation: the return of Christ to Earth amidst a series of catastrophes heralding the end of the world, the Last Judgement and the reconciliation of Christians with God.

Y is for Yorkshire

1 What did the Romans name their settlement at York?

2 What are the three main ingredients of Yorkshire pudding?

3 Which Yorkshire breed of dog is the largest of the terriers and was originally known as the 'Waterside' or 'Wharfedale' Terrier?

4 Sheffield is situated at the confluence of the Don and which other river?

5 Which Yorkshire cricketer scored his hundredth century at Headingley in 1977 in a Test match against Australia?

6 In which Civil War battle, which took place seven miles west of York on 2 July 1644, did Cromwell's army defeat that of Prince Rupert?

7 Which Quaker chocolate manufacturer from York founded three charitable trusts which support research and development in the fields of housing, social care and social policy?

8 What is the name of the home ground of York City FC?

9 The remains of which twelfth-century Cistercian abbey stand just outside Ripon in North Yorkshire?

10 Who founded the Viking settlement of York (Jórvík) in 875–6?

11 In Yorkshire dialect, what does 'to caffle' mean?

12 Which notorious citizen of York was born in Stonegate, baptised at the nearby church of St Michael-le-Belfrey in 1570 and hanged in London in 1606?

13 With which football club did the Yorkshire County Cricket Club share its ground from 1855 to 1973?

14 Which regiment, formed in 1688, has its headquarters and museum in Richmond, North Yorkshire?

15 At which castle near Leyburn, built in 1399, was Mary Queen of Scots held captive for six months in 1568–9?

16 In 1138 Thurstan, Archbishop of York, led an army which defeated which Scottish king at the Battle of the Standard, just outside Northallerton?

17 In 1699 which two architects designed Castle Howard, the location of the 1981 ITV series *Brideshead Revisited*?

18 Who was the leader of the 'Pilgrimage of Grace', the Yorkshire uprising in 1536 provoked by the Dissolution of the Monasteries?

19 Who was the first Duke of York, the founder of the House of York?

20 What was the name of the Icelandic warrior-poet who visited the court of the Norse King of York, Eirík Blood-Axe, in 948, and only escaped with his life by composing in his honour a heroic eulogy known as the 'Head Ransom'?

Y is for Yorkshire   Answers

1 **Eboracum**. The Romans occupied the site from AD 71 to 400.

2 **Milk, flour and eggs**.

3 **Airedale Terrier**.

4 **Sheaf**, from which it takes its name.

5 **Geoffrey Boycott** (b 1940). He went on to make 191. In all, he scored 151 centuries in first-class cricket.

6 **Marston Moor**.

7 **Joseph Rowntree** (1836–1925). The Joseph Rowntree Foundation includes the Joseph Rowntree Model Village, Charitable and Reform Trusts, each of which operates independently.

8 **Bootham Crescent**.

9 **Fountains Abbey**.

10 **Hálfdan**, son of Ragnar Loðbrók (Hairy-Breeks).

11 **To hesitate**.

12 **Guy Fawkes**. There is a plaque on the bookshop which occupies the site of the house in which Guy Fawkes was born in Stonegate.

13 **Sheffield United** (at Bramall Lane). Since 1973 Yorkshire have played at Headingley, Leeds.

14 **The Green Howards**. The headquarters are in the tower of Holy Trinity church in the Market Place. The name 'Green Howard' was originally a nickname from the colour of the facings on the scarlet uniform of the regiment, and was first used in 1744 to distinguish between two regiments with colonels named Howard; the other one was known as the 'Buffs'.

15 **Bolton Castle**. The castle was built in 1378–99 by Richard Scrope (Lord Chancellor of England from 1378 to 1380 and 1381 to 1382). When Mary Queen of Scots arrived in England from Scotland in 1568, she landed at Workington, and travelled to Carlisle. Sir Henry Scrope, 9th Lord Scrope of Bolton (Captain of Carlisle) was at court at the time, but hurried north with Sir Francis Knollys (Treasurer of Elizabeth of England's household) to take charge of her; they took her to Bolton Castle on 16 July.

16 **David I** (c 1080–1153). The battle got its name from the standard, a tall mast with the banners of the bishops of Durham, Ripon and York fixed to its top and mounted on a four-wheeled cart, which was trundled on to the battlefield.

17 **John Vanbrugh** and **Nicholas Hawksmoor**, commissioned by Charles, 3rd Earl of Carlisle (1669–1738).

18 **Robert Aske** (c 1501–37). After capturing York the rebels disbanded in the belief that they would be pardoned. However, 200 were executed, including Aske himself, who was hanged, drawn and quartered in York.

19 **Edmund of Langley** (1341–1402), the fifth son of Edward III. He had previously been made Earl of Cambridge (1362).

20 **Egil Skallagrímsson** (c 910–90). He is the eponymous hero of one of the greatest of the Icelandic sagas, *Egil's Saga*, written in the 1230s by the saga-historian and statesman Snorri Sturluson, author of *Heimskringla* (The History of the Kings of Norway).

General Knowledge

1 Which town in West Yorkshire has given its name to a type of liquorice lozenge made there since the sixteenth century and bearing the impression of a castle?

2 By what name is Mrs Anne Laurence better known?

3 In a 1995 poll conducted by the BBC radio programme *The Bookworm*, which poem did the people of the United Kingdom choose as their favourite?

4 To which modern country did the Roman province of Lusitania roughly correspond?

5 Which football team won the European Champions Cup three times in succession from 1974?

6 Which American film actor played himself in the 1955 war film biography *To Hell And Back*?

7 In the symbols used on clothing labels, what is meant by a crossed-out triangle?

8 What was the name of the spacecraft in which Yuri Gagarin of the USSR made the first human space flight on 12 April 1961?

9 The title of which 1972–3 BBC2 series, set around a taverna in a holiday resort in Crete frequented by British expatriates, refers to the travellers in Homer's *Odyssey* who ate a plant which made them forget their families and lose all desire to go home?

10 Which Czech village was destroyed on 10 June 1942 by the Nazis in retaliation for the assassination of Reinhard Heydrich, deputy leader of the SS?

11 The name of which 1960s rock group was also the place where monks in procession to St Paul's Cathedral on Corpus Christi day finished their paternoster?

12 On the ruins of which Aztec city was Mexico City founded?

13 If an animal is an operculate, what physical characteristic does it have?

14 Who was the sculptor of *Newton* (1995), on the piazza of the new British Library at St Pancras, London?

15 Which London club was formed in 1700 by Whigs who dined at the house of the pastry cook Christopher Cat?

16 Which English artillery officer gave his name to a shell, originally used in the First World War, which contained small shot and an explosive charge to scatter the shot as well as fragments of the shell casing?

17 Which day of the year used to be known jocularly as St Distaff's Day?

18 In which molten metal is 'float glass' usually floated?

19 Which early-seventeenth-century British surgeon and teacher of anatomy and surgery wrote *Anatomy of the Human Body* and *Osteographia*, both of which were used as texts by anatomy students for nearly a century?

20 Who was the alleged witch, born in 1488 in a cave close to the mysterious 'Petrifying Well' near Knaresborough, North Yorkshire, who predicted events such as the Great Fire of London and the defeat of the Spanish Armada?

General Knowledge   Answers

1 **Pontefract** (Pontefract cakes).

2 **The Princess Royal** (b 1950). In 1992 she married Timothy Laurence (b 1955).

3 *If* (1910) by Rudyard Kipling (1865–1936).

4 **Portugal**. The name comes from the people who lived there, the Lusitani.

5 **Bayern Munich**. In the finals they beat Atletico Madrid 4–0 in 1974 in a replay after a 0–0 draw, Leeds United 2–0 in 1975 and St Etienne 1–0 in 1976.

6 **Audie Murphy** (the most decorated GI in the Second World War).

7 **Do not use bleach**.

8 **Vostok 1**. The flight lasted 1 hour and 48 minutes.

9 *The Lotus Eaters*. The lotus-eaters (*Lotophagi*) ate the fruit of the lotus tree; this made them want only to live in idleness in Lotus-land.

10 **Lidice**. In 1947 a new village was created nearby. A museum, a monument and an international rose garden mark the site of the original village.

11 **Amen Corner**. The processions began in Paternoster Row with the Lord's Prayer, which ended as the monks reached the end of the Row, where they said 'Amen'. (Amen Corner was destroyed in an air raid in 1940.)

12 **Tenochtitlán**, which began as a settlement on islands in Lake Texcoco, and was named after the legendary patriarch Tenoch, whose name was also given to the Aztecs themselves (Tenochca). The Aztecs were also known as Mexica, which gave rise to the name of the modern city and the country.

13 **Gills**.

14 **Eduardo Paolozzi** (b 1924). The statue was inspired by William Blake's 1795 print *Newton*.

15 **The Kit-Cat Club**. The Club's secretary was the publisher Jacob Tonson (1656–1737), at whose house, Barn Elms, the Club later began to meet. Members included William Congreve, Sir John Vanbrugh, the Duke of Somerset and Sir Robert Walpole. A threequarter-length portrait came to be known as a 'kit-cat' from those painted by Sir Godfrey Kneller of the Club's members. Now in the National Portrait Gallery, London, they measure 91 × 71 centimetres – they all fitted into Tonson's dining room.

16 **Henry Shrapnel** (1761–1842). The shell had a time-fuse to set off the explosive charge towards the end of its flight, near to the opposing troops. During the Second World War it was found that a more powerful charge could break up the iron casing of the shell so effectively that it was not necessary to fill it with shot.

17 **7 January**, the day after Twelfth Night: so called because it was the day when women returned to their daily occupations after the Christmas revelries.

18 **Tin**. A thin layer of glass is poured straight from the furnace on to the surface of a bath of molten tin, on which it floats while cooling. The result is a perfect finish which avoids the need to grind plate glass. The process was invented by Sir Alastair Pilkington (1920–95).

19 **William Cheselden** (1688–1752).

20 **Mother Shipton** (née Ursula Sontheil), who even forecast her own death in 1561. Magical powers were attributed to her because objects left in the waters of the Petrifying Well appeared to turn to stone; in fact, the water there has a high concentration of dissolved minerals which are deposited on the objects.

Z is for Zoology

1 The name of which breed of dog means 'badger dog' in German?
2 Which is the smallest mammal in the world?
3 What kind of animal was featured in Gavin Maxwell's 1960 best-seller, *A Ring of Bright Water*, which was made into a 1969 film starring Virginia McKenna and Bill Travers?
4 What kind of animal is a quagga?
5 Which collective term is used to refer to animals which feed on the remains of dead animals or plants?
6 Which Australian bird is known as the 'laughing jackass'?
7 Which pigment is obtained from cuttlefish and squid?
8 How does a female chameleon signal her readiness for mating?
9 What physical characteristic do pinnipeds have?
10 What name is given to a young salmon which has been to the sea only once?
11 What name is given to a larva of the salamander which never develops fully because of a hormone deficiency, although it can breed?
12 The name of which Russian explorer was given to the wild horse which he discovered in western Mongolia in the late 1870s and which was the last remaining species of wild horse to survive into the twentieth century?
13 What kind of animal is a boomslang?
14 Which woodland bird performs a 'roding' display flight in the breeding season?'
15 What characterises stags which are referred to as 'hummels'?
16 The larva of which insect is the rat-tailed maggot?
17 Which wading bird, a member of the sandpiper family, has the Latin name *Calidris canutus*?
18 Which two scientists led the team at the Roslin Institute in Edinburgh which cloned Dolly the sheep in February 1997?
19 Which member of the *anura* order of amphibians was once used in pregnancy tests?
20 After which marine animal is L'Anse aux Meadows in Newfoundland named?

Z is for Zoology

1 **Dachshund**. It was used in Germany as a hunting dog which could pursue the prey (particularly the badger) into its burrow.

2 **The pygmy shrew**. Savi's pygmy shrew (*Suncus etruscus*); some have been known to weigh only two grams.

3 **Otter**. The book describes his life with two pet otters in his cottage in the west Highlands of Scotland. The title is from a poem by Kathleen Raine.

4 **Zebra**. It is also known as Burchell's zebra, or bonte quagga (*Equus quagga*).

5 **Detrivore**.

6 **Kookaburra** (*Dacelo gigas*). It is a member of the kingfisher family and is so named because its call sounds like fiendish laughter. It has also been named 'the bushman's clock', as it is heard very early in the morning and just after sunset.

7 **Sepia**. This dark brown liquid is excreted from the ink sac, near the anus, to create a 'smoke screen' which helps the creature to escape from predators.

8 **She changes her colour and/or pattern**; she changes again when she has had enough. A chameleon's changes in colour are affected by factors such as light and temperature and by emotions, but not, as is commonly supposed, by the colour of the animal's surroundings (for camouflage).

9 **Fins for feet**: for example, seals and walruses.

10 **Grilse**. The stages of a salmon's life are i) egg, ii) alevin (yolk sac), iii) fry, which move down the river toward the sea, iv) parr, v) smolt, which adjust to the salt water conditions near the sea, vi) grilse, and vii) kelt (after it has spawned).

11 **Axolotl**. The name axolotl is also given to any fully grown larva of the genus *Ambystoma* which has not yet lost its external gills.

12 **Nikolai Przhevalski** (1839–88). It was named Przhevalski's horse (*Equus caballus przhevalskii*).

13 **Snake**. It is found in savannas throughout sub-Saharan Africa where it lies in wait in a tree for chameleons or birds. Its venom is fatal to humans; minuscule amounts cause haemorrhages.

14 **Woodcock**. At dusk the male makes croaking sounds as it flies in a low path over the treetops. It also makes spiralling flights of up to 60–90 metres in height, followed by a fluttering drop back to the starting point, accompanied by a sweet whistling. This is repeated for about 30 minutes.

15 **They have no antlers**. The term is also used for cattle without horns.

16 **Hoverfly**. A species of hoverfly named the drone fly (*Eristalis tenax*) lays its eggs in drains and polluted water. The larva is aquatic; the 'rat-tail' is a snorkel-like tube which enables it to get air from above the surface.

17 **Knot**. Knots can be recognised by their feeding habits: they stand almost body-to-body on the shore, and move along the ground as if in one piece.

18 **Ian Wilmut** and **Keith Campbell**.

19 **Clawed toad** (*Xenopus laevis*). It was found that young female South African claw-toed tree toads laid eggs when injected with minute quantities of a human hormone found in the urine of pregnant women.

20 **Jellyfish**. It is a corruption of the French *L'Anse aux Méduses* (Cove of Jellyfish). During excavations from 1961 to 1968 the Norwegian archaeologists Helge and Anne Stine Ingstad discovered an eleventh-century Norse settlement there.

General Knowledge

1 To which group of animals do the cayman and the gavial belong?
2 Which actress was covered in gold paint in the 1964 James Bond film *Goldfinger*?
3 In which book of the Bible is the Plague of Frogs described?
4 What is the county town of Derbyshire?
5 For which county team did the Bedser twins play first-class cricket?
6 Which pop-singing puppet duo created by Jan and Vlasta Dalibor had their own weekly show on BBC television from 1960 to 1968?
7 Which artist is known for his silk-screen images of Marilyn Monroe?
8 In which country are the mountains which, it is believed, Ptolemy named the Mountains of the Moon?
9 What are the names of the three auditoria of the National Theatre?
10 If a plant is latifoliate, what characteristic does it have?
11 Which aerospace manufacturer produced the *Flying Fortress*, a prototype of which was first flown in 1935?
12 Which book opens with the words 'Of late years, an abundant shower of curates has fallen upon the north of England'?
13 What is the name of the house designed by Richard Norman Shaw for the first Lord Armstrong between 1870–85 – the first in the world to have lights powered by hydro-electricity?
14 Which English engineer developed a safety lamp for miners at the same time as Humphrey Davy?
15 Which city in Sudan, the scene of a battle in 1898, was the residence of the Mahdi?
16 In which geographical feature is a caldera found?
17 Who was the co-founder (with Herbert Gruhl) of the German Green party in 1979 and became one of the best-known Green MPs in the world?
18 Which English poet and anthologist founded the *Poetry Review* in 1912 and the Poetry Bookshop in London in 1913?
19 Whose law states that equal volumes of gas contain equal numbers of molecules when at the same temperature and pressure?
20 What was the name of the legendary Norwegian sea-monster which 'awoke' in the title of the 1953 science-fiction novel by John Wyndham?

General Knowledge Answers

1 **Crocodile**. The cayman is found in South America and the gavial in northern India.

2 **Shirley Eaton**.

3 *Exodus*: 'So Aaron stretched out his hand over the waters of Egypt; and the frogs came up and covered the land of Egypt'. (*Exodus* 8: 6)

4 **Matlock**, on the banks of the River Derwent.

5 **Surrey**. Both Eric and Sir Alec Bedser (b 1919) were bowlers for the county team; Alec also bowled for England.

6 **Pinky and Perky**.

7 **Andy Warhol** (Andrew Warhola, 1926–87).

8 **Uganda** (Ruwenzori Range). The highest, Margherita Peak, rises to 5,119 metres.

9 **Cottesloe, Lyttelton and Olivier**.

10 **Broad leaves**.

11 **Boeing**: the *B-17 Flying Fortress* – so named because of the thirteen 0.50-calibre machine-guns which bristled from it in all directions. During the Second World War it was used by US forces for high-level daylight bombing over Europe.

12 *Shirley* (1849), by Charlotte Brontë (1816–55), who married her father's curate, the Reverend Arthur Bell Nicholls.

13 **Cragside**, near Rothbury in Northumberland. The water with which the electricity is generated is stored in artificial lakes in the grounds of the house.

14 **George Stephenson** (1781–1848), who named his lamp 'the Geordie'. The lamps were developed independently in 1815. In 1813 the Irish physician William Clanny had also made a safety lamp for use in coal mines, and before that the German naturalist Alexander Von Humboldt had invented one in the 1790s.

15 **Omdurman**. The title 'Mahdi' means, in Arabic, 'Guided One' and the holder of it is regarded as a 'restorer of the faith' (Islam). Major-General (later Lord) Herbert Kitchener led the victorious British forces in the Battle of Omdurman, gaining this territory from Abh Allah and the Mahdists and establishing British dominance in Sudan.

16 **A volcano**. It is a crater formed when the summit cone of a volcano collapses.

17 **Petra Kelly** (1947–92).

18 **Harold Monro** (1879–1932), author of poems such as *Milk for the Cat* (1914), *Strange Meetings* (1917) and *Bitter Sanctuary* (1933).

19 **Avogadro** (Amedeo Carlo Avogadro of Turin, 1776–1856). Avogadro proposed the law in 1811, but it was not generally accepted until after 1858, when the Italian chemist Stanislao Cannizzaro set out a logical system of chemistry based on it.

20 **The Kraken** (*The Kraken Wakes*, which was published in the USA as *Out of the Deeps*).

A is for Architecture Questions

1 In which city is the Dome of the Rock mosque?
2 What is the name of the classical rotunda which was built as a pagan temple in Rome and is now a Christian place of worship?
3 Which American architect designed the house named 'Falling Water' which was built in 1936–7 in Bear Run, Pennsylvania?
4 Which two architects designed the present Houses of Parliament?
5 What name was given to the extension to the Louvre, designed by Ieoh Ming Pei and built in 1983–93?
6 In church architecture what name is given to a semi-circular recess beyond the chancel, containing the altar?
7 What is the name of the huge three-tiered Roman aqueduct built in AD 14 between Uzès and Nîmes in France?
8 Which British architect designed the 1995–9 alterations to the Reichstag (the German Parliament) in Berlin, for which he was awarded the Pritzer Architecture Prize?
9 What are voussoirs?
10 Which architect designed the dome of the cathedral of Santa Maria del Fiore in Florence, which was built between 1418 and 1436?
11 What name is given to the wall of a mosque which faces Makkah (Mecca)?
12 Which bridge in England, designed by Robert Adam and built in 1769–74, was inspired by the Ponte Vecchio in Florence (1345)?
13 Where in Scotland is there a replica of the Colosseum of Rome known as McCaig's Tower?
14 Which graduate of Oxford University designed the Sheldonian Theatre in Oxford in 1662, which was named after Bishop Gilbert Sheldon of London, a former Warden of All Souls?
15 Which school of modern architecture in Germany was closed by the Nazis in 1933?
16 On the bank of which river is the Taj Mahal situated?
17 In 1929 which prestigious New York hotel was demolished to make way for the Empire State Building, designed by Shreve, Lamb and Harmon Associates and built in 1931?
18 Who was the Spanish architect of the new Scottish Parliament at Holyrood in Edinburgh?
19 Which structure in Brussels, built for the World Exposition of 1958, consists of nine spheres, linked by struts, to represent the atomic structure of iron magnified 165 billion times?
20 The subject of which 1964 novel by William Golding is the building of a medieval cathedral?

A is for Architecture Answers

1 **Jerusalem**. It was built in 688–92.

2 **The Pantheon**. It was begun in 27 BC; it is thought to have been a classical Roman temple – rectangular with a gabled roof supported by a colonnade on all sides. It was completely rebuilt by Hadrian between AD 118 and 128 and in 609 it was dedicated as the Church of the Santa Maria Rotonda, or ad Martyres, which it remains.

3 **Frank Lloyd Wright** (1869–1959). 'Falling Water' was built directly over a waterfall and has bare natural rock as a floor surface in the living room.

4 **Charles Barry** (1795–1860) and **Nicholas Pugin** (1812–52). The buildings were constructed between 1834 and 1860.

5 **The Pyramid**, a metal and glass construction which allows light into the underground extensions beneath the Napoleon Court and is set into a triangular lake.

6 **Apse**.

7 **Pont du Gard**.

8 **Sir Norman Foster** (b 1935).

9 **Wedge-shaped blocks** (usually of stone) which are used to form an arch.

10 **Filippo Brunelleschi** (1377–1446).

11 **Qibla wall**. Qibla is the direction of Makkah; the qibla wall is marked by a niche named the *mihrab*.

12 **The Pulteney Bridge**, which was built to connect Bath with the new suburb of Bathwick across the River Avon.

13 **Oban**. It was built by a banker named John McCaig between 1897 and 1900 as a memorial to his family and to provide employment for local people. It is known locally as 'McCaig's Folly'.

14 **Christopher Wren** (1632–1723).

15 **Bauhaus** ('Building House'), founded by Walter Gropius in 1919.

16 **Jumna** (or Jamuna).

17 **The Waldorf Astoria**. The new Waldorf Astoria stands in Park Avenue.

18 **Enric Miralles** (1955–2000), in partnership with RMJM Scotland (formerly Robert Matthew, Johnson-Marshall & Partners).

19 **The Atomium**, designed by André Waterkeyn.

20 *The Spire*. The builder is a priest who believes he has been ordered by God to build a spire which defies all reasonable calculations and measurements.

General Knowledge

1 Which Italian-style resort on the coast of Gwynedd in Wales was designed in 1925 by Clough Williams-Ellis?

2 What is the name of the Norwegian Parliament?

3 Which cocktail is a mixture of tequila, lime juice and an orange-flavoured liqueur, served in a glass rimmed with salt?

4 What is the name of the hot south wind which blows on to the European coast of the Mediterranean?

5 Which television series began as a series of six adaptations of *The Adventures of a Black Bag* by A. J. Cronin?

6 In which English city did the new L. S. Lowry Arts Centre open in April 2000?

7 Which First World War German fighter ace gave his name to an aerial turning manoeuvre – a half-loop followed by a half-roll?

8 *The Bell Jar* (1963) was the only novel of which American poet?

9 Which English scientist designed computers in the 1820 and 1830s named the 'Difference Engine' and the 'Analytical Engine'?

10 Who made his debut as a film writer and director with the 1992 film *Reservoir Dogs*, in which he also acted?

11 Which common wild flower is known in Scotland as Stinking Willie?

12 Which 1954 play by Brendan Behan was about life in an Irish prison on the eve of an execution?

13 What was the term for a printer's errand-boy and a boy who took the printed sheets off the press?

14 Who was the father of Cleopatra's first child, born in 44 BC?

15 What kind of animal is a wapiti?

16 Which 1878 music-hall song by G. W. Hunt, popularised by the singer 'The Great Macdermott' (Gilbert Farrell), gave rise to the term 'jingoism' for bellicose patriotism?

17 Which principle, first enunciated by the German physicist Werner Heisenberg in 1927, attempts to define unpredictability – that the behaviour of individual components cannot be forecast by reference to known laws?

18 In 1909 Edward VII was the first reigning British monarch to own a Derby winner; what was the name of the horse?

19 In culinary terms, what is zabouska?

20 Which architect designed the Crystal Palace for the Great Exhibition of 1851?

General Knowledge   Answers

1 **Portmeirion**, which was the setting for the 1967–8 ITV series *The Prisoner*.

2 **Storting**, constituted at Eidsvoll in 1814. It evolved from the ancient Altings (general assemblies) in different districts around the country. These were combined between 1263 and 1280 and remained in force until Frederik III, king of the Danish-Norwegian union, introduced absolute monarchy in 1660.

3 **Margarita**.

4 **Sirocco**, which comes from North Africa as a dry wind and picks up moisture as it crosses the Mediterranean. It brings rain and fog.

5 *Dr Finlay's Casebook*. It was so successful during its initial run in 1962 that another six series were commissioned right away. The programme continued until 1969.

6 **Salford**, the home-town of Laurence Stephen Lowry (1887–1976). In 1997 Michael Wilford and Partners (the successor of James Stirling, Michael Wilford and Associates) was commissioned to design and build The Lowry.

7 **Max Immelmann** (1890–1976).

8 **Sylvia Plath** (1931–63).

9 **Charles Babbage** (1791–1871). His designs were forgotten until his unpublished notebooks were discovered in 1937. In 1991 British scientists built 'Difference Engine No. 2', based on these notes.

10 **Quentin Tarantino** (b 1963), who went on to win the Paume d'Or at the Cannes Film Festival and an Academy Award for Best Original Screenplay with his second film, *Pulp Fiction*.

11 **Ragwort** (*Senecto jacobaea*). The plant has an unpleasant smell when crushed or bruised. It was named after William, Duke of Cumberland, known as 'the Butcher' because of the cruelty with which his forces treated the survivors of the Battle of Culloden in 1746. In England the pink garden flower *Dianthus barbatus* was named Sweet William after the same man.

12 *The Quare Fellow*.

13 **Printer's devil**.

14 **Julius Caesar**. Cleopatra named the boy Caesarion (in full, Ptolemy Philopator Philometor Caesar). He was joint ruler of Egypt with Cleopatra from 44 to 30 BC, and was killed by Octavian (later the emperor Augustus) after Cleopatra's death in 30 BC.

15 **Elk** (the American elk, *Cervus canadensis*).

16 *We don't want to fight, but by Jingo if we do!* Jingo became a nickname for supporters of Disraeli's resistance to the Russian advance on Turkey during the Russo-Turkish War (1877–8):

> *We don't want to fight, but by Jingo if we do,*
> *We've got the ships, we've got the men, and got the money too.*
> *We've fought the Bear before, and while we're Britons true,*
> *The Russians shall not have Constantinople.*

17 **The Uncertainty Principle**.

18 **Minoru**. It had already won the 2,000 Guineas but failed to win the Triple Crown when it was well beaten in the St Leger by Bayardo.

19 **A Russian hors-d'œuvre**.

20 **Joseph Paxton** (1801–65).

B is for **Business**

1 Which bread was first marketed in 1887 as 'Smith's patent Germ Bread'?

2 Which soap manufacturers set up a model industrial village on the Wirral in Cheshire which they gave the same name as one of their products?

3 IBM, the name of the computer manufacturing company, is an abbreviation of what?

4 Which German-born British economist wrote *Small is Beautiful* in 1973, in which he argued that the cost of higher living standards brought about by capitalism was a deterioration of culture, and that large industries and large cities would drain the Earth's limited resources?

5 What is the name given to the Paris Stock Exchange?

6 For which occasion were Fortnum & Mason's famous food hampers first produced?

7 Which trade name was devised for the children's construction set first marketed as 'Mechanics Made Easy' in 1901?

8 Which great Scottish economist argued that if everyone pursued his or her self-interest, a 'guiding hand' ensured that the general result was in the best interest of society?

9 Which British prime minister first introduced income tax, in 1798, to pay for the Napoleonic Wars?

10 In the name Tesco, from whose names do 'TES' and 'CO' come?

11 In 1955 which product was the first to be advertised on British television?

12 In 1947 the American research physicist Chester Carlson founded which company to sell the office machine he had invented?

13 Which company was founded in England in 1555 'for the Discovery of Regions, Dominions and Places Unknown'?

14 Which principle propounds the theory that all members of a hierarchy rise to their own levels of incompetence?

15 What are the meanings of the two Danish words from which the trade name Lego originates?

16 Which petroleum company grew from the nineteenth-century London curio shop of Marcus Samuel which began selling barrels of paraffin oil?

17 The investigation into the share-buying and -selling of which Chancellor of the Exchequer became known as the 'Marconi Affair'?

18 Against which tax laws did Richard Cobden and John Bright form a campaign in 1838?

19 According to the 'comparative value' theory of the English economist David Ricardo, to what is the value of any product roughly equal?

20 In 1842 which London writer and publisher started the first privately funded 'circulating library' for which users paid a subscription?

B is for **Business**

1 **Hovis**. The name 'Hovis' was the result of a competition to think up a better name for the bread; the winner (Herbert Grime) devised it from the Latin *hominis vis* ('strength of a man').

2 **Lever Bothers** (William Lever, later Lord Leverhulme, and James Darcy Lever). 'Sunlight' soap was first manufactured in 1885, and Port Sunlight was created in 1888 adjacent to the factory.

3 **International Business Machines**. The company was first registered in 1911 (when it incorporated three smaller companies which made punch-card tabulators and other office products) as the Computer Tabulating Recording Company, and adopted the name IBM in 1924.

4 **Ernst Schumacher** (1911–77).

5 **La Bourse** (in full La Bourse des valeurs).

6 **The Great Exhibition of 1851**.

7 **Meccano**, which was invented by Frank Hornby of Liverpool; he changed the name to Meccano in 1907.

8 **Adam Smith** (1723–90).

9 **William Pitt the Younger** (1759–1806). The tax (6d in the pound, ie 2.5 per cent) was scrapped at the end of the war, but Sir Robert Peel reintroduced it in 1842 at 7d in the pound (less than 3 per cent) for a limited period of three years. It was never discontinued.

10 **The company's founder, John Cohen, and T. E. Stockwell, his tea-supplier**. John Cohen began the business as a market stall in London in the 1920s.

11 **Gibbs toothpaste**.

12 **Xerox**, from the Greek *xēros* (dry). Chester Carlson had first made a xerographic photocopy in 1937, having been exasperated by the unsatisfactory wet systems then in use. The company is now the Rank-Xerox Corporation.

13 **The Muscovy Company**, whose first governor was Sebastian Cabot (1474–1557). It was the first English joint-stock company to retain its capital rather than paying it out after every voyage.

14 **The 'Peter Principle'**, named after the American educationist Laurence J. Peter (1919–90). *The Peter Principle*, written with Raymond Hull, was published in 1969.

15 **Play well** (*leg godt*).

16 **Shell**. In 1878 Marcus Samuel junior (1853–1927) took over his father's shop, which imported Oriental shells, and began to import and sell paraffin oil. He began to operate tankers to the Far East and set up oil depots and eventually oil wells and refineries in Borneo. In 1897 he formed a separate company for his oil interests, which he named Shell Transport and Trading Company.

17 **David Lloyd George**, who, in 1912, had bought shares in the US Marconi company at a preferential rate through the managing director of the company, Godfrey Isaacs. Meanwhile, Marconi UK shares soared in value because of a government contract to build radio stations.

18 **The Corn Laws**, introduced in 1815, which taxed imported wheat and grain. The Corn Laws were repealed in May 1846.

19 **The value of the labour which has gone into producing it**.

20 **George Mudie**, who bought thousands of copies of popular books and sent them to shops which would organise a lending system. Mudie's library continued until 1937.

General Knowledge Questions

1 Which two Oxford graduates founded lastminute.com in April 1998 and hit the headlines with their share flotation in March 2000?

2 Which breed of horse, dating back to 1580, is traditionally ridden at the Spanish Riding School in Vienna?

3 In which Welsh town is the Theatre Clwyd?

4 What is the term for plants which produce shoots one year and flower, produce seeds and die the following year?

5 Jimmy Hill gave up his job as manager of which football club in 1967 to become an ITV sports commentator?

6 Which annual publication first appeared in 1868 'containing an Account of the Astronomical and other Phenomena and A vast Amount of Information respecting the Government, Finances, Population, Commerce and General Statistics of the various Nations of the World'?

7 Which African capital city is named after a nineteenth-century American president?

8 What is the name of the process by which a solid substance changes into a gas without first becoming a liquid?

9 What is the motto of the BBC?

10 What was the original name of President Tito of Yugoslavia?

11 The 'Swing Riots' of 1830–33 concerned which workers?

12 In Greek mythology who took out the family chariot before he had learned to drive it, and came to grief?

13 Which Scottish writer resurrected the caddish Harry Flashman from *Tom Brown's Schooldays* in a series of 'Flashman' novels?

14 Who painted *And When Did You Last See Your Father?*, now in the Walker Art Gallery, Liverpool?

15 What characterises someone referred to as a 'Bob Acres'?

16 Who composed the opera *Mitridate*?

17 Which 'spaghetti Western' was based on the 1961 film *Yojimbo* (The Bodyguard) by the Japanese director Akira Kurosawa?

18 In academia where would one find a scholium (plural scholia)?

19 Which lighthouse designer was swept away in his lighthouse in a storm in November 1703?

20 According to Say's Law of Markets, what does a rise in the supply of goods produce?

General Knowledge Answers

1 **Martha Lane Fox** and **Brent Hoberman**.

2 **Lipizzaner**. The name of the breed comes from the Austrian imperial stud at Lipizza, near Trieste; it has six strains, named from their foundation sires: Pluto, Conversano, Neapolitano, Favory, Maestoso, and Siglavy.

3 **Mold** (*Yr Wyddgrug*).

4 **Biennial** (for example, campanula, primula and wallflower).

5 **Coventry City**.

6 **Whitaker's Almanack**, first compiled by Joseph Whitaker (1820–95).

7 **Monrovia**, capital of Liberia, which was named after James Monroe (1758–1831), the fifth President of the USA (1817–25). Monrovia was founded by the American Colonisation Society in 1822 as a home for liberated slaves.

8 **Sublimation**. Solid ammonium chloride and arsenic 'sublime' when heated.

9 **Nation shall speak unto nation**. It was thought up by teacher Montague John Rendell (1862–1950) in a competition held by the BBC in 1927.

10 **Josip Broz** (1892–1980). Tito had been a partisan leader in the Second World War. He was the first prime minister of the new Yugoslav federal republic in 1945, and then president from 1953; he was made president for life in 1974.

11 **Agricultural labourers**, who were concerned about the new threshing machines which threatened their livelihood. The promoters of the 'Swing Riots' were named 'Captain Swing', who became a legendary character and was immortalised in a poem:

> *The neighbours thought all was not right,*
> *Scarcely one with him ventured to parley,*
> *And Captain Swing came in the night,*
> *And burnt all his beans and barley.*

(from *Ingoldsby Legends: 'Babes in the Wood'* by R. H. Barham)

12 **Phaeton**, who overturned the chariot of his father Helios (the Sun) and caused widespread drought and devastation in Africa. The light, four-wheeled phaeton carriage was named after him.

13 **George MacDonald Fraser** (b 1925).

14 **William Frederick Yeames** (1835–1918). He was one of the seven members of the St John's Wood School, a group of Victorian artists who specialised in 'history' paintings. *And When Did You Last See Your Father?*, which he painted in 1878, depicts a young boy being questioned by Parliamentary officials during the English Civil War.

15 **Cowardice**, after the character of that name in *The Rivals* (1775) by Richard Brinsley Sheridan (1751–1816); his courage always 'oozed out at his fingers' ends'.

16 **Mozart**.

17 *A Fistful of Dollars* (1964).

18 **As a commentary or annotation**, especially on a classical text. The word is derived from the Greek *skholion* (*skholē*: disputation).

19 **Henry Winstanley**, in the first Eddystone lighthouse, a wooden structure which was built in 1696–9 on the Eddystone Rocks, off Plymouth.

20 **An increase in demand for them**. Jean-Baptiste Say (1767–1832) formulated this law in 1803 and, until the Great Depression, it was generally believed to be true. Nowadays economists apply it only to barter economies.

C is for **Cricket**

1 What name was given to the annual cricket match between the best amateurs and best professionals which began in 1806 and was discontinued in 1962 when the distinction between amateurs and professionals was abolished?

2 Why was the first Test of the 1998 series between the West Indies and England discontinued after just over an hour?

3 In 1864 how were the rules of cricket altered with regard to bowling?

4 In which country did cricket teams compete annually for the Plunket Shield from 1906 to 1975?

5 The term 'googly' was coined during the 1903–4 MCC tour of Australia to describe a new kind of delivery by which bowler?

6 Which England cricketer's wife wrote *Another Bloody Tour* in 1987?

7 Where and when was the first-ever Test match played?

8 Who were the two almost invincible Australian batsmen against whom the England team used 'bodyline bowling' during the 1932–3 tour of Australia?

9 What is the maximum width permitted for a cricket bat?

10 In the 1960s which West Indian cricketers were known as 'the three Ws'?

11 Before Len Hutton, who was the first former professional cricketer to captain England, in 1946–7?

12 Which two England cricket captains appeared in the 1939 Alexander Korda film *The Four Feathers*?

13 Which West Indian cricketer wrote the cricket-based novels *Bonaventure* and *The Flashing Blade*?

14 In 1984 which prime minister said that he wanted everyone in his country to play cricket because 'cricket civilises people and creates good gentlemen' and 'I want ours to be a nation of gentlemen'?

15 In 1928 which cricketer (later the High Commissioner for Trinidad and Tobago in Britain) became the first West Indian player to achieve the double of 1,000 runs and 100 wickets in a single season?

16 What was the name of the first women's cricket club (formed in 1887), which survived until 1957?

17 Which scorecard printer at the Oval published *The Young Cricketer's Guide* annually from 1849 to 1866 and *The English Cricketers' Trip to Canada and the United States* in 1859?

18 In 1994 which batsman set two records: the highest individual scores in Test matches and in first-class cricket?

19 Which Marxist writer (the author of *England for All* and *The Evolution of Revolution*) played cricket for Sussex from 1863 to 1868?

20 Which unusual venue for amateur cricket, which has been played on by teams from yachting clubs and Parkhurst prison, can be used on only two days each year?

C is for **Cricket**

1 **Gentlemen v. Players.**

2 The pitch (at Sabina Park in Kingston, Jamaica) was deemed too dangerous. Play had been interrupted six times while batsmen had been treated for blows to the hand, elbow and head. After the seventh injury the teams agreed a draw.

3 **Overarm bowling was allowed.** In 1835 the MCC had already altered the rules to allow the hand to be raised as high as the shoulder. The first overarm bowlers were Willes (Kent), Broadbridge (Hambleden) and Walker (Sussex). The story goes that Willes' sister Christina had used the technique when playing against him (because her skirt impeded underarm bowling); she bowled him out and he resolved to try it for himself.

4 **New Zealand.** The trophy was donated by Lord Plunket, who was Governor-General of New Zealand from 1904 to 1910.

5 **Bernard Bosanquet.** It was described as an offbreak with a leg-break action.

6 **Frances Edmonds**, wife of Phil Edmonds (b 1951).

7 **Melbourne in 1877.** Australia (245 and 104) beat England (196 and 108) by 45 runs.

8 **Don Bradman** (b 1908) and **Bill Ponsford** (1900–91).

9 **10.8 centimetres** (4½ inches). The length of the bat (including the handle) must be not more than 96.5 centimetres (38 inches).

10 **Frank Worrell** (1924–67), **Everton Weekes** (b 1925), and **Clyde Walcott** (b 1926).

11 **Walter Hammond** (1903–65), who turned amateur in 1938 in order to be eligible to play for England.

12 **C. Aubrey Smith** (1863–1948) and **Archie Maclaren** (1871–1944). C. Aubrey Smith appeared in numerous films, including *Dr Jekyll and Mr Hyde* (1941) and *The Adventures of Mark Twain* (1944). He organised Sunday cricket games for Hollywood actors, including David Niven, Boris Karloff and Laurence Olivier. The pitch on which they played at Griffith Park became known as the C. Aubrey Smith Cricket Ground. The story goes that when Smith heard that Laurence Olivier had arrived in Hollywood, he sent him a note: 'There will be cricket practice tomorrow at 4 pm. I trust I shall see you there.'

13 **Sir Garfield Sobers** (b 1936).

14 **Robert Mugabe** (b 1924), Prime Minister of Zimbabwe from 1980 to 1987 and the country's first executive president from 1987.

15 **Learie Constantine**, Lord Constantine of Maraval and Nelson (1901–71).

16 **The White Heather Club**. The Women's Cricket Association was not founded until 1926.

17 **Fred Lillywhite.**

18 **Brian Lara.** On 18 April, in Antigua, he scored 375 to beat Garfield Sobers' 365 not out Test record (set in 1958); and on 6 June, at Edgbaston (playing for Warwickshire against Durham), he scored 501 not out to beat Hanif Mohammed's first-class record of 497 not out.

19 **Henry Hyndman** (1842–1921).

20 **Bramble Bank**, in the Solent, which is covered by water except for about an hour on the spring and autumn equinoxes. It was used for cricket in the early 1900s until 1922, and the tradition was revived in 1954 by the yachtsman Uffa Fox.

General Knowledge Questions

1 Which cricketer (who also played football for Arsenal and England) made a series of *Brylcreem* advertisements just after the Second World War?

2 For what does the acronym ERNIE stand?

3 Which British monarch was known as the 'Sailor King'?

4 Who wrote in 1762, 'Man was born free and everywhere he is in chains'?

5 In which European art galleries are the two versions of Leonardo da Vinci's *Virgin of the Rocks*?

6 In a suit of armour, which part of the body was protected by a greave?

7 What name is given to a positive electrode?

8 Which classic 1939 Hollywood film derives from Maupassant's short story *Boule de Suif*?

9 What is the term for an outwork which defended the entrance of a castle or fortified town, or for a double fortified tower over a gate or bridge?

10 In which European city is the International Museum of the Reformation, which includes statues of John Knox and John Calvin?

11 Which French dramatist was originally named Jean-Baptiste Poquelin?

12 The interior of which continent was explored by Gregory Blaxland in 1813, John Oxley in 1818 and Charles Sturt in 1829–30?

13 James Brooke, an ex-employee of the East India Company, and his descendants, ruled which independent state on the island of Borneo between 1841 and 1946?

14 Which bird in flight is the symbol of St John the Apostle?

15 Which city is famed for its Temple of the Emerald Buddha?

16 At which battle between British and Zulu forces in South Africa in 1879 did a small British force win eleven Victoria Crosses?

17 What two lines come after these, from a 1950 song by Stephen Weiss and Bernie Baum:

> *Put another nickel in;*
> *In the nickelodeon,*

18 What kind of insects belong to the order *Odonata*?

19 Who provided the speaking voice of Tex Tucker ('Two-Gun Tex of Texas') in the 1960 ITV children's puppet western series *Four Feather Falls*?

20 Which poet wrote the following lines on a cricket match in *Vitae Lampada* in 1897:

> *There's a breathless hush in the Close tonight –*
> *Ten to make and the match to win –*
> *A bumping pitch and a blinding light,*
> *An hour to play and the last man in.*
> *And it's not for the sake of a ribboned coat,*
> *Or the selfish hope of a season's fame,*
> *But his Captain's hand on his shoulder smote –*
> *'Play up! play up! and play the game!'*

General Knowledge

1 **Dennis Compton** (1918–97).
2 **Electronic Random Number Indicator Equipment**, the electronic equipment used to select the winning numbers of Premium Bonds, which were introduced in 1956.
3 **William IV** (1765–1837, r 1830–37).
4 **Jean-Jacques Rousseau** (1712–78), in his *Social Contract*.
5 **The Louvre, Paris** and **the National Gallery, London**. The painting was commissioned as an altarpiece for the church of San Francesco Grande in Milan. The Paris version was painted in about 1483–6 and the National Gallery version in 1506–08.
6 **The lower part of the leg**.
7 **Anode**, from the Greek *ánodos* (way). A negative electrode is named the cathode, from the Greek *cáthodos* (going down).
8 *Stagecoach*. The script was based on *Stage to Lodsburg* by Ernest Haycox (published in *Collier's* magazine) which in turn was derived from *Boule de Suif* ('Ball of Tallow', written in 1880).
9 **Barbican**.
10 **Geneva**. Both John Knox and John Calvin influenced the growth of Protestantism in Geneva in the 1540s and 1550s.
11 **Molière** (1622–73).
12 **Australia**.
13 **Sarawak**. The sultan made him Raja of Sarawak as a reward for his assistance against rebel tribes. With the help of local forces, James Brooke mounted a vigorous campaign against piracy around the coasts of Sarawak, during which he repelled attacks from Chinese opium smugglers. His nephew, Charles Johnson (who changed his name to Brooke), succeeded him. The last of the dynasty was Charles Vyner, who ceded Sarawak to Britain in 1946.
14 **Eagle**. The feast day of St John is 27 December.
15 **Bangkok**. King Rama I (1737–1809, r 1782–1809) of Bangkok had the Temple of the Emerald Buddha built. The Emerald Buddha is, in fact, carved from green jade.
16 **Rorke's Drift**.
17 *All I want is loving you*
 And music, music, music.
 'Nickelodeon' was the name given to early juke boxes. It was first used for a type of cinema, to which admission was five cents (one nickel). The first nickelodeon was opened in Pittsburgh in 1905 by John P. Harris and Harry Davies.
18 **Dragonflies** (including damselflies). True dragonflies have two dissimilar pairs of wings which are held out horizontally at right angles to the body when at rest; they have stouter bodies and a stronger flight than damselflies. Damselflies have slender bodies and two pairs of similar wings which are held vertically over the abdomen when at rest; they have a fluttering flight.
19 **Nicholas Parsons**. The singing voice of Tex Tucker was that of Michael Holliday.
20 **Henry Newbolt** (1862–1938).

D is for Dance

1 What is the meaning of 'bolshoi' in the Bolshoi Ballet?

2 Who was Fred Astaire's dancing partner in the 1957 film *Silk Stockings*?

3 Who were the principal male and principal female dancers of the 1994 show *River Dance* when it opened at the Point Theatre, Dublin?

4 In the fourteenth and fifteenth centuries what name was given to the dance of a skeleton or corpse leading people to the grave in order of social precedence?

5 Where in England is the traditional 'Furry Dance' held annually in May?

6 What name was given to the form of dance which originated in the USA in the 1970s and consisted of disjointed robotic movements and acrobatic spins carried out while balancing on the head or back?

7 Who was the first presenter of the BBC television programme *Come Dancing*?

8 What was the name of Stravinsky's first ballet, which was first performed in 1910 and which he abbreviated and reorchestrated as a suite, having described it as 'too long and patchy'?

9 Which former ballet dancer was the first director of the Royal Ballet (previously Sadler's Wells Ballet, which she had founded in 1931)?

10 Which form of dancing often features characters from the Robin Hood stories, along with Bavian the fool, Malkin the clown and a hobby horse?

11 What is the meaning of the word 'ballet'?

12 Who were the three principal dancers in the 1948 film *The Red Shoes*?

13 Which ballet dancer's 1998 autobiography was entitled *Life in Dance*?

14 Who composed the ballets *Billy the Kid* in 1939 and *Rodeo* in 1942?

15 In the sixteenth century which Lord Chancellor was nicknamed 'the Dancing Chancellor' because he attracted the notice of Queen Elizabeth by his graceful dancing during a masque at court?

16 Which was the last ballet directed by Rudolf Nureyev, in 1992?

17 What is a *bayadère*?

18 From a poem by which seventeenth-century poet does the phrase 'trip the light fantastic' come?

19 Who composed *Le Bourgeois Gentilhomme* (1670), one of the first recorded ballets?

20 Which American jazz musician composed and recorded *Black Bottom Stomp* in the late 1920s?

D is for Dance

1 **Great.** The Bolshoi Ballet was founded in 1776; the first recruits were from the orphanage where the ballet company used to hold classes.

2 **Cyd Charisse.** *Silk Stockings* was based on the 1939 film *Ninotchka*, starring Greta Garbo and Melvyn Douglas.

3 **Michael Flatley** and **Jean Butler**. Michael Flatley gained a place in the *Guinness Book of Records* for the speed at which he could tap-dance: 35 taps per second.

4 *Danse Macabre* or **Dance of Death**.

5 **Helston** in Cornwall. It is part of an ancient spring festival, dating from pre-Christian times in which townsfolk dance through the streets. One explanation of the name of the dance is that 'Furry' could be a corruption of the Latin *feriae* (festivals).

6 **Break dancing.**

7 **McDonald Hobley.** *Come Dancing* began in 1949 as a series of ballroom dancing lessons, with the steps demonstrated by Syd Perkins and Edna Duffield. In 1959 it changed its format to a series of dancing competitions for amateurs.

8 *The Firebird*.

9 **Dame Ninette de Valois** (Edris Stannus, b 1898). She was Director of the Royal Ballet from 1956 to 1963.

10 **Morris dancing**, which was originally a military dance of the Moors (Moriscos), from whom it takes its name.

11 **A little dance** (from the Italian *balletto*).

12 **Moira Shearer, Leonide Massine** and **Robert Helpmann**.

13 **Darcey Bussell** (b 1969).

14 **Aaron Copland** (1900–90).

15 **Sir Christopher Hatton** (1540–91).

16 *La Bayadère* (1877) by Léon Minkus. Rudolf Nureyev, who was born in 1939, died in 1993.

17 **A Hindu professional dancing girl**, employed for both religious dances and for entertainment. In Rudolf Nureyev's 1992 production of *La Bayadère*, Elisabeth Platel danced the part of Nikiya, the temple dancer.

18 **John Milton** (1608–74) in *L'Allegro* (1645):
> *Sport that wrinkled Care derides,*
> *And Laughter holding both his sides.*
> *Come, and trip it as ye go*
> *On the light fantastic toe,*
> *And in thy right hand lead with thee,*
> *The mountain nymph, sweet Liberty.*

19 **Jean-Baptiste Lully** (1632–87) in collaboration with Molière. Lully himself danced the part of the Mufti when the ballet was first performed in Chambord, France.

20 **Jelly Roll Morton** (1890–1941).

General Knowledge

1 With which member of the Royal Ballet did Diana, Princess of Wales, dance on the stage of the Royal Opera House in 1985, while the Prince of Wales watched from the royal box?

2 In which nineteenth-century English novel are Becky Sharp and her school-friend Amelia Sedley the contrasting main characters?

3 On which African river is the Kariba Dam?

4 Which rock star, originally named Paul Gadd, used many stage-names including Paul Raven and Paul Monday?

5 Which large sea-bird is sometimes known as the 'mollymawk' because of its awkwardness on land?

6 Which perfume house launched *Youth Dew* in 1952?

7 Which species of whale is sometimes known as a 'grampus'?

8 Whom did George Robertson succeed as Secretary-General of NATO in 1999?

9 The churches in Ravenna in northern Italy are renowned for what kind of decoration?

10 Which dynasty ruled Turkey from the fourteenth century to the end of the First World War?

11 Which ITV series was shown in France as *Chapeau Melon et Bottes de Cuir*?

12 In Islam, what is the Adhan?

13 Which sweets were specially invented for Fleetwood trawlermen by a local pharmacist, James Lofthouse?

14 Which biennial sporting competition was instituted by Sir Myles Watt in 1957?

15 What does the word 'Balaam' represent in printers' jargon?

16 Bonfire Red, Harvest Moon and Showgirl are varieties of which garden plant?

17 What was the machine named 'Thor', designed by Alva J. Fisher in the USA between 1907 and 1910?

18 In Irish literature of the eighth and ninth centuries, from whose beauty did Cathbad the seer prophesy would arise 'a sharp sword to split apart the Tree of Ulster'?

19 Which fourteenth-century bishop and Chancellor of England remodelled Winchester Cathedral?

20 Which former journalist and art critic began to organise concerts of Russian music in 1908, which developed into the Ballets Russes?

General Knowledge   Answers

1 **Wayne Sleep**. They danced a three-minute routine to the pop song *Uptown Girl* (a pastiche of a song by the Four Seasons) recorded in 1983 by Billy Joel.

2 *Vanity Fair*, written in 1847–8 by William Makepeace Thackeray.

3 **Zambezi**. The 128-metre-high dam (completed in 1959), which created Lake Kariba, stands in Kariba Gorge on the border between Zambia and Zimbabwe.

4 **Gary Glitter** (b 1940).

5 **Albatross**. 'Mollymawk' derives from the Dutch *Mallemok*, from *mal* (silly) and *mok* (gull).

6 **Estée Lauder**.

7 **The killer whale** (*Orcinus orca*). The approximate maximum length and weight of the male are 9.5 metres and 5,000 kilograms. The female is usually much smaller.

8 **Xavier Sólana** of Spain, who had been Secretary-General since 1995.

9 **Mosaic**. Examples from the sixth century include the basilica of Sant'Apollinaire Nuovo and the church of San Vitale, which houses the National Museum of Antiquities.

10 **Ottoman**. The first Ottoman sultan was Osman I (*c* 1259–*c* 1326), the ruler of Anatolia, a Turkmen principality; the last was Mehmet VI Vahideddin (1861–1926, r 1918–22).

11 *The Avengers*. The translation of the French title is *Bowler Hat and Leather Boots*.

12 **The call to prayer**.

13 **Fisherman's Friends**. Lofthouse's descendants donated one penny for every packet sold during 1990–92 to the Royal National Lifeboat Institution.

14 **The Admiral's Cup**. Sir Myles Watt was the 'admiral' of the Royal Ocean Racing Club of Great Britain. The competition consists of six races (five until 1987) for teams of three yachts, culminating in the 975-kilometre Fastnet Cup Race.

15 **Nonsensical matter kept in type to fill up odd spaces**. It is an allusion to 'talking like Balaam's ass'. (Balaam's ass had refused to carry him to Moab, where he was going to curse the Israelites, and where he would have been killed had he proceeded. The ass was given the power of speech: 'Am I not thine ass, upon which thou hast ridden ever since I was thine unto this day? Was I ever wont to do so unto thee?' (Numbers 22:30)

16 **Poppy** (*Papaver*). They are all oriental poppies.

17 **The first electric washing machine**.

18 **Deirdre of the Sorrows**, the heroine of *The Fate of the Sons of Usnech* (*Oidheadh Chloinne Uisneach*).

19 **William of Wykeham** (1324–1404), Bishop of Winchester, who built New College, Oxford, and founded Winchester College in 1382.

20 **Sergey Diaghilev** (1872–1929).

E is for **Engineering**

1 Which ancient Greek mathematician invented a device known as a 'screw' for moving materials, which is still in use as a water pump?

2 Which fifteenth-century artist and inventor designed the 'ornithopter', a flying machine which used flapping wings to imitate the flight of birds, and an aerial screw – the predecessor of the helicopter?

3 Which British motor company built the Interceptor?

4 What is the name of the tunnel under the Tsugaru Strait which links the Japanese islands of Hokkaido and Honshu?

5 Which American industrialist designed the sleeping car for railways in 1865?

6 Which American suspension bridge, designed by Leon Moisseiff, collapsed within four months of its opening in 1940?

7 In 1915 which aircraft engineer built the J-1 Blechesel ('Sheet Metal Donkey') – the first successful all-metal aircraft?

8 What kind of vehicle (the first of its kind) did the architect William Kent make for the 3rd Duke of Devonshire in 1733 and which is still on display at Chatsworth House?

9 The grandfather of which Scottish writer was one of the pioneers of the planning and building of lighthouses in nineteenth-century Scotland?

10 What kind of gear has the axles of its toothed wheels at an angle to one another (for example to transfer the vertical rotation of a windmill to the horizontal rotation of a millstone)?

11 What name is given to a bridge (dating from prehistory) constructed from stone piers with slabs of stone spanning them?

12 Which piece of office equipment did Milwaukee newspaper editor Christopher Latham Sholes invent with Carlos Glidden and Samuel Soulé in 1868?

13 Undershot, overshot and breastshot are types of what kind of mechanical device?

14 Which science fiction writer, in his 1972 book *The Lost Worlds of 2001*, wrote 'Any sufficiently advanced technology is indistinguishable from magic'?

15 Which aeronautical engineer designed the Schneider Trophy-winning Supermarine S6 seaplanes and the Spitfire?

16 What was the name of the first commercial hovercraft, designed by Sir Christopher Cockerell?

17 What is the name of the process in which metal particles are compressed into a solid body under heat lower than melting point?

18 Which seventeenth-century German engineer invented the vacuum pump?

19 With which innovation in transport in the 1830s is the English surgeon and inventor Sir Goldsworthy Gurney associated?

20 Which cabinet-maker and locksmith was so sure of the security of the lock he made in 1784 that he issued the following challenge: 'The Artist who can make an Instrument that will pick or Open this Lock, shall Receive 200 Guineas The Moment it is produced'?

E is for **Engineering**

1 **Archimedes** (c 287–212 BC).
2 **Leonardo da Vinci** (1452–1519), after whom the airport in Fiumicino, Rome, is named.
3 **Jensen**.
4 **The Seikan Rail Tunnel**, which is the longest tunnel in the world. It is 53.8 kilometres long, 23.3 kilometres of which are under the sea.
5 **George M. Pullman** (1831–97).
6 **The Tacoma Narrows Bridge**, across the Narrows of the Puget Sound, which linked the Olympic Peninsula with the mainland of Washington State. In a fairly gentle wind (about 68 kilometres per hour) the 853-metre main span twisted and broke up.
7 **Hugo Junkers** (1859–1935).
8 **A baby's perambulator**. It was designed to be pulled by a dog.
9 **Robert Louis Stevenson** (1850–94). His grandfather, Robert Stevenson (1772–1850), was the First Engineer of the Northern Lighthouse Board and was responsible for constructing 23 Scottish lighthouses. He also acted as a consulting engineer for roads, bridges, harbours, canals and waterways. Robert Louis Stevenson's father, Thomas Stevenson, two of his uncles and his great-grandfather were also lighthouse engineers.
10 **Bevel gear**. The toothed edges of the wheels are bevelled so that they can mesh at an angle.
11 **Clapper bridge**.
12 **The typewriter**. In 1864 Sholes and Soulé were granted a patent for a page-numbering machine. Glidden, a mechanic who had come across an account of a writing machine devised by John Pratt of London, suggested that they adapt the device to become a letter-printing machine – a typewriter.
13 **Waterwheel**. In an undershot wheel, water enters below the centre of the wheel; in an overshot wheel it enters the wheel above the centre; and in a breastshot wheel it enters at the ten o'clock or two o'clock position, usually into bucket-shaped paddles.
14 **Arthur C. Clarke** (b 1917).
15 **Reginald J. Mitchell** (1895–1937).
16 **SR.N1**, built by Saunders Roe (owned by Westland). It successfully crossed the English Channel from Calais to Dover on 25 July 1959.
17 **Sintering**.
18 **Otto von Guericke** (1602–86). He demonstrated the vacuum pump before Emperor Ferdinand III in 1654 by fitting two large metal hemispheres together, pumping out the air from inside them and hitching two teams of eight horses to them to attempt to pull the hemispheres apart. The horses could not move them, but once the air was allowed back inside, the hemispheres fell apart.
19 **Steam-driven stagecoaches**. Following the success of George Stephenson's *Rocket* in 1829, Gurney built a steam-powered road vehicle which he drove from London to Bath and back at a speed of 24 kilometres per hour.
20 **Joseph Bramah** (1748–1814). The lock defied all challenges for 67 years until Alfred Hobbs, a mechanic, succeeded after 51 hours' work spread over 16 days. The complexity of the lock meant that it could be produced in quantity only with a set of precisely engineered machine tools.

General Knowledge Questions

1 Which small French car, first designed in 1939, is affectionately known as 'the Tin Snail'?

2 In cricket where is a yorker pitched to land?

3 Which fortified wine is particularly associated with the River Douro?

4 According to the nursery rhyme, how many miles was it to Babylon?

5 Which American writer wrote the following similes in his detective stories: 'I belonged in Idle Valley like a pearl onion in a banana split', 'She was as cute as a washtub' and 'The voice got as cool as a cafeteria dinner'?

6 In which group of islands in Britain were the Churchill Barriers constructed during the Second World War to protect the British fleet anchored there?

7 Which cartoonist created George and Gaye Gambol, who appeared in the *Daily Express* from 1951 to 1994?

8 Which pair of nineteenth-century showmen ran *The Greatest Show on Earth*, a presentation of circus acts, a menagerie and a collection of freaks?

9 Which two 1986 films, directed by Claude Berri and both starring Yves Montand, Daniel Autieul and Elisabeth Depardieu, were inspired by a two-part novel by Marcel Pagnol whose plot centres on a subterranean spring in Provence?

10 Who was the narrator for the 1999 BBC1 series *Walking with Dinosaurs*?

11 Who was the first Prime Minister of the Australian Commonwealth, from 1901 to 1903?

12 Which Paris fashion house produced the perfume with the aggressive-sounding name *Ma Griffe* (My Claw), which is advertised by a picture of a woman with long fingernails embracing an apparently naked man with long green scratches across his back?

13 What is the more familiar name for potassium nitrite as used in fertilisers, explosives and glass-making?

14 Which architect designed the Queen's House at Greenwich (built between 1616 and 1635), which is now part of the National Maritime Museum?

15 Which King of Scots was succeeded by his stepson, Lulach?

16 Who painted *The Rev Robert Walker Skating on Duddingston Loch* in 1784?

17 Which centuries-old English contest requires a married couple to take the following oath:

> *You doe swear by custom of confession*
> *That you ne're made Nuptiall Transgression,*
> *Nor since you were married man and wife,*
> *By household brawles or contentious strife*
> *Or otherwise in bed or at boarde,*
> *Offended each other in*
> *Deed or in Word. . .*

18 The name of which wind instrument comes from the Latin word for a young bull?

19 What kind of animal, found in parts of north Africa, is an addax?

20 Which railway engineer designed the locomotives *Sans Pareil*, which took part in the Rainhill Trials in 1829, and *Royal George*?

General Knowledge

1 **The Citroën 2CV** ('*Deux cheveaux*' : two horse-power). The company was founded by André Citroën (1878–1935). The aim was to produce an economical means of transport, simple to drive and maintain, which could carry four adults (wearing hats and clogs), along with 50 kilograms of potatoes, in comfort on even the poorest roads; alternatively, with the back seats removed, the car could accommodate a bale of hay.

2 **On, or just inside, the crease.**

3 **Port**, which is named after the town of Oporto where it is aged and bottled.

4 **Three-score and ten:**
>   *How many miles to Babylon?*
>   *Three-score and ten.*
>   *Can I get there by candle-light?*
>   *Yes, and back again.*
>   *If your heels are nimble and light,*
>   *You may get there by candle-light.*

5 **Raymond Chandler** (1888–1959). The first simile is from *The Long Goodbye* (1953) and the other two are from *Farewell My Lovely* (1940).

6 **The Orkneys**, in Scapa Flow, an area of sheltered water bounded by the islands of Mainland, South Ronaldsay and Hoy. Old ships had been scuppered to block access by German submarines, but a U-boat slipped through these defences and sank HMS *Royal Oak* in 1939. Winston Churchill had every access filled in with concrete blocks. The barriers are now used as pedestrian causeways between the islands.

7 **Barry Appleby** (1910–96).

8 **Phineas T. Barnum** (1810–91) and **James Bailey** (1847–1906).

9 *Jean de Florette* and **Manon des Sources**.

10 **Kenneth Branagh** (b 1960).

11 **Sir Edmund Barton** (1849–1920), a high-court judge who had headed the committee which drafted the Commonwealth Constitution Bill 1900.

12 **Carven**, which specialised in couture for 'the petite'. *Ma Griffe* was created in the year the company opened (1944).

13 **Saltpetre.**

14 **Inigo Jones** (1573–1652). The queen was Anne of Denmark (1574–1619), wife of King James VI & I.

15 **Macbeth** (1005–57, r 1040–57).

16 **Sir Henry Raeburn** (1756–1823). The painting hangs in the National Gallery of Scotland and is featured on many of its publicity posters.

17 **The Dunmow Flitch**, which Chaucer mentioned in *The Tale of the Wife of Bath*. A couple can win a flitch of bacon by proving that they are happily married. The contest is now held every four years at Dunmow in Essex.

18 **Bugle** (from *buculus*).

19 **An antelope**, which is now in danger of extinction. It used to range the Sahara region in groups of about 20 to 25, but in 1998 fewer than 250 remained.

20 **Timothy Hackworth** (1786–1850). The other four contestants at the Rainhill Trials were: *Novelty*, built by John Braithwaite and John Ericsson, *Perseverance*, built by Timothy Burnstall, T. S. Brandreth's *Cyclopede* (an ingenious locomotive propelled by a horse on a treadmill) and, of course, the winner, Robert Stephenson's *Rocket*.

F is for **Films**

1 Which 1949 film, based on a novel by Graham Greene, topped the 1999 British Film Institute poll of the favourite films of the twentieth century?

2 From which 1942 film do the following quotations (spoken by Orson Welles) come: 'I am, have been and only will be one thing – an American', and 'Mr Carter, if the headline is big enough, it makes the news big enough'?

3 Who was the animator of the Mickey Mouse cartoon films created by Walt Disney?

4 What name was given to the video system (now obsolete) developed by Sony in the 1970s?

5 For what do the initials VHS stand?

6 Which veteran Welsh-born actor, who died in a road accident in December 1999, played the gadget-minded Q in 17 James Bond films?

7 Which British film actor was educated at Sandhurst and served as an army officer in the Second World War before going to Hollywood, where he was registered as a film extra as 'Anglo-Saxon type 2008'?

8 In the 1988 film *A Fish Called Wanda*, John Cleese plays a barrister whose name is the real name of which film star?

9 What name was given to the cinema technique invented by Fred Waller in which three synchronised projectors each project a third of the picture on to a wide, curving screen?

10 Who directed the 1999 film *Tea with Mussolini*?

11 What name was given to the group of formidable English expatriate women in the film *Tea with Mussolini*?

12 Which record-breaking swimmer, who was selected for the cancelled 1940 Olympics in Helsinki, was the *Million Dollar Mermaid* in the 1952 film about the swimming career of the Australian swimmer Annette Kellerman?

13 Whose abdication in the seventeenth century was the subject of the 1974 film *The Abdication*?

14 In the 1966 film *Blowup* what is blown up?

15 In the 1933 Marx Brothers film *Duck Soup*, of which imaginary country did Rufus T. Firefly (played by Groucho) become president?

16 In the 1962 film, directed by Anthony Kimmins, what was *The Amorous Prawn*?

17 In which 1960 film did Michael Todd Jr introduce 'Smell-O-Vision', a system devised by Hans Laube as 'Scentovision' in which scents, piped to individual seats in the cinema, were synchronised with the action?

18 Which 1973 film about a bird, based on a book by Richard Bach and directed by Hall Bartlett, shows no human beings apart from some fishermen in a boat during the opening sequence?

19 Who dubbed the singing voice of Lauren Bacall in the 1944 film *To Have and Have Not*?

20 In the 1939 film *Gone with the Wind*, Olivia de Havilland is shown holding a baby who grew up to marry Raquel Welch. Who was he?

F is for **Films** Answers

1 *The Third Man*, directed by Carol Reed. The novel was not published until 1950.

2 *Citizen Kane* (1941).

3 Ub Iwerks (1907–71).

4 Betamax, derived from the Japanese *betabeta* ('all over') combined with 'max' from the English 'maximum', because the whole area of the tape could be used, without any of the 'guard bands' or empty spaces of earlier types. It proved less popular than its contemporary, VHS, developed by the Matsushita Corporation.

5 Video Home System.

6 Desmond Llewelyn (1914–99).

7 David Niven (1909–83).

8 Cary Grant (Archibald Leach).

9 Cinerama, which was first presented in *This is Cinerama* in 1952 and used in the same year in *How the West Was Won*. Because of the expense of the projectors it was superseded in the late 1960s by Panavision (a form of Cinemascope).

10 Franco Zeffirelli (b 1923).

11 Scorpioni.

12 Esther Williams (b 1923), who was nicknamed 'America's Mermaid'.

13 Queen Kristina of Sweden (1626–89), the daughter of Gustav II Adolf. She succeeded him in 1632 and then stunned Europe by abdicating in 1654 in favour of her cousin Karl X Gustav, whom she had refused to marry.

14 A photograph. A photographer, played by David Hemmings, surreptitiously photographs a couple embracing in a park, enlarges the pictures and finds evidence of a murder.

15 Freedonia.

16 A guest house in a converted military headquarters in Scotland.

17 *Scent of Mystery*. Although smells had been used (with a system named 'Aromarama') in the 1959 film *Behind the Great Wall*, they were added after the film had been made and conveyed through the cinema's normal air-conditioning system to complement the film.

18 *Jonathan Livingston Seagull*, which was nominated at the Academy Awards for Best Cinematography and Editing.

19 Andy Williams. Lauren Bacall had such a deep speaking voice that no suitable female singer could be found.

20 Patrick Curtis, who appeared as the infant Beau Wilkes, the son of Melanie Hamilton Wilkes (Olivia de Havilland).

General Knowledge

1 Which early Hollywood film star, originally named Gladys Mary Smith, was known as 'America's Sweetheart'?

2 Who owned the chocolate factory in Roald Dahl's 1964 children's story *Charlie and the Chocolate Factory*?

3 For what does the acronym BUPA stand?

4 A pantry was originally used for the storage of which foodstuff?

5 What is the name given to parallel beams which stretch from one wall to another in a building to support the floors?

6 Whom did Jack Dempsey, 'the Manassa Mauler', defeat in 1919 to win the world heavyweight boxing title?

7 Samuel Hahnemann (1755–1843) was the founder of which branch of 'alternative' medicine?

8 Under what pseudonym did William Connor write a column for the *Daily Mirror* from 1935 until his death in 1967?

9 Which Buckinghamshire village is used as the location for the BBC comedy TV series *The Vicar of Dibley*?

10 *Lutra lutra* is a carnivorous water-dwelling animal, better known as what?

11 Which French village on the edge of the Forest of Fontainebleau gave its name to a nineteenth-century school of landscape painters?

12 In which Lincolnshire town, the birthplace of Isaac Newton, did Oliver Cromwell establish his headquarters in 1643?

13 In the Aston Martin DB series, for what do the letters DB stand?

14 What did Locks of St James's, the hatters, make in 1850 for William Coke, a Norfolk landowner who asked for a hat with a lower crown?

15 Which commodity is measured in cords?

16 Which play opens with the words of Parker, the butler: 'Is your ladyship at home this afternoon?'

17 In ancient Rome what was the name of the annual fertility festival celebrated on 15 February?

18 Which member of the sandpiper family of waders is named after its ring of colourful fluffed-out tail feathers?

19 What is the line which comes after the following, in the 1938 poem *On a Sundial* by Hilaire Belloc:

   I am a sundial, and I make a botch . . .

20 What was the name of the bookseller played by Hugh Grant in the 1999 film *Notting Hill*?

General Knowledge Answers

1 **Mary Pickford** (1893–1979).
2 **Willie Wonka.**
3 **British United Provident Association**, formed in 1947 from 17 British provident associations with the aim of providing improved healthcare.
4 **Bread.** The word comes from the Old French *paneterie* (bread cupboard or box) which, in turn, was derived from the Latin *panis* (bread).
5 **Joists.**
6 **Jess Willard.**
7 **Homeopathy.**
8 **Cassandra** (the name of the legendary daughter of King Priam of Troy, a prophet of doom who was never believed).
9 **Turville**, where the church of St Mary becomes St Barnabas' church. Turville was also the setting for the films *Chitty Chitty Bang Bang* and *101 Dalmatians.*
10 **Otter.**
11 **Barbizon.** Members of the Barbizon school included Jean-François Millet and Théodore Rousseau.
12 **Grantham**, which was also the birthplace of Margaret Thatcher in 1925.
13 **David Brown.** Sir David Brown (1904–93), originally from a Yorkshire engineering family, bought Aston Martin (founded by Lionel Martin and Robert Bamford in 1932). 'Aston' came from the racing circuit at Aston Clinton near Aylesbury where Martin had won several car races. The Two Litre Sports (later nicknamed 'DB1') was produced soon afterwards; the first car to be marketed with David Brown's initials was the DB2 in 1950.
14 **A bowler** (known as a 'Derby' in the USA).
15 **Wood** (cut wood for fuel). A cord is equivalent to a stack measuring $4 \times 4 \times 8$ feet (128 cubic feet). It is subdivided into cord feet, which measure $4 \times 4 \times 1$ feet. A short cord is a 4×8 foot stack of pieces shorter than four feet, and a long cord is a similar stack of pieces longer than four feet. A face cord is a 4×8 foot stack of pieces one foot long. It was so named because a cord was used to tie the wood into a bundle.
16 *Lady Windermere's Fan* (1892) by Oscar Wilde.
17 **Lupercalia.** The name was derived from Lupercus, a Roman god of flocks. Lupercal was also the name of the cave were Romulus and Remus were said to have been suckled by a wolf (Latin *lupus*) and where people gathered for the festival.
18 **Ruff** (the female is known as a reeve).
19 *Of what is done much better by a watch.*
20 **William Thacker.**

G is for Games

1 The name of which board game, based on the Indian game 'Pachisi', is a Latin word meaning 'I play'?

2 In the pencil and paper game of 'Battleships' how many squares does a cruiser occupy?

3 Which Chinese game, whose name means 'sparrow', did Joseph P. Babcock introduce to the USA in about 1919?

4 In poker what is a 'dead man's hand'?

5 The name of which water sport comes from an older version in which players rode barrels painted like horses and struck the ball with sticks?

6 Of which game was 'battledore' a forerunner?

7 In *Alice's Adventures in Wonderland* which game did the Red Queen invite Alice to play when they first met?

8 Which London thoroughfare is the name of a type of croquet game which used to be played there before the street was built in the seventeenth century?

9 The phrase 'according to Hoyle', meaning 'on the greatest authority', originally referred to the rules of which game?

10 Which sport did the Apple Tree Gang introduce to the USA in 1888?

11 Which very old game, which is still played, was once known as 'Fippeny Morrell' and was described as follows in 1626: 'Thrice three stones, set in a crossed square, where he wins the game that can set his three in a row'?

12 Which Flemish artist painted *Children's Games* in 1560?

13 What type of game are Grandfather's Clock, Klondike and Lovely Lucy?

14 The Paris art gallery Jeu de Paume, opened in 1947, occupies a building built by Napoleon III to house courts for which game?

15 Which game did the knight play against death in the 1957 Ingmar Bergman film *The Seventh Seal*?

16 In which board game, invented by Albert Lamorisse, do two to six players throw five dice to attack and counter-attack one another's armies placed in 42 countries on six continents, with the aim of taking over the world?

17 Which Japanese designer created Game Boy for Nintendo?

18 In Shakespeare's *Antony and Cleopatra*, which game did Cleopatra prefer to listening to music?

19 An action in which game is known as 'fulking'?

20 Which two American journalists invented Trivial Pursuit in 1979?

G is for Games Answers

1 **Ludo.**

2 **Three.** A submarine occupies one square, a destroyer two and a battleship four.

3 **Mah jong.** The sparrow ('bird of 100 intelligences') appears on one of the 144 tiles used in the game, which is thought to have originated in China in the 1870s.

4 **A hand of mixed eights and aces.** The story goes that the American frontiersman 'Wild' Bill Hickok (James Butler Hickok, 1837–76) was holding such a hand when he was shot dead by Jack McCall during a poker game in the Number Ten saloon in Deadwood in the Black Hills of Dakota.

5 **Water polo.** The sport, for teams of seven, originated in Britain in 1870. The United Kingdom was the first Olympic gold-medal winner in Paris in 1900 and subsequently in 1908, 1912 and 1920.

6 **Badminton,** which is named after the home of the Dukes of Beaufort in Gloucestershire, where it was first played in about 1873. A version of badminton named 'poona' had also been played in the 1860s by British army officers in India.

7 **Croquet.** The mallets were flamingos, the balls were hedgehogs, and the Red Queen's soldiers bent double to form the arches.

8 **Pall Mall,** from the Italian *palla* (ball) and *maglio* (mallet). Pall mall (also known as 'pell mell') was played on the site of The Mall, too.

9 **Whist.** In 1742 Edmond Hoyle wrote *A Short Treatise on the Game of Whist*, which became the standard authority on the game.

10 **Golf.** The Apple Tree Gang was a name given to John Reid and his Scottish friends in 1892, when they moved to their six-hole 'course' at Yonkers. They had begun playing golf at another 'course' at Yonkers in 1888.

11 **Nine Men's Morris.**

12 **Pieter Brueghel the Elder** (*c* 1525–69). The painting, which includes more than 200 children playing 80 different games, hangs in the Kunsthistorisches Museum in Vienna.

13 **Patience** (a card game for one player).

14 **Real Tennis.** '*Jeu de paume*' means 'game of the palm' (real tennis was played without racquets, like fives). In 1986 the contents of the Jeu de Paume were transferred to the newly converted Musée d'Orsay (formerly a railway station). The Jeu de Paume is now used for temporary exhibitions.

15 **Chess.**

16 **Risk.** The game was first marketed by Parker Brothers in 1959 under a name devised by one of their sales people (R – I – S – K were the initials of his grandchildren).

17 **Gumpei Yokoi** (1941–97), who was killed in a road accident.

18 **Billiards.** Act II, Scene v:

Cleopatra: *Give me some music; music, moody food*
      Of us that trade in love.

All: *The music ho!*
      [*Enter Mardian the Eunuch*]

Cleopatra: *Let it alone; let's to billiards.*

19 **Marbles.** It means 'shooting' the marble, which is placed on the thumb, held there by the tip of the forefinger and then flicked with the thumb.

20 **Chris Haney** and **Scott Abbott.**

General Knowledge

1 What is the name of the French game, similar to bowls, which is sometimes called 'jeu de boules'?

2 Which cartoon character has a dog named Gnasher?

3 From whom did Mohammed Ali (as Cassius Clay) take the world heavy-weight boxing title at Miami Beach in 1964 and subsequently retain it in a rematch at Lewiston in Maine?

4 Which 'myco-protein' food is produced by a mould which feeds on carbo-hydrates such as potatoes and rice?

5 Which queen's dolls' house, created by Lutyens, is on display at Windsor Castle?

6 Which ports are situated at the north and south ends of the Suez Canal?

7 Which bewhiskered bungler, who first appeared on BBC television in *Sunday Night at the London Palladium* in 1960, was played by Richard Hearne?

8 Which singer, known as 'the king of skiffle', recorded *My Old Man's a Dustman*, which entered the UK charts at Number 1 in 1960?

9 Who played the title role in Steven Spielberg's 1998 war film *Saving Private Ryan*?

10 The first 'Frisbees' were the empty containers for what?

11 Which book opens with the words 'The past is a foreign country: they do things differently there'?

12 Who was the founder of the Mughal empire?

13 Which was the first football club (as distinct from a school or university club) to be founded (in 1857) and whose rules were merged with those of the Football Association in 1878 to form a common set of rules for all teams?

14 In Shakespeare's *Hamlet* which herb did Ophelia give for remembrance and which flower for thoughts?

15 Who wrote the music for the hymn *Onward Christian Soldiers*?

16 What is the name of the 'virtual pet', which in Japanese means 'lovable egg', designed by Naoharu Yamashina?

17 Which English playwright collaborated with André Previn in the 1977 'play for actors and orchestra' *Every Good Boy Deserves Favour*?

18 What is the common name for D_2O (deuterium oxide)?

19 The sinking of which ship near Plymouth in 1782, with the loss of about 800 lives, inspired William Cowper to write a poem which opens as follows:

Toll for the brave –
The brave! That are no more:
All sunk beneath the wave,
Fast by their native shore.

20 Who was the first women's world chess champion from 1927 until her death in 1944?

General Knowledge   Answers

1 **Pétanque**, which is derived from the very old French game of 'jeu Provençal boules'. The players take turns throwing or rolling a ball (*boule*) to land as close as possible to the jack (*cochonnet*).

2 **Dennis the Menace**, who first appeared in the *Beano* in 1951. Gnasher (an 'Abyssinian Wire-haired Tripe Hound') joined him in 1968, and they were promoted to the cover of the *Beano* in 1974.

3 **Sonny Liston** (1932–70).

4 **Quorn**, which was produced after the discovery of a tiny mushroom-like organism, which occurs naturally in soil, growing in a field near Marlow in Buckinghamshire. Quorn was first marketed in a vegetable pie in 1986 by Marlow Foods Ltd.

5 **Queen Mary** (Mary of Teck, 1867–1953). Sir Edwin Landseer Lutyens designed the dolls' house in 1921. It was completed in 1924, and 1,617,556 people went to see it at the Wembley Exhibition. Numerous manufacturers made miniature replicas of their products for the dolls' house, including Dunhill, who supplied tiny pipes and packets of tobacco, and Bryant and May, who provided a minute box of matches to accompany them.

6 **Port Said** and **Suez**. Port Said (*bur Said*), whose site is mainly on reclaimed land, was founded in 1859. Suez (*as-Suways*) is on the site of the Greek town of Clysma, which became the Muslim city of Kolsum in the seventh century.

7 **Mr Pastry**.

8 **Lonnie Donegan** (b 1931). *My Old Man's a Dustman* was an adaptation of the ribald Liverpool folk song *My Old Man's a Fireman on the Elder Dempster Line*.

9 **Tom Hanks** (b 1956).

10 **Pies**. In 1948 Fred Morrison noticed students at Yale throwing empty saucer-shaped containers of pies (from the Frisbie Pie Company) to one another. He manufactured a plastic version which he first marketed as 'Morrison's Flyin' Saucer', and later changed its name to 'Frisbee'.

11 *The Go-Between* (1953), by L. P. Hartley, which was made into a film starring Julie Christie and Alan Bates in 1971.

12 **Babur** (Zahir-ud-din Muhammad, 1483–1530), a descendant of Genghis Khan and of Timur (Tamerlane).

13 **The Sheffield Club**.

14 **Rosemary** and **pansy**:
   There's rosemary, that's for remembrance; pray, love, remember: and there is pansies, that's for thoughts.
   (*Hamlet*, Act IV, Scene v)

15 **Sir Arthur Sullivan** (1842–1900) in 1872. The words had been written by Sabine Baring-Gould in 1865.

16 **Tamagotchi**. Naoharu Yamashina (c 1918–97) founded the Bandai company, which also produced the Mighty Morphin Power Rangers.

17 **Tom Stoppard** (b 1937).

18 **Heavy water**. It is water made up of deuterium (the hydrogen isotope whose mass is twice that of ordinary hydrogen) and oxygen. It is used as a coolant in nuclear reactors.

19 The *Royal George* (*On the Loss of the Royal George*).

20 **Vera Menchik Stevenson** (1906–44). She was still world champion when she died during an air raid in London.

H is for Humour

1 In the *Daily Mirror* cartoon what is the name of Andy Capp's long-suffering wife?

2 Who provided the voice of Count Jim Moriarty in *The Goon Show*?

3 *Now – Something Else*, in 1986, was the first television series of which comedian and impressionist?

4 Who created the 'Muppets'?

5 In which of Shakespeare's comedies does the clown Touchstone appear?

6 Which former Royal Marine, teacher, social worker and photographer wrote the humorous novels *Porterhouse Blue* (1973) and *Blott on the Landscape* (1975), both of which were made into television series?

7 Which comedian and former rabbi was originally named Yacov Moshe Maza?

8 In which establishment does Herman Munster work?

9 Which ancient Greek dramatist is known as 'The Father of Comedy'?

10 Which ITV comedy duo lived at 46 Peacock Crescent, Hampton Wick?

11 In 1772 which scientist discovered laughing gas?

12 Which English dramatist wrote the 1599 comedy *The Shoemaker's Holiday*?

13 Which comedy duo performed a sketch based on *Mastermind* in which the specialised subject was 'Answering the Question Before Last'?

14 What was the title of William Hanna and Joe Barbera's first *Tom and Jerry* cartoon film?

15 In which comedy for music do the characters Marschallin (the wife of the field marshal), Oktavian, Sophie, Baron Ochs and Faninal appear?

16 What is the fourth line of the following quatrain:
    My name is George Nathaniel Curzon
    I am a most superior person,
    My cheek is pink, my hair is sleek;

17 Which comedian rebutted Freud's study of comedy with the words: 'He might know his theory, but Freud never went on in the second house at the Glasgow Empire'?

18 Which music-hall performer was known as 'The Prime Minister of Mirth'?

19 Which 1936 play by Ian Hay popularised the phrase 'funny peculiar or funny ha ha'?

20 Which American humorist and cartoonist, in 1960, defined humour as 'emotional chaos remembered in tranquility'?

H is for Humour

1 **Flo.** Andy Capp was created by Reg Smythe in 1958.

2 **Spike Milligan** (b 1918).

3 **Rory Bremner** (b 1961).

4 **Jim Henson** (1936–90), who coined the name from 'marionette' and 'puppet'. They made their first appearance in the children's television series *Sesame Street* in 1971. *The Muppet Show* began in 1976.

5 *As You Like It* (1599).

6 **Tom Sharpe** (Thomas Ridley, b 1928).

7 **Jackie Mason** (b 1930), whose first television appearance was on *The Steve Allen Show*.

8 **Goodbury & Grave Funeral Home.**

9 **Aristophanes** (*c* 450–385 BC).

10 **George and Mildred Roper** (played by Brian Murphy and Yootha Joyce), in the series *George and Mildred*, which was a spin-off from *Man About the House*.

11 **Joseph Priestley** (1733–1804). Its scientific name is nitrous oxide (N_2O). It was given the name laughing gas because, when inhaled, it produces a feeling of exhilaration (followed by unconsciousness, hence its use as an anaesthetic).

12 **Thomas Dekker** (*c* 1572–*c* 1632).

13 **Ronnie Barker** and **Ronnie Corbett**. The sketch, written by David Renwick (the writer of the television series *One Foot in the Grave*) is, to my mind, the most brilliant of all the many *Mastermind* take-offs. Ronnie Barker told me he thought it the funniest sketch the two Ronnies ever did.

14 *Puss Gets the Boot* (1940).

15 *Der Rosenkavalier* (The Knight of the Rose), composed in 1909–10 by Richard Strauss.

16 *I dine at Blenheim once a week*. Lord Curzon of Kedleston the British Foreign Secretary in the 1920s, had been elected president of the Oxford Union in 1880 and made a fellow of All Souls College in 1883. His contemporaries resented his ability to make friends in high places, and the verse was circulated. He later wrote: 'Never has more harm been done to one single individual than that accursed doggerel has done to me.'

17 **Ken Dodd** (b 1927). Audiences at the Glasgow Empire were notorious for giving visiting comedians a hard time.

18 **Sir George Robey** (1869–1954), a versatile entertainer who sang comic songs and appeared in humorous sketches and revues. He wrote and appeared in the revue *Bits and Pieces* (1927) and even played the part of a pantomime dame in *Jack and the Beanstalk* and Falstaff in *Henry IV Part I*.

19 *The Housemaster* (Act III):
   Chris: *That's funny.*
   Button: *What do you mean, funny? Funny peculiar or funny ha ha?*

20 **James Thurber** (1894–1961), quoted in the *New York Post* on 29 February 1960.

General Knowledge

1 According to the Liverpool comedian Ken Dodd what are mined in Knotty Ash?

2 Which two horse races make up the 'autumn double'?

3 By what name is the plant *Lawsonia inermis*, commonly used in hair colouring, better known?

4 The Martyrs' Memorial in Oxford commemorates which three bishops who were martyred in 1555–6?

5 Who was the first woman in space?

6 In which city is the CN Tower, the world's tallest free-standing structure?

7 Which vitamin is a fat-soluble naphthoquinone compound found in green leafy vegetables and essential in enabling the blood to clot?

8 Who won the first Academy Award for Best Actress, in 1928, for her performance in *Sunrise – A Song of Two Humans*?

9 In Egyptian mythology who were the parents of the falcon-headed Sun God, Horus?

10 Which piece of domestic equipment was invented by Josephine Cockran in 1886?

11 What is meant by the Latin phrase *mutatis mutandis*?

12 In mathematics, what does the symbol consisting of three short, horizontal parallel lines ($\equiv$) mean?

13 In Mozart's *The Magic Flute* which character is Pamina's mother?

14 For what do the initials BSA, in the name of the motorcycle manufacturer, stand?

15 What name is given to snakes such as the bushmaster, copperhead and moccasin which have a sensory organ between the nostril and the eye which detects infra-red radiation and thus enables them to find warm-blooded prey?

16 From which source did P. D. James take the title of her 1989 book *Devices and Desires*?

17 For what kind of art was Henricus Van Meegeren principally known in the late 1930s and early 1940s?

18 In Hilaire Belloc's *Cautionary Verses*, what had Sarah Byng refused to do which led to her being tossed into a thorn bush by a bull?

19 Marien Ngouabi, who was assassinated in 1977, was president of which African country?

20 What was the name of the sharp-tongued DSS official who dealt with the frequent claims made by the Boswells in the BBC 1 series *Bread*?

General Knowledge   Answers

1 **Jam butties** (jam sandwiches). Knotty Ash is a real suburb of Liverpool – in fact, Ken Dodd lived there. Residents of Knotty Ash are often met with disbelief when they give their addresses when booking hotels.

2 **The Cambridgeshire** and **the Cesarewitch**, flat races at Newmarket.

3 **Henna**, whose leaves contain a substance which reacts with the keratin in human hair and skin to form a bright pigment.

4 **Hugh Latimer** (c 1485–1555), **Nicholas Ridley** (c 1500–55) and **Thomas Cranmer** (1489–1556).

5 **Valentina Tereshkova** of the USSR in *Vostok 6*, which was launched on 16 June 1963 and completed 48 orbits in 71 hours. She had no pilot training, but her accomplishment as an amateur parachutist gained her a place as a trainee cosmonaut (the Russian term for 'astronaut') in 1961.

6 **Toronto**, Canada. The Canadian National Tower (built in 1976) is an observation and broadcasting tower, 553 metres high. The tallest supported structure is a television broadcasting tower (built in 1963), between Fargo and Blanchard in North Dakota, which is 629 metres high.

7 **Vitamin K**, which was discovered in 1929 and given the name vitamin K for 'Koagulation vitamin'.

8 **Janet Gaynor** (Laura Gainor, 1906–84).

9 **Isis and Osiris**. In the myth of Osiris, Seth murdered Osiris in an attempt to claim the royal throne of Egypt. Horus fought Seth to avenge his father and injured Seth's left eye (the Moon), which was healed by the god Thoth. This became a mythical explanation for the phases of the Moon.

10 **A dishwasher**. In Josephine Cockran's hand-cranked dishwasher the crank made the machine spray soapy water over the crockery. Its purpose was to avoid breakage rather than to save time. The first electrically powered dishwasher appeared in 1922.

11 **Having made the necessary changes**.

12 **Identical with**. The symbol meaning 'not identical with' has three parallel lines with a vertical or oblique line running across them ($\neq$).

13 **The Queen of the Night**.

14 **Birmingham Small Arms**, an engineering company established in 1873. It manufactured guns, bicycles and small cars as well as motorcycles.

15 **Pit viper**. The sensory organ is the 'pit'.

16 *The Book of Common Prayer*, 1662:
  We have erred, and strayed from Thy ways like lost sheep. We have followed too much the devices and desires of our own hearts.

17 **Forgery**. He specialised in Vermeers, one of which (*Christ at Emmaus*) was bought by the Boymans Museum in Rotterdam in 1937. He was arrested and imprisoned for selling art treasures to the Nazis. To clear himself he painted another Vermeer to prove that his paintings were forgeries, and he was given a twelve-month sentence for forgery.

18 **To learn to read**. She climbed the gate into a field, ignoring the warning on the nearby sign: 'BEWARE THE VERY FURIOUS BULL'. The lesson she learned was not that she should learn to read but that she should avoid signs, whatever they might say, and that 'literature breeds distress'!

19 **Congo**. Marien Ngouabi was the third president of Congo since it gained its independence in 1960.

20 **Martina** (played by Pamela Power).

I is for Information Technology Questions

1 Who founded Microsoft with Bill Gates?

2 In computer games what kind of creature is 'Sonic'?

3 Who coined the term 'global village' in 1962?

4 For what is 'bit' a shorthand term?

5 In 1993 BSkyB launched the first national shopping television channel in Britain. By which three letters is it known, and for what do they stand?

6 How is twenty-one written in binary numbers?

7 What is the popular name for a small wafer of semiconductor material which forms the base for an integrated circuit?

8 What was the name of the educational computer toy with a speech synthesiser, produced by Texas Instruments in 1978 for teaching spelling?

9 What are Empire Monkey, Pretty Park, Concept and Melissa?

10 In whose honour was the high-level computer language Ada named?

11 What was advertised in the first interactive British television commercial, shown on Channel 4 on 26 March 2000?

12 The name given to what kind of mechanism is derived from a Czech word, coined in 1920 by the dramatist Karel Čapek, meaning 'compulsory service'?

13 Ninetails, Pikachu, Vileplume and Weepinbell are types of what?

14 In computer terminology, what is a nibble?

15 Barclays Bank in Enfield was the first bank in the world to have which piece of technological equipment?

16 As what is *Cognoscenti v. Intelligentsia* better known?

17 Between 1937 and 1942 which American theoretical physicist built the first electronic digital computer?

18 What was the name of the first British-built electronic digital computer?

19 What was the name of the first commercial computer produced in the USA which was used for forecasting the 1952 election results?

20 Which English poet wrote the following lines in 1974:
Official designs are aggressively neuter,
The Puritan work of an eyeless computer.

I is for Information Technology   Answers

1 **Paul Allan.** Bill Gates wrote his first software program at the age of 13 and, while still at school, worked with a group of programmers to computerise the school's wages system. They founded Traf-O-Data, a company which sold traffic-counting systems. In 1975, at the age of 19, Gates joined his friend Paul Allen to develop software for the first microcomputers.

2 **A hedgehog,** produced by Sega.

3 **Marshall McLuhan** (1911–80), in *The Gutenberg Galaxy*: 'The new electronic interdependence recreates the world in the image of a global village.'

4 **Binary digit.**

5 **QVC (Quality, Value, Convenience),** which was launched in October 1993.

6 **10101.**

7 **Chip.**

8 **Speak and Spell.**

9 **Computer viruses.**

10 **Augusta Ada King,** Countess of Lovelace (1815–52), the daughter of Lord Byron. She had worked as an assistant to Charles Babbage in the development of his Analytical Engine and is credited with being the world's first computer programmer. The United States Department of Defence developed the language, the first version of which was completed in 1979.

11 **Chicken Tonight cooking paste.**

12 **Robot** (*robota*). Karel Capek's robots, in his play *R.U.R.* (*Rossum's Universal Robots*), were artificial beings designed to perform mechanical tasks.

13 **Pokémon,** computer-generated characters in games produced by Nintendo.

14 **A half-byte** (4 consecutive bits).

15 **An automatic cash-dispenser.**

16 *Hamster Dance* (1999), the electronically produced music by the Cuban Boys.

17 **John V. Atanasoff** (1903–95), who built a prototype which was working by October 1939, and then began work on the Atanasoff-Berry Computer, or ABC (named after Atanasoff and his assistant, Clifford E. Berry), but the outbreak of the Second World War interrupted work on it. Meanwhile, John Mauchly, who was influenced by Atanasoff's work, built the ENIAC computer (Electronic Numerical Integrator And Calculator); but a landmark court case ruled that Atanasoff, and not Mauchly, was the originator of the electronic digital computer.

18 **Colossus,** which was built (independently of Atanasoff's work) at Bletchley Park in Buckinghamshire and was in use by December 1943. Colossus was designed to decipher codes generated by German devices known as the Enigma and the Geheimschreiber (secret writer) during the Second World War.

19 **UNIVAC 1,** which correctly forecast a win for Dwight D. Eisenhower against Adlai E. Stevenson.

20 **Sir John Betjeman** (1906–84) in *The Newest Bath Guide*.

General Knowledge

1 Which term was coined for the informal canon of good behaviour to which Internet users should adhere?

2 By what stage name was the music-hall performer Maxwell George Lorimer known?

3 The name of which dynasty of English monarchs comes from the yellow flowering broom?

4 What is the meaning of the German word *Meerschaum*, the name given to a type of tobacco pipe?

5 Emperor is the largest, and pott is the smallest, size of what?

6 What is the title of the music which introduces the radio quiz *Brain of Britain*?

7 What does an orrery demonstrate?

8 In medieval armour which part of the body did a hauberk protect?

9 On which John Wyndham novel were the 1960 and 1995 films *Village of the Damned* based?

10 In April 2000 who were selected by a panel of cricket experts as Wisden's five greatest players of the twentieth century?

11 For which discovery did immunologist and pathologist Karl Landsteiner receive the 1930 Nobel Prize for physiology or medicine?

12 The motto of which newspaper is 'All the news that's fit to print'?

13 Which British aircraft designer created the Hawker Hurricane in 1935?

14 A variety of which plant is known as 'Stinking Corpse Lily' because it looks and smells like decaying carrion?

15 Which National Trust property was the location for Mr Darcy's home (Pemberley) in the BBC's 1995 adaptation of Jane Austen's *Pride and Prejudice*?

16 What is commemorated by the Hindu festival of Janmashtami?

17 According to James K. Stephen what happens when 'the Rudyards cease from kipling'?

18 Who took the pictures for one of the first photographically illustrated books to be published, *Pencil of Nature*, in 1844?

19 What advice did Dame Nellie Melba give to fellow singer Dame Clara Butt before her departure for a tour of Australia?

20 Which chess computer made history by beating a grand master (Gary Kasparov) by a score of 3.5 to 2.5 in a series of games in 1997?

General Knowledge   Answers

1 **Netiquette.** 'Net.abuse' is a breach of netiquette.

2 **Max Wall** (1908–90).

3 **Plantagenet,** from an Old French word for a sprig of broom, which came from the Latin *planta* (sprig) and *genista* (broom). Plantagenet was taken as a surname by Geoffrey, Count of Anjou (father of Henry II), who used to wear a spring of broom. The story goes that this habit began when he stooped to retrieve his hat which had fallen off while he was out hunting and scooped up some broom flowers with it.

4 **Sea-foam,** from *Meer* (sea) and *Schaum* (foam or scum). The bowls of Meerschaum pipes are made from this clay mineral (hydrated magnesium silicate), which is found in soft greyish-white masses resembling sea-foam. It is also known as sepiolite because of its resemblance to the bones of the cuttlefish (*Sepia*). It is common in the areas around the Black Sea.

5 **Writing and drawing papers.** Emperor = 72 × 48 inches and pott = 15 × 12½ inches.

6 *Eine Kleine Nacht Musik* by Mozart.

7 **The movement of the Earth and other bodies in the Solar System.** It was invented in about 1700 by George Graham, a renowned watch-maker who made instruments for the Astronomers Royal Edmond Halley and James Bradley, and for Charles Boyle, 4th Earl of Orrery, after whom he named the device.

8 **The neck and shoulders.** It comes from a Frankish word *halsberg*; *hals* (neck) and *berg* (protect).

9 **The Midwich Cuckoos** (1957), in which all the inhabitants of, and anyone passing through, a small village mysteriously fall asleep for several hours. Before long every woman of child-bearing age turns out to be pregnant. Their children have telepathic powers and a high intelligence, and seem to share a collective mind. The interference of aliens is suspected.

10 **Don Bradman** (Australia, b 1908), **Jack Hobbs** (England, 1882–1963), **Vivian Richards** (West Indies, b 1952), **Garfield Sobers** (West Indies, b 1936) and **Shane Warne** (Australia, b 1969).

11 **The ABO system of blood typing,** which helped to make blood transfusion safe.

12 **The *New York Times*.** The motto was thought up by Adolph S. Ochs (1858–1935) when he took over the newspaper in 1896.

13 **Sir Sydney Camm** (1893–1966), who was chief designer for Hawker Siddeley Aviation from 1925 until his death. The Hurricane was his first monoplane.

14 *Rafflesia* (named after Sir Stamford Raffles, who discovered it). *Rafflesia arnoldii* is the world's largest flower; it can measure more than a metre across and can weigh as much as seven kilograms. Its appearance and smell attract the flies which pollinate it.

15 **Lyme Park,** Cheshire.

16 **The birth of Krishna.**

17 **The Haggards ride no more** (in his poem, *To R.K.*, written in 1891).

18 **William Henry Fox Talbot** (1800–77).

19 **'Sing 'em muck! It's all they can understand!'**

20 **Deep Blue** (IBM).

J is for **Japan**

1 Which 1987 film, directed by Bernardo Bertolucci, was about the life of Pu Yi (Hsuan T'ung)?

2 What name was given to the ancient Japanese warrior caste (*bushi*), but came to be used for all members of the warrior class which rose to power in the twelfth century and dominated the Japanese government until the Meiji Restoration in 1868?

3 What are the names of Tokyo's two airports: international and domestic?

4 Who was the longest-reigning monarch in Japan's history?

5 Against which football team did Manchester United play in Japan in November 1999 to win the Intercontinental Cup?

6 Which trend-setting Japanese fashion designer, who started a shop named Jungle Jap in 1970, retired in 1999?

7 *Kabuki* and *Nō* are types of what?

8 In which Japanese city were about 200,000 buildings destroyed, 6,000 people killed and another 30,000 injured by the 'Great Hanshin Earthquake' in 1995?

9 Which Japanese city was the location of the 1998 Winter Olympics?

10 What is the name of the Japanese alcoholic drink made from fermented rice?

11 The autobiography of which Japanese film director, who died in 1998, was entitled *Gama no Abura* ('Something like an autobiography')?

12 What is the English name given to the sea known in Japanese as *Nihon-Kai*, in Russian as *Yaponskoye More* and in Korean as *Tonghae*?

13 Which country's naval fleet was annihilated by the Japanese fleet at the Battle of Tsushima in 1905?

14 Which two ports serve the cities of Tokyo and Osaka (and Kyoto)?

15 Which American-held island fortress at the entrance to Manila Bay in the Philippines fell to the Japanese in May 1942?

16 Which Greek-born novelist and writer, author of the children's story *The Boy who Drew Cats*, became a citizen of Japan and wrote about the customs, religion and literature of his adopted country?

17 What is the meaning of the word 'geisha'?

18 What is the term applied to the political changes in Japan which returned power to the imperial house in 1868?

19 Which sixteenth-century aesthete at the court of the military dictator Toyotomi Hideyoshi codified the tea ceremony into a style known as *wabi* ('deliberate simplicity in daily living'), which is still popular in Japan?

20 What are the *Koji-ki* and the *Nihon-shoki*?

J is for Japan Answers

1 *The Last Emperor*. Hsuan T'ung (1906–67) was the last emperor of China, who was deposed in 1912 and in 1932 became governor (and, in 1934, emperor) of the Japanese state of Manchuguo. *The Last Emperor* is based on his book *From Emperor to Citizen* (1964).

2 *Samurai*.

3 **Narita** and **Haneda**.

4 **Emperor Hirohito** (Michinomiya Hirohito, 1901–89, Emperor from 1926), whose posthumous name was Showa. He was succeeded by his eldest son, Crown Prince Akihito.

5 **Palmeiras** of Brazil. Manchester United won 1–0. Because of its reputation for violence among spectators the competition, between the winners of the European Cup and the South American Copa Libertadores, has been held in the East since 1980.

6 **Kenzo** (Kenzo Takada, b 1940).

7 **Drama.** *Kabuki* is the popular theatre. Its name comes from *ka* (singing), *bu* (dancing) and *ki* (acting). The more aristocratic *Nō* has a more formal style and courtly language.

8 **Kobe**. The earthquake measured 7.2 on the Richter scale.

9 **Nagano**, in the Japanese Alps (*Nihon Arupusu*) in Honshu.

10 *Sake*. It is often mistakenly called a wine because of its appearance and alcoholic content (up to 18 per cent), but it is made in a two-step process similar to that for brewing beer.

11 **Akira Kurosawa**, who was born in Tokyo in 1910. His autobiography was published in serial form in 1978 in the daily paper *Yomiuri Shimbun*.

12 **The Sea of Japan**.

13 **Russia**. The ships of Admiral Togo Heihachiro destroyed the Russian Baltic fleet under the command of Admiral Zinovy Petrovich Rozhestvensky in the Tsushima Strait, off the coast of south-eastern Japan.

14 **Yokohama** and **Kobe**.

15 **Corregidor**.

16 **Lafcadio Hearne** (Patricio Lafcadio Tessima Carlos Hearne, 1850–1904). His books include *Exotics and Retrospective* (1898), *In Ghostly Japan* (1899), *Shadowings* (1900), and *A Japanese Miscellany* (1901).

17 **Art person.** The arts learned by geishas include singing, dancing and playing the *samisen* (a type of lute). Many geishas are also adept at flower arranging, calligraphy and performing the tea ceremony. The geisha system is thought to have emerged in the seventeenth century to provide a class of entertainers of a different type to courtesans and prostitutes.

18 **The Meiji Restoration** (Enlightened Rule).

19 **Sen Rikyu** (1522–91). He set up a tea school which was also a kind of finishing school for soldiers from the provinces. Sen Rikyu had such a profound influence on artistic standards and social etiquette that he has been considered one of the most outstanding figures of Japanese cultural history.

20 **Histories of Japan** combined with fables. *Koji-ki* (712) means 'Records of Ancient Matters' and *Nihon-shoki* (eighth century) means 'Chronicles of Japan').

General Knowledge

1 What was the name of the town in which Gilbert and Sullivan's *The Mikado* was set?

2 In the traditional song which begins 'A frog he would a-wooing go', who says 'Heigh ho!'?

3 Which comedian's catchphrase was 'Hello playmates!'?

4 On clothing labels what is the meaning of a symbol consisting of a circle within a square, crossed out?

5 Which English League football team is nicknamed 'The Posh'?

6 Who played the part of the murderer John Christie in the 1971 film *Ten Rillington Place*?

7 Which eighteenth-century French innovation (also the name for a type of small, delicate writing table) was a term for a method of gilding furniture and clocks?

8 In which television game show, hosted by Ted Rogers and hostesses known as 'The Gentle Secs', were the losers presented with a 'Dusty Bin'?

9 Which jockey rode seven winners at Ascot on Saturday 28 September 1996?

10 Whose painting, exhibited in 1874, gave rise to the term Impressionism?

11 Who wrote the 1974 musical play *John, Paul, George, Ringo . . . and Bert*?

12 By what title is *A Dictionary of Arts and Sciences* (1768–77), the work of two Edinburgh printers named Andrew Bell and Colin Macfarquhar, now known?

13 From an old name for which country did Horace Walpole coin the term 'serendipity' for happy finds made by chance?

14 Which American test pilot was the first to break the sound barrier, in 1947, when he flew the Bell X-1 rocket research aircraft at 670 miles per hour?

15 Which two products are obtained from the tall cane-like variety and from the female plant of the short, branchy variety of *Cannabaceae sativa*?

16 In the mathematical formula $E = mc^2$, what is 'c'?

17 In which art form was Donald McGill a specialist in the early twentieth century?

18 Who was the hero of the songs and ballads of the Fenian Cycle (also known as Fionn Cycle or Ossianic Cycle)?

19 Which term was coined by environmentalists in the 1990s for a strip of land sown with perennial grasses to create an environment in which aphid-eating insects can thrive?

20 In traditional Japanese dress, what is an *obi*?

General Knowledge Answers

1 **Titipu.**

2 **Anthony Rowley:**

> *A frog he would a-wooing go,*
> *Heigh ho! says Rowley,*
> *Whether his mother would let him or no.*
> *With a roly, poly, gammon and spinach,*
> *Heigh ho! says Anthony Rowley.*

3 **Arthur Askey** (1900–82).

4 **Do not tumble dry.**

5 **Peterborough United**, who play at London Road.

6 **Richard Attenborough** (b 1923).

7 **Ormolu.** Bronze or brass were frequently used instead of genuine gilding.

8 *3–2–1.* The star prize was a car.

9 **Frankie (Lanfranco) Dettori.**

10 **Claude Monet** (1840–1926). The term 'Impressionism' was coined, from the title of the painting *Impression: soleil levant*, by the journalist Louis Leroy writing in the satirical magazine *Le Charivari* in 1874.

11 **Willy Russell** (b 1947).

12 *Encyclopaedia Britannica.* The first part of it was published in December 1768 and the whole work was completed in 1771. It consisted of three volumes containing 2,391 pages, four folded leaves of unnumbered tables, and 160 copperplates engraved by Andrew Bell. It has been published in the USA since the American publishers, Horace E. Hooper and Walter M. Jackson, bought *Britannica* from Adam and Charles Black in 1901.

13 **Sri Lanka** (Ceylon), which was known as Serendib as early as AD 361. Horace Walpole's inspiration, about which he wrote to Horace Mann in 1754, came from a Persian fairy tale, *The Three Princes of Serendip*, whose heroes often made discoveries by chance.

14 **Charles (Chuck) Yeager** (b 1923). He also flew the Bell X-1 A at more than twice the speed of sound in 1953.

15 **Hemp** (from the tall cane-like variety) and **cannabis** (from the short branchy variety).

16 **The speed of light.** According to Einstein's Theory of Relativity, mass and energy are equivalent and interchangeable quantities, the equivalence being expressed by his famous equation in which 'm' is an object's mass.

17 **Postcards.** He specialised in outsize women wearing bathing suits at the seaside with their skinny henpecked husbands, and in captions with double meanings.

18 **Finn MacCumhaill (MacCool).** He led a band of warriors, huntsmen and poets, the Fianna Éireann, during the reign of Cormac mac Airt in the third century.

19 **Beetle bank.** It is one of the methods, introduced in the 1990s, by which farmers are encouraged to manage their land in an environmentally sensitive way.

20 **A wide sash or belt.** It is made of satin or a stiff silk material and secures the kimono. The size of a woman's *obi* is about 370 centimetres long and 25 centimetres wide; a man's *obi* is about threequarters of that length and one-sixth of the width. The *obi* is wound around the waist over the kimono and tied at the back.

K is for **Kitchen**

1 What are the principal ingredients of kedgeree?

2 Which American politician quoted his 'military jester', Harry Vaughan, when he said in 1952, 'If you can't stand the heat, get out of the kitchen'?

3 Who is the chef of *Le Manoir aux Quat' Saisons* in Great Milton, Oxfordshire?

4 From which family of fish does caviare come?

5 From what is the French brandy known as Calvados made?

6 Who wrote the 1999 recipe book *A Taste of India*?

7 What kind of fish is soaked in brine and then strung from wooden slats and lightly smoked to produce the Great Yarmouth speciality, bloaters?

8 What is the common name for the herb *Petroselinium crispum*, which is used for garnishing and flavouring foods?

9 Which foodstuff was the first to be rationed during the First World War?

10 What are morels, ceps and blewits?

11 'Jamaica pepper' and 'pimento' are alternative names for which spice?

12 In the dish 'Angels on horseback', what are wrapped in bacon and served on hot buttered toast?

13 Which frothy sweet drink, popular in Georgian England, was traditionally made by milking a cow into a bowl of sweetened wine or brandy (or other spirit)?

14 If a dish is devilled what has been done to it?

15 What name is given to a double loin of beef?

16 Which food ingredient, made from seaweed, is used as a vegetarian alternative to gelatine for setting jellies?

17 In Chaucer's *Canterbury Tales*, which pilgrim's table manners did he describe as follows:
> *At mete well y-taught was she withalle:*
> *She let no morsel from hir lippes falle,*
> *Nor wet hir fingers in hir sauce deepe;*
> *Well could she carry a morsel and well keepe*
> *That no drop ne fill upon hir brest.*

18 What is smoked to produce the Icelandic speciality *hangikjöt*?

19 For what is a mandolin used in the kitchen?

20 What is the name of the French chef who wrote the 1857 book *Culinary Campaign in the Crimea*?

K is for **Kitchen** Answers

1 **Fish and rice.** The dish originated in India and its name is a corruption of the Hindi and Sanskrit words *khicri* and *khicca*.

2 **Harry S. Truman** (1884–1972).

3 **Raymond Blanc.** The restaurant opened in 1984.

4 **Sturgeon.** Caviare is prepared by pickling and salting the roe.

5 **Apples.**

6 **Madhur Jaffrey.**

7 **Herring.**

8 **Parsley.**

9 **Sugar.** Sugar supplies fell short of demand in 1916, and in 1917 a form of rationing was introduced; to buy sugar, people had to register with a grocer. Grocers received supplies of sugar which were equivalent to the rations of their registered customers. In 1918 a national rationing scheme was introduced in which everyone received a ration book containing separate coupons for meat, butter or margarine, sugar and lard.

10 **Edible fungi** (mushrooms).

11 **Allspice.**

12 **Oysters.** '*Devils* on horseback' are prunes wrapped in bacon and served on toast.

13 **Syllabub.** A more modern way to make it is to infuse the rind of two lemons in 300 millilitres of sweet white wine (or any combination of white wine, medium sherry and brandy). Leave it overnight, remove the rind and add the juice of the lemons. Pour the mixture into a bowl, together with 300 millilitres of whipping cream and up to one tablespoon of sugar and about half a teaspoon of nutmeg. Whisk well and pour the syllabub into glasses. Refrigerate for several hours and serve once the cream and wine or spirit have separated.

14 **It has been highly spiced.**

15 **Baron.** A loin of beef comes from the area between the ribs and the tail. A baron is a double loin (ie it has not been split at the backbone). The equivalent cut of lamb is known as a saddle. Sirloin of beef is from above the loin (from the Old French *surlonge*). The mistaken spelling 'sir-' has given rise to stories in which the beef was 'knighted', for example by James VI & I. In turn, these stories have led to others about the nobility of the 'baron' of beef.

16 **Agar-agar.** Gelatine is made by the prolonged boiling of the bones and tissues of fish and other animals.

17 **The Prioress.**

18 **Lamb.** The word *hangikjöt* means, literally, 'hung meat'.

19 **Slicing vegetables.** It is a rectangular base to which a blade is fixed horizontally. The gap between the base and the blade can be adjusted to alter the thickness of the slices produced by rubbing the vegetable up and down the mandolin.

20 **Alexis Soyer** (1809–58). He was born in Meaux, France, and became the chef of the Reform Club in London in 1837. In 1855 he went to the Crimea, where he introduced the 'Soyer stove' for use in the preparation of food for the British forces.

General Knowledge

1 Which US Labrador fur trader set up a frozen food business in 1924 after noticing how the people there preserved food for the winter?

2 For what is AWACS the acronym?

3 Which singer rose to fame in the revue *Mr Tower of London* in 1923 and became known for songs such as *Wish Me Luck as You Wave Me Goodbye* and *The Biggest Aspidistra in the World*?

4 From which species of goat is mohair obtained?

5 The names of which cartoon husband and wife pair were used in army slang for pairs of medals which are usually worn together, such as the British War Medal and the Victory Medal?

6 In Paris what are Franklin D. Roosevelt, Louis Blanc and Étienne Marcel?

7 The popular name of which rare butterfly comes from the London borough in which it was first discovered in the United Kingdom?

8 For what do the letters P & O in the shipping line stand?

9 Who composed the Academy Award-winning song *Moon River* for the 1961 film *Breakfast at Tiffany's*?

10 In fairy folklore what was the occupation of Mab?

11 Who instituted the Thames 'Head of the River' race in 1926?

12 What was the pen-name of the nineteenth-century author Maria Louisa de la Ramée?

13 In the 1971 BBC1 television programme *The Wombles*, what was the name of the Wombles' cook?

14 Which king did Colonel Qaddafi depose in 1969?

15 What is the crime of 'embracery'?

16 Which French word is used for a type of enamelling in which a pattern is marked on to a surface by thin metal strips soldered on to it, and the resulting compartments are filled in with coloured enamels?

17 From which American Nobel Prize winner's *Lectures on Physics* were the books *Six easy Pieces* and *Six not-so-easy Pieces* compiled?

18 Of which Irish province were the MacCarthys hereditary kings?

19 Which three pairs of comedians made up the Crazy Gang?

20 From what is mock turtle soup made?

General Knowledge   Answers

1 **Clarence Birdseye** (1886–1956). Birdseye froze packaged food between two refrigerated metal plates. He was not the first to produce frozen foods, but his process was very efficient and preserved the original taste of foods such as fish, fruits and vegetables.

2 **Airborne Warning And Control System**, a mobile, long-range radar surveillance and control system for air defence which was first used in 1977.

3 **Gracie Fields** (Grace Stansfield, 1898–1979).

4 **Angora**. Mohair is derived from the Arabic word *mukayyar* (to select).

5 **Mutt and Jeff**. They were the creations of the American cartoonist Bud Fisher (1884–1954).

6 **Metro stations**. The first was named after the US president Franklin Delano Roosevelt (1882–1945, president 1933–45). Louis Blanc (1811–82) was a utopian socialist, noted for his theory of 'social workshops' (workshops controlled by the workers). Étienne Marcel (*c* 1316–58) was a Paris bourgeois leader, who played a major part in the Paris Revolution of 1355–8.

7 **Camberwell beauty** (*Nymphalis antiopa*). It is known as the 'mourning cloak' in the USA.

8 **Peninsular and Oriental**. The shipping line was founded in 1837 as the Peninsular Steam Navigation Company and ran a mail service between Britain and the Iberian Peninsula.

9 **Henry Mancini** (1924–94).

10 **Midwife**. In Shakespeare's *Romeo and Juliet* she is the fairies' midwife, who delivers sleeping men of their innermost wishes in the form of dreams.

11 **Steve Fairbairn**. The Head of the River Race is a winter race for eights over the ½-mile course from Mortlake to Putney (part of the University Boat Race course in reverse). Steve Fairbairn devised it for crews preparing for summer regattas.

12 **Ouida** (1839–1908). She took the name from a childish mispronunciation of 'Louisa'. Her novels include *Held in Bondage* (1863) and *A Village Commune* (1881).

13 **Madame Cholet**.

14 **King Idris I** (1890–1983), the first king of Libya when it gained its independence in 1951. After Colonel Muammar al-Qaddafi (b 1942) led an army which took over the government, Idris was given political asylum in Egypt, where he stayed until his death.

15 **Attempting to influence a jury by improper means**. The offence is now dealt with as 'contempt of court'.

16 **Cloisonné** (a *cloison* is a compartment).

17 **Richard Feynmann** (1918–88), who was awarded the Nobel Prize for physics in 1965 for his work on quantum electrodynamics, along with Julian Schwinger of the United States and Tomonaga Sin-Itiro of Japan.

18 **(South) Munster**. In 1127 Kerry was divided to form the O'Brien kingdom of Thomond (North Munster) and the MacCarthy kingdom of Desmond (South Munster).

19 **Bud Flanagan** (1896–1968) and **Chesney Allen** (1894–1982), **Jimmy Nervo** (1890–1975) and **Teddy Knox** (1896–1974), **Charlie Naughton** (1887–1976) and **Jimmy Gold** (1886–1967).

20 **Calf's head**. When turtles were in short supply and became too expensive, calf's head was found to be a useful substitute.

L is for **Literature**

1 Which character in a children's book yearns for his 'dulce domum' thus:
   *... the home he had been so happy to get back to after his day's work.
   And the home had been happy with him, too, evidently, and was missing him, and wanted him back, and was telling him so, through his
   nose, sorrowfully, reproachfully, but with no bitterness or anger; only
   with plaintive reminder that it was there, and wanted him.*

2 In Dickens' *David Copperfield*, what is the name of the obsequious and
   scheming clerk who frequently claims ''Umble, I'm very'?

3 Which nineteenth-century novel was first published under the title of *The
   Weaver of Raveloe*?

4 The final chapter of which eighteenth-century novel begins as follows:
   *Thus, gentle reader, I have given thee a faithful History of my Travels
   for Sixteen Years, and above Seven Months; wherein I have not been so
   studious of Ornament as Truth.*

5 Which African-American writer, originally named Marguerite Johnson, has
   written a series of autobiographical books including *I Know Why the
   Caged Bird Sings* (1970), *The Heart of a Woman* (1981) and *Even the Stars
   Look Lonesome* (1998)?

6 What is the name of the family which lives at Cold Comfort Farm, in the
   1932 novel of that title by Stella Gibbons?

7 In Henry Fielding's *History of Tom Jones, a Foundling*, written in 1749, in
   whose bed was the baby Tom Jones found?

8 Which Canadian writer wrote the 1985 novel *The Handmaid's Tale*, about
   a society of the future in which the role of women is only to produce
   babies?

9 What was the title of D. H. Lawrence's first published novel?

10 Which American journalist, fashion critic and novelist wrote the 1988 best-
   seller *Bonfire of the Vanities*?

11 Which Oxford don and writer of science fiction and children's novels also
   wrote books on religious subjects, such as *The Screwtape Letters* (1940)?

12 Which book opens with the words '"Take my camel, dear," said my aunt
   Dot, as she climbed down from this animal on her return from High Mass'?

13 What was the pen-name of the Scottish novelist James Leslie Mitchell who
   wrote the trilogy *A Scots Quair*?

14 Which Nigerian writer and minority rights activist, who was hanged for
   promoting Ogoni nationalism, wrote *A Novel in Rotten English* in 1985?

15 From which source did Thomas Hardy take the title of his novel *Far From
   the Madding Crowd*?

16 In Homer's *Odyssey*, what was the name of the sorceress who lived on the
   island of Aeaea and turned Odysseus's companions into swine?

17 *Heimskringla* (The History of the Kings of Norway), *The Poetic Edda* (a
   manual of Norse mythology for poets) and *Egil's Saga* were all written by
   which thirteenth-century Icelandic chieftain and historian?

18 Who was the German-born author of the anti-war novel, *Im Westen nichts
   Neues* (*All Quiet on the Western Front*), published in 1929?

19 In Chaucer's *Canterbury Tales*, who was the keeper of the Tabard Inn?

20 Who is the only Icelandic novelist to have won the Nobel Prize for
   literature, in 1955?

L is for **Literature**   Answers

1 **Mole** in *The Wind in the Willows* (1908) by Kenneth Grahame. *The Wind in the Willows* is my all-time favourite book. It was the first book my mother and I read together – to improve our English – after the family moved from Iceland to Scotland in 1930.

2 **Uriah Heep.**

3 *Silas Marner* (1861) by George Eliot.

4 *Gulliver's Travels* (1726) by Jonathan Swift (1667–1745).

5 **Maya Angelou** (b 1928).

6 **Starkadder.**

7 **Squire Allworthy.**

8 **Margaret Atwood** (b 1939). *The Handmaid's Tale*, which was shortlisted for the Booker Prize, was made into a film starring Natasha Richardson, Robert Duvall and Faye Dunaway in 1990.

9 *The White Peacock* (1911).

10 **Tom Wolfe** (b 1931).

11 **C. S. Lewis** (Clive Staples Lewis, 1898–1963).

12 *The Towers of Trebizond* (1956) by Rose Macaulay (Dame Emilie Rose Macaulay, 1881–1958). The novel, set in Turkey, is about a woman who is determined to start an Anglican mission in Turkey.

13 **Lewis Grassic Gibbon** (1901–35). The three novels were entitled *Sunset Song* (1932), *Cloud Howe* (1933) and *Grey Granite* (1934). They chronicle the life of a crofter's daughter from the Mearns of Kincardineshire named Chris Guthrie of Kinraddie. *Sunset Song* was serialised in a highly acclaimed 1971 BBC television production starring Vivien Heilbron.

14 **Ken Saro-Wiwa** (Kenule Beeson Saro-Wiwa, 1941–95). He also wrote a series of humorous books about 'Basi and Company', satirising Nigerians whose main aim in life was to make money with the minimum effort, on which a popular Nigerian television series was based.

15 **Thomas Gray's** *Elegy Written in a Country Churchyard* (1751):
Far from the madding crowd's ignoble strife
Their sober wishes never learned to stray;
Along the cool sequestered vale of life
They kept the noiseless tenor of their way.

16 **Circe** (from the Greek *kirkos*, meaning 'falcon'). The spell did not affect Odysseus because he had an antidote – a magic herb known as moly (possibly a form of lily) given to him by the god Hermes.

17 **Snorri Sturluson** (1179–1241).

18 **Erich Maria Remarque** (1898–1970). The 1930 film of the book won an Academy Award for Lewis Milestone (Best Picture Director).

19 **Harry Bailley.**

20 **Halldór Laxness** (1902–98). He wrote several epic novels of Icelandic life, including *Independent People* (1934–5), *World Light* (1937–40) and *Iceland's Bell* (1943–9). I have had the pleasure of translating five of his novels into English.

General Knowledge Questions

1 What is the name of the multi-coloured elephant in the children's books by David McKee?

2 Which Member of Parliament is nicknamed 'the Beast of Bolsover'?

3 Which seventeenth-century woodcarver, known for his carvings of acanthus leaves, fruit, flowers, acorns and cherubs' heads, produced many of the carvings in St Paul's cathedral?

4 What is the name of the Pope's official summer residence?

5 The computer language BASIC is an acronym for what?

6 What is the name of the small, submarine-shaped toy musical instrument which produces sounds similar to those of a comb and tissue paper?

7 In which village in Gwynedd, North Wales, is the grave of a hound which, according to local legend, belonged to Llewelyn the Great (Llewelyn ap Iorwerth)?

8 What are the names of the two islands in the Seine in the centre of Paris?

9 What are the names of the two racecourses at Newmarket?

10 What name, from the Dutch meaning 'mumblers', was given to the followers of John Wycliffe in the fourteenth century?

11 What was the former name of the building which now houses the Tate Modern on the South Bank of the Thames, opposite St Paul's cathedral?

12 For what forenames do the initials F. W. stand in Woolworths?

13 By what name is the edible fruit of the plant *Lycopersicon esculentum*, a member of the nightshade family (*Solanaceae*), better known?

14 The members of which string quartet were Norbert Brainin (violin), Sigmund Nissel (violin), Martin Lovett (cello) and Peter Schidlof (viola), until Schidlof died in 1987?

15 What name is given to the curved mark (~) which is placed above a letter to indicate its pronunciation: for example, in Spanish, to indicate that 'n' is pronounced 'ny'?

16 What name is given to the last of the seven canonical hours for prayer?

17 Which German physicist, in 1827, formulated the law of electrical resistance which is named after him?

18 In which 1949 film did Alec Guinness play eight parts?

19 The defence of which Scottish castle against English forces in the fourteenth century was led by 'Black Agnes'?

20 In the 1911 novel by Max Beerbohm, what effect does Zuleika Dobson have on the young men at Judas College, Oxford?

General Knowledge · Answers

1 **Elmer.**

2 **Dennis Skinner** (b 1932). The nickname comes from his constituency and his savage comments in the House.

3 **Grinling Gibbons** (1648–1741). He was born in Rotterdam and moved to England in about 1667, where his talents were brought to the attention of Charles II, who appointed him to the Board of Works.

4 **Castel Gandolfo.** The palace overlooks Lake Albano in the Alban Hills to the south of Rome.

5 **Beginners' All Symbolic Instruction Code.**

6 **Kazoo.** The user hums or sings into the opening at one end of the instrument, rather than blowing it. This makes a paper or polythene membrane vibrate to produce a buzzing sound.

7 **Beddgelert.** The name comes from the Welsh *bedd* (grave) and the hound's name, Gelert. According to legend, Llewelyn (1173–1240) had left his baby son in the care of his faithful hound, but returned to find the animal with blood dripping from its jaws, and no sign of his son. He killed the hound in his grief and then found the baby close to the body of a wolf which the dog had killed.

8 **Île de la Cité and Île St-Louis.** The Île de la Cité is the ancient centre of the city; eight bridges link it to the banks of the Seine and a ninth leads to the Île Saint-Louis to the south-east.

9 **The Rowley Mile** and the **July Course.** The Rowley Mile course is used in the spring and autumn and the July course is used in the summer.

10 **Lollards.**

11 **Bankside Power Station.** The building was originally designed by Sir Giles Gilbert Scott and built between 1947 and 1960. The alterations to convert it were designed by the Swiss architects Herzog and de Meuron.

12 **Frank Winfield** (Franklin Winfield Woolworth, 1852–1919).

13 **Tomato.** The leaves and roots of the plant are poisonous, like most plants of the *Solanaceae* family; they contain neurotoxin solanine.

14 **The Amadeus Quartet.**

15 **Tilde.** The word is derived from the Latin *titulus* (title).

16 **Compline.** The others are: matins, prime, tierce, sext, nones and vespers.

17 **Georg Ohm** (1787–1854). Ohm's law states that the resistance, or the ratio of voltage to current, for an electric circuit at a fixed temperature is usually constant. The Ohm is the unit of measurement for resistance.

18 *Kind Hearts and Coronets.* The film is about an heir to a dukedom who overcomes numerous obstacles to his inheritance and is tried for a murder of which he is innocent. Alec Guinness plays, in turn, each member of the ancestral family.

19 **Dunbar.** Agnes, Countess of Dunbar, was the wife of Patrick, Earl of Dunbar and March; her nickname came from her swarthy colouring. In her husband's absence she defended Dunbar Castle with a small garrison of archers and servants when it was besieged by an English expeditionary force in 1338. After each day's bombardment the countess and her ladies-in-waiting paraded along the battlements and ostentatiously wiped away with their kerchiefs the debris created by the mangonels.

20 **They commit suicide by drowning themselves in the Isis** because of their unrequited infatuation with her.

M is for **Mathematics**

Questions

1 When two dice are rolled, what total has the highest probability of being produced?

2 Which Greek mathematician wrote *Elements* in about 300 BC?

3 What name is given to a triangle which has no equal sides?

4 What is the Arabic equivalent of the Roman numeral MMCDLXXXIV?

5 What does the mathematical sign ∞ represent?

6 An acre (from the Latin *ager*, meaning 'field') used to be the area of land a yoke of oxen could plough in a day; which English king standardised it as a piece of land which was 40 rods long and 4 rods wide?

7 What name is given to a diagram which shows relationships between sets as shown below:

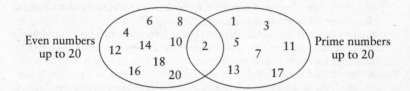

Even numbers up to 20   Prime numbers up to 20

8 Which Scottish mathematician and theological writer first devised logarithms?

9 What is the name of the mathematical game in which any number of objects (such as counters) is divided arbitrarily into several piles; two players take turns to remove any number of objects from any one of the piles, and the player who removes the last object wins?

10 What name is given to a rectangular strip of paper or other material whose ends have been joined after first giving one of them one half-twist?

11 Which English mathematician and Episcopal minister invented the slide rule in about 1622?

12 Which Swiss mathematician invented logarithms independently of John Napier and published his table of antilogarithms in 1620?

13 In which country was the metric system devised?

14 What are the next eight numbers in the Fibonacci series?
1, 1, 2, _, _, _, _, _, _, _, _.

15 What is multiplied by π (pi = 3.1416) to calculate the surface area of a sphere?

16 Which English mathematician and physicist was appointed Warden of the Mint in 1696 and then Master of the Mint in 1699?

17 What name is given to a whole number which equals the sum of its proper divisors (ie, divisors including 1 but excluding the number itself)?

18 What number is a googol?

19 Which British mathematician was awarded the 1995–6 Wolf Prize for his solution of the mathematical problem known as 'Fermat's Last Theorem'?

20 Which mathematical innovation did Simon Stevin of Holland introduce to Europe in his short pamphlet *La Disme* in 1585?

M is for Mathematics   Answers

1 **Seven**. There are six ways in which to make seven: $1 + 6$, $6 + 1$, $2 + 5$, $5 + 2$, $4 + 3$ and $3 + 4$.

2 **Euclid**.

3 **Scalene**.

4 **2,484**. MM = 2,000, CD = 400, LXXX = 80 and IV = 4.

5 **Infinity**.

6 **Edward I** (1239–1307, r 1272–1307). A rod is equivalent to 16½ feet: one acre = 660×66 feet (43,560 square feet, or 4,840 square yards).

7 **Venn diagram**. It was named after John Venn who used it in his work, although he did not invent it; similar diagrams had been used by Gottfried Leibniz and Leonhard Euler.

8 **John Napier** (1550–1617). His first work on logarithms, *Mirifici Logarithmorum Canonis Descriptio* (Description of the Marvellous Canon of Logarithms), was published in 1614.

9 **Nim**. It is an extremely skilled game, in which the players have to work several moves ahead to ensure that they leave their opponent with no option but to remove the penultimate counter.

10 **Möbius strip**. The strip has only one face and remains in one piece when split down the middle along its length. The German mathematicians August Ferdinand Möbius and Johann Benedict Listing discovered it independently, in 1858.

11 **William Oughtred** (1574–1660).

12 **Joost Bürgi** (1552–1632). He was court watch-maker to Duke Wilhelm IV of Hesse-Kassel and worked in the royal observatory, where he developed geometrical and astronomical instruments.

13 **France**. It was devised by a group of twelve scientists appointed by the French National Assembly in 1791.

14 **3, 5, 8, 13, 21, 34, 55, 89**. Each number is the sum of the two which precede it. The series was devised by the Italian mathematician Leonardo Fibonacci (*c* 1170–1240) to solve a puzzle about the breeding rate of rabbits.

15 **The diameter squared**.

16 **Sir Isaac Newton** (1642–1727).

17 **A perfect number**: for example, 6 $(1 + 2 + 3 = 6)$ and 28 $(1 + 2 + 4 + 7 + 14 = 28)$. The next two perfect numbers are 496 and 8,128. Most numbers are either 'abundant' or 'deficient'. In an abundant number, the sum of its proper divisors is greater than the number: for example, 24 $(1 + 2 + 3 + 4 + 6 + 8 + 12 = 36)$. In a deficient number, the sum of its proper divisors is smaller than the number: for example 32 $(1 + 2 + 4 + 8 + 16 = 31)$.

18 10^{100}. The term was coined by the American mathematician Edward Kasner, at the suggestion of his thirteen-year-old son. A googolplex is 10^{googol} (the number 1 followed by 10^{100} zeros).

19 **Andrew Wiles** (b 1953). 'Fermat's last theorem' was really a long-standing conjecture, posed in the third century by Diophantus (that there are no positive integer solutions of $xn + yn = zn$ for $n > 2$). Richard Taylor helped Wiles to fill in a few gaps in the solution which he proposed in 1993; it was completed by 1995.

20 **Decimal fractions**.

General Knowledge

1 What name is given to a solid figure which has twelve edges, all of equal length and at right angles to one another?

2 In the BBC children's television series *Watch with Mother* what was the name of Andy Pandy's rag doll friend?

3 What name is given to the outermost layer of the skin?

4 In electronics, for what do the letters LED stand?

5 On which Caribbean island is the holiday resort of Montego Bay?

6 'The writing on the wall' has come to mean anything which heralds disaster; who, in the Bible, interpreted the writing on the wall?

7 Which French phrase implies that the privilege of rank imposes obligations of honour and responsibility?

8 Which late-fifteenth-century fresco by Leonardo da Vinci is in the refectory of the monastery of Santa Maria delle Grazie in Milan?

9 Which sport is played at 'Billy Williams' Cabbage Patch'?

10 Which of Shakespeare's plays ends with the words: 'Go bid the soldiers shoot'?

11 *Ricinus communis* used to be in common use as a treatment for digestive disorders. What is the more common name of this plant?

12 After which emperor of Ethiopia do Rastafarians take their name?

13 What was the first film in which Greta Garbo was heard speaking?

14 Which composer's String Quartet in D major is nicknamed the Frog Quartet because of the 'croaking' theme in the finale?

15 What was the name of Helen Keller's teacher, who helped her to overcome her inability to see, hear or speak and to communicate with others, and who accompanied her to Radcliffe College and on worldwide lecturing tours?

16 Which Scottish chemist, in 1895, discovered the presence of helium in the Earth's atmosphere and was awarded the Nobel Prize for chemistry in 1904 for his work on inert gases?

17 By what other name is the Battle of Chevy Chase, which was fought between the English and the Scots in 1388, known?

18 Which cartoonist created Colonel Blimp in 1934 for the *Evening Standard*?

19 Which figure of speech was named after a fourteenth-century Archbishop of Canterbury who extorted taxes for Henry VII from both the rich and the poor?

20 A prime number is a whole number which can be divided only by itself and by 1; what name is given to whole numbers greater than 1 which are not prime numbers?

General Knowledge Answers

1 **Cube.**

2 **Looby Loo.** The series was first shown in 1950.

3 **Epidermis.**

4 **Light-emitting diode:** a semiconductor diode which emits infra-red or visible light when an electric current is passed through it.

5 **Jamaica.** It lies on the site of an Arawak village visited by Christopher Columbus; Spanish traders named it Bahía de Manteca (Butter Bay), probably because lard ('hog's butter') was one of the main commodities bought and sold there.

6 **Daniel.** A mysterious hand appeared, writing on the wall of the chamber in which Belshazzar was feasting:

> ... MENE, MENE, TEKEL *and* UPHARSIN. *This is the interpretation of the thing:* MENE; *God hath numbered thy kingdom and finished it.* TEKEL; *thou art weighed in the balances, and art found wanting.* PERES; *thy kingdom is divided and given to the Medes and Persians.*

(Daniel, 5:25–28)

7 *Noblesse oblige.*

8 *The Last Supper* (*c* 1497).

9 **Rugby.** It is the nickname given to the English Rugby Football Union's ground at Twickenham. Billy Williams (1860–1951) acquired the site, a former market garden, in 1907.

10 *Hamlet* (spoken by Fortinbras).

11 **Castor oil.**

12 **Haile Selassie I** (Prince Ras Tafari, 1892–1975). He was emperor from 1930 until he was deposed in 1970, after taking Ethiopia into the League of Nations and the United Nations and making Addis Ababa the major centre for the Organisation of African Unity. He was a Coptic Christian and Rastafarians regard him as a divine being and the champion of black people.

13 *Anna Christie*, in 1930. She won an Academy Award for Best Actress.

14 **Haydn.**

15 **Anne Sullivan** (1866–1936). She had impaired vision herself, and had learned the manual alphabet in order to communicate with others.

16 **Sir William Ramsay** (1852–1916). In 1894 he isolated argon with Lord Rayleigh and in 1898, with other scientists, he discovered krypton, neon and xenon. In 1900 he isolated radon and demonstrated that it was an inert gas.

17 **The Battle of Otterburn** (Northumberland). Sir Henry Percy, eldest son of the Earl of Northumberland, led an English force which fought against a Scottish army led by James, Earl of Douglas. The battle is immortalised in ballads such as the English *Ballad of Chevy Chase* and the Scots *Ballad of Otterburn*.

18 **Sir David Low** (1891–1963).

19 **Morton's fork** (after John Morton, *c* 1420–1500). He told people who appeared rich that they must easily be able to afford to contribute, and accused those who appeared poor of having concealed wealth. The phrase 'Morton's fork' is now applied to any two-pronged attack.

20 **Composite numbers.** A composite number is the product of two whole numbers, each greater than 1. By repeated factorisation, every composite number can be expressed as the product of primes, some of which may be repeated. For example, $147 = 7, 21 = 7, 7, 3$.

N is for **Natural History**

1 Blindworm is a misnomer – the animal is not a worm; what is it?

2 Which crop is attacked by the Colorado beetle?

3 By what name is the houseplant *Saintpaulia* better known?

4 Which area is to be designated as Scotland's first National Park?

5 The 1988 film *Gorillas in the Mist* is the life story of which anthropologist, who was murdered in 1985 after spending eighteen years observing, and trying to protect, gorillas which inhabit a small area in the Virunga mountains on the border of Rwanda?

6 What type of tree are sessile, Turkey, English and Mirbeck's?

7 To which animal did Robert Burns address the following lines in 1785:

> *Wee, sleekit, cow'rin', tim'rous beastie,*
> *O, what a panic's in thy breastie!*
> *Thou need na start awa sae hasty,*
> > *Wi' bickering brattle [scamper]!*
> *I wad be laith to rin an' chase thee,*
> > *Wi' murd'ring pattle [a type of spade]!*

8 Chewing gum was originally made from a product of which tree?

9 Conifers are gymnosperms; what does the word 'gymnosperm' mean?

10 Which animal was toasted by the Jacobites during the reign of Queen Anne as 'the little gentleman in velvet', and why?

11 The name of which environmental organisation is abbreviated to CCW?

12 What kind of living things does a mycologist study?

13 Which mammals were the subject of the English conservationist Jane Goodall's 1971 book, *In the Shadow of Man*?

14 What is the name for the seed-bearing part of a flower comprising the ovary, stigma and style?

15 In 1946 which ornithologist and artist established the Severn Wildlife Trust at Slimbridge in Gloucestershire?

16 In Australia what kind of animal is known as a wobbegong?

17 What is the collective name for a group of foxes?

18 What is the name of Britain's only wild parrot?

19 What kind of birds were reared by Benedictine monks from 1393 in Abbotsbury in Dorset and are still protected there?

20 In 1998 which insect was celebrated at a first-ever festival in its honour in Argyll?

N is for Natural History

1 **A lizard** (*Anguis fragilis*). It isn't blind either.
2 **Potato.** The beetle (*Leptinotarsa*) was a native of semi-desert areas of Colorado, feeding on the buffalo burr plant; when potatoes were introduced it adapted itself to this newly abundant diet.
3 **African violet.**
4 **Loch Lomond and the Trossachs.**
5 **Dian Fossey** (1932–85). Sigourney Weaver played the role of Dian Fossey, for which she won an Academy Award for Best Actress.
6 **Oak.**
7 **A mouse** (*To a Mouse*). The phrase 'the best-laid schemes of mice and men' comes from the poem, in which the poet's plough destroys the field-mouse's nest:

> *The best-laid schemes o' mice an' men*
> > *Gang aft a-gley [often go awry],*
> *An' lea'e us nought but grief an' pain,*
> > *For promis'd joy.*

8 **Chicle, sapodilla** or **naseberry** (*Achras zapota*), which is native to Central America. Chevron-shaped incisions are made in the bark so that the latex can ooze out. It is boiled to make the gum base for chewing gum; synthetic products have now been developed to use in its place.
9 **Naked seed** (ie, not enclosed in a fruit). In an angiosperm (flowering plant), the seeds are enclosed by mature ovaries (fruits).
10 **The mole** (because William III, who took the throne from the last Jacobite king, James VII & II during the 'Glorious Revolution' of 1688, broke his collar bone and died after his horse stumbled on a molehill).
11 **Countryside Council for Wales.**
12 **Fungi**, a group which includes mushrooms and yeasts. Mycology is relevant to medicine (penicillin, streptomycin and tetracycline), the dairy, wine and baking industries and in the production of dyes and inks. Medical mycology is the study of fungus organisms which cause disease in humans.
13 **Chimpanzees.** Jane Goodall (b 1934) became the scientific director of the Gombe Wildlife Research Institute in Tanzania in 1967. She discovered that chimpanzees modify various natural objects for use as tools and weapons and demonstrated that they hunt other animals for meat.
14 **Pistil.**
15 **Sir Peter Scott** (1909–89).
16 **A shark** of the *Orectolobidae* family.
17 **A skulk.**
18 **Ring-necked (or rose-ringed) parakeet.**
19 **Mute swans.** The monastery, the Abbey of St Peter, was built in the eleventh century by Orc, a Christian steward of Canute. In 1538 Sir Giles Strangways, the commissioner appointed by Henry VIII to administer the surrender of the monastery, land and holdings, bought it, including the Swannery. Five hundred years and fifteen generations later the land still belongs to his family.
20 **The midge.** The Midge Festival featured presentations and displays about the midge and its habitat; it included local folklore as well as scientific information and even workshops in which children could make insect masks to wear at the grand procession at the Midge Fair.

General Knowledge

1 Of what kind of tree is General Sherman (named after a union leader in the American Civil War) the largest known living specimen?

2 The trademark of which Wigan-born music-hall singer was his ukulele?

3 Who was the Roman god of sleep?

4 In publishing, for what does the abbreviation ISBN stand?

5 Which cricketer holds the record for the most first-class centuries?

6 The phrase 'the Affluent Society' was popularised by whose 1958 book of that title?

7 Which follower of St Francis of Assisi (whose feast-day is 11 August) is the patron saint of television?

8 What did Percy Shaw invent in 1934, which are still useful to motorists?

9 One of the many idioms which Shakespeare introduced into English is 'salad days'; by which character is it said, and in which play?

10 Which American naturalist wrote the 1962 book *Silent Spring*, about the effects of synthetic pesticides on the food chain?

11 Who is the creator of the 'Lost Consonants' feature in the *Guardian*?

12 If a dish is served 'à la Crécy', with which vegetable has it been cooked or garnished?

13 What is known as 'gerrymandering'?

14 Which king of England was married in Cyprus?

15 Which pre-Raphaelite artist painted *Flaming June*, which is now in the Museo de Arte de Ponce in Puerto Rico?

16 Which classic piece of photographic equipment was designed in 1924 by Oskar Barnack for use in his mountaineering holidays in the Alps?

17 What was the city of Oslo named between 1877 and 1925?

18 In the First World War, who were known as 'Ally Sloper's Cavalry'?

19 According to the old 'Iron Law of Wages', what happens when wages rise above subsistence level?

20 What is 'Will o' the wisp'?

General Knowledge Answers

1 **Giant sequoia** or **redwood** (*Sequoiadendron giganteum*). General Sherman, in Sequoia National Park, California, is 83 metres high and the circumference at its base is 31 metres.
2 **George Formby** (1905–61).
3 **Somnus** (the Greek god of sleep was Morpheus).
4 **International Standard Book Number.** The ten digits identify the country of publication, publisher, title, edition and volume number.
5 **Jack Hobbs** (1882–1963). Wisden gives 197 as Jack Hobbs' total number of centuries, but the Association of Cricket Statisticians gives 199.
6 **J. K. Galbraith** (b 1908).
7 **St Clare** (1194–1253). She was abbess of the Poor Clares, founded by St Francis. She was designated the patron saint of television by Pope Pius XII in 1958 because while she was in her cell on Christmas day, 1252, she 'saw and heard' Mass being held in the church of St Francis at Assisi.
8 **'Cats' eyes'.** Percy Shaw (1890–1976) ran a small road-repair business in Halifax and set up a factory to manufacture the self-cleaning reflective road studs he named 'cats' eyes'; he became a millionaire.
9 **Cleopatra** in *Antony and Cleopatra*:
> My salad days,
> When I was green in judgement . . .

(Act I, Scene v, to Charmian, while Mark Antony is in Rome after the death of his wife Fulvia.)
10 **Rachel Carson** (1907–64). While working as a marine biologist she also wrote *The Sea Around Us* (1951) about marine pollution.
11 **Graham Rawle.**
12 **Carrot.** The area around Crécy-en-Ponthieu in northern France is famous for its carrots.
13 **The redrawing of electoral boundaries.** It was named after Elbridge Gerry (1744–1814), governor of Massachusetts, who redrew election boundaries in 1812 in order to keep control for his own (Republican) party, creating oddly shaped electoral districts. The word 'gerrymander' was coined by Benjamin Russell, editor of the Boston *Sentinel*. The artist Gilbert Stuart showed him a map he had drawn of the new boundaries with the shape of one district depicted as a salamander: 'Better say a gerrymander,' said Russell.
14 **Richard I** ('The Lionheart', 1157–99, r 1189–99), who married Berengaria of Navarre at Limassol in 1191.
15 **Frederic Leighton** (Lord Leighton of Stretton, 1830–96) in 1895.
16 **The Leica camera,** the first precision miniature camera to become available commercially.
17 **Kristiania.**
18 **The Army Service Corps,** which provided transport for troops and supplies. Ally Sloper was a comic figure created by Charles Ross and Marie Duval, which first appeared in *Judy* (1867–76).
19 **The birthrate rises and so there is soon a greater workforce which, in turn, forces wages down to subsistence level.** Modern trends have disproved this law, which was defined in about 1817 by David Ricardo (1772–1823).
20 **A flame-like glow** seen in marshland and caused by the spontaneous combustion of decaying vegetation.

O is for **Operas**

1 In the television commercials which launched the Fiat Strada, the feverish activity of the factory's production line was accompanied by the music of *Largo al factotum*, from which opera?

2 Which Czech composer wrote *The Bartered Bride* between 1863 and 1866?

3 In which opera by Verdi is there a scene in a blacksmith's forge featuring *Chi del gitano* (*Chorus of the Gypsies*), popularly known as 'the Anvil Chorus'?

4 What is the name of Igor Stravinsky's only full-length opera?

5 In which opera by Bizet do Zurga and Nadir fall in love with the priestess Leïla?

6 Who are the heroine and her husband in Beethoven's opera *Fidelio*, whose full title is *Fidelio or Married Love*?

7 On which three plays by Shakespeare did Verdi base operas?

8 Which opera is set in Catfish Row, Charleston, in the 1920s?

9 When Mascagni's *Le Maschere* was first performed in Milan in 1901, which tenor sang the part of Florindo?

10 Which was the last of Gilbert and Sullivan's light operas, produced at the Savoy Theatre in 1896?

11 Which English composer wrote the opera *The Mask of Orpheus*, first performed in London in 1986?

12 Which novel by Sir Walter Scott is the source of an opera by Donizetti?

13 In Verdi's *Aida* what is the name of the commander of the Egyptian army who is entombed alive because he refuses to forget Aida?

14 Which opera by Wagner features the Dance of the Apprentices?

15 Who wrote the 1897 opera *Mozart and Salieri*?

16 The 1957 opera *Die Harmonie der Welt* (*The Harmony of the World*) by Paul Hindemith features which German astronomer?

17 Which opera by Gian Carlo Menotti, frequently shown on television at Christmas, is based on the fifteenth-century painting *The Adoration of the Magi* by Heironymus Bosch?

18 Who wrote the poem on which Benjamin Britten's 1945 opera *Peter Grimes* is based?

19 Which opera by Prokofiev was the first to be performed at the Sydney Opera House after it opened in 1973?

20 The first opera of which English composer was *Hugh the Drover*, a pastoral idyll set in the Napoleonic Wars and first performed in 1924?

O is for Operas

1 *The Barber of Seville* (1816) by Gioachino Rossini.

2 Bedřich Smetana (1824–84).

3 *Il Trovatore* (1853).

4 *The Rake's Progress* (1951), based on the series of engravings of the same title by William Hogarth in 1733–5.

5 *The Pearl Fishers* (1863). The *Pearl Fishers' Duet* is one of the great tenor/baritone duets in opera – and my own personal favourite.

6 Leonore and Florestan.

7 *Macbeth* in 1847, *Othello* (*Otello*) in 1887 and *The Merry Wives of Windsor* (*Falstaff*) in 1893.

8 *Porgy and Bess* (1952) by Du Bose Heyward and Ira Gershwin. Catfish Row is the main setting of the love triangle involving Bess, Porgy and Crown, which ends with the murder of Crown by Porgy. By the time Porgy is released from jail because of lack of evidence, Bess has gone to New York with a new lover, Sporting Life, but Porgy sets off to find her.

9 Enrico Caruso (1873–1921).

10 *The Grand Duke* (or *The Statutory Duel*).

11 Sir Harrison Birtwistle (b 1934).

12 *The Bride of Lammermoor* (1819) was the source of *Lucia di Lammermoor* (1835).

13 Radamès. Aida has already hidden herself in the tomb so that she can die with him.

14 *Die Meistersinger von Nürnberg* (1868).

15 Nicolay Rimsky-Korsakov (1844–1908). Pushkin had already written a 'little tragedy' (in 1830) based on the rumour (which appears to have had no foundation) that Antonio Salieri (1750–1825) had poisoned Mozart, his near-contemporary. The opera has Salieri comparing Mozart's genius with his own ability and deciding that such a gift is, in fact, destructive to musical tradition. He decides that he must poison Mozart's wine in order to ensure the future of music.

16 Johannes Kepler (1571–1630). The opera is set during the Thirty Years' War and compares the different quests for harmony in the universe of Kepler and General Albrecht Wallenstein (Commander-in-Chief of Frederick V's forces). At the end of the opera Kepler is transformed into the Earth and Wallenstein into Jupiter.

17 *Amahl and the Night Visitors*. It was the first opera ever written for television (NBC in the USA), and was first performed on 24 December 1951.

18 George Crabbe (1754–1832). *The Borough*, written in 1810, is a collection of 24 tales which includes *Peter Grimes; the Outcast*:

> *Where the small eels that left the deeper way*
> *For the warm shore, within the shallows play;*
> *Where gaping mussels, left upon the mud,*
> *Slope their slow passage to the fallen flood; –*
> *Here dull and hopeless he'd lie down and trace*
> *How sidelong crabs had scrawled their crooked race . . .*

19 *War and Peace* (1942, based on Tolstoy's 1869 novel).

20 Ralph Vaughan Williams (1872–1958).

General Knowledge

1 What does the word 'opera' mean?

2 Which race-horse, ridden by Walter Swinburn, won the Epsom Derby by ten lengths in 1981 and, in the same year, went on to win the Irish Derby and the King George VI and Queen Elizabeth Diamond Stakes at Ascot?

3 What is the common name of the fruit *Ananas comosus*, which is native to tropical and sub-tropical America and was introduced by the Portuguese to their colonies in Saint Helena, Africa and India in the sixteenth century?

4 What is the common name for allergic rhinitis?

5 In Richmal Crompton's *William* books, what is the name of the girl who persists in joining the 'Outlaws' despite their attempts to discourage her?

6 What was the married name of Isabella Mary Mayson, who published *The Book of Household Management* serially in 1859–60?

7 What term is used in law for a document which modifies a will?

8 By what name was the .45 calibre submachine gun invented in the United States by John Thompson commonly known?

9 Who appeared for five minutes playing the part of Cardinal Wolsey in the 1966 film *A Man For All Seasons*?

10 By what name is the fourteenth-century church of St Botolph in Boston, Lincolnshire, commonly known?

11 What kind of tree is depicted in the foreground of Vincent van Gogh's 1889 painting *Starry Night*?

12 Which beat group, whose leader set out to amuse audiences while the three guitarists performed syncopated routines intended as a send up of the Shadows, had hits in the 1960s with *I'm Telling You Now* and *You Were Made For Me*?

13 What are Euchre, Pinochle and Piquet?

14 The aurochs is the ancestor of which domesticated animals?

15 Which member of the Women's Social and Political Union threw herself under the hooves of George V's horse during the 1913 Derby?

16 The word 'snob' means someone with aspirations but no claim to gentility. At Cambridge University it used to refer to a townsman. To what kind of worker did it once refer?

17 Which alkaline metallic element, first isolated by Sir Humphrey Davy in 1807, is so reactive that it is not found in its free state in nature?

18 In which play, which opened at the Donmar Warehouse Theatre in September 1998, did Nicole Kidman play all five female roles and Iain Glen all five male roles?

19 Which mountain to the west of Damascus on the Lebanon/Syria border, historically known by the names Sirion and Senir, was a sacred landmark in Hittite, Palestinian and Roman history, and marked the north-western limit of the Israelite conquests led by Moses and Joshua?

20 Which operatic tenor made his debut in 1961 as Rodolfo in *La Bohème* at the Teatro Reggio Emilia in Italy?

General Knowledge

1 **Works.** It is the plural of the Latin noun *opus*.

2 **Shergar,** owned by the Aga Khan. Shergar was stolen from the Aga Khan's Irish stud and killed by members of the IRA in 1983.

3 **Pineapple.** By the end of the sixteenth century, cultivation of pineapples had spread over most tropical areas, including some of the islands of the South Pacific.

4 **Hayfever** (sometimes called rose fever). In people who are allergic, contact with pollen releases histamine; this irritates the small blood vessels and mucus-secreting glands.

5 **Violet Elizabeth Bott** (the daughter of the *nouveau riche* Mr Bott of 'Bott's Digestive Sauce').

6 **Mrs Beeton** (1836–65).

7 **Codicil.**

8 **Tommy gun.** It was first used for military purposes by the US Marines in Nicaragua in 1928.

9 **Orson Welles** (1915–85). The film won Academy Awards for Best Picture, Best Director (Fred Zinneman), Best Actor (Paul Scofield in the title role, Sir Thomas More) and Best Adapted Screenplay (Robert Bolt adapted his own 1960 play), as well as Best Color Cinematography and Best Color Costume Design. Robert Shaw (as Henry VIII) was nominated for Best Supporting Actor and Wendy Hiller for Best Supporting Actress (as Alice More, wife of Sir Thomas).

10 **The Boston Stump.** It is the tallest parish church in England (83 metres). The top of the tower was designed as a 'lantern'; it was lit at night as a beacon for ships.

11 **Cypress.** The painting now hangs in the Museum of Modern Art, New York.

12 **Freddie and the Dreamers.**

13 **Card games.** Euchre is played with one pack of cards with the twos and eights removed; it has elements of whist and bridge – play follows the rules of whist, but it has a bidding system. Pinochle is played with two packs (with all cards from two to eight removed) and Piquet with one pack (with twos and sixes removed); both have a complicated system of collecting sets of cards to secure points, and require a high level of skill.

14 **Cattle.** The aurochs (*Bos primigenius*) was a European wild ox which survived in central Poland until 1627 but is now extinct. It was black, with spreading, forward-curving horns, and its height to the shoulder was about 1.8 metres.

15 **Emily Davison** (1872–1913).

16 **Cobbler.**

17 **Sodium** (Na).

18 *The Blue Room*, adapted by David Hare from Arthur Schnitzler's 1912 play *Reigen* (*Round Dance*), which was also the basis for the 1950 French film *La Ronde*.

19 **Mount Hermon** (*Jabal Ash-Shaykh*). At 2,814 metres, it is the highest point on the east coast of the Mediterranean Sea. Since the Arab–Israeli War of June 1967, about 100 square kilometres of Mount Hermon's southern and western slopes have been part of the Israeli-administered Golan Heights.

20 **Luciano Pavarotti** (b 1935).

P is for **Pop and Rock Music** Questions

1 The name of which singing group, formed in 1973, was an acronym of the initials of its four members?

2 Which American singer recorded *Roll Over Beethoven* in 1957?

3 Of which instrument was Robert Moog a pioneer in 1967?

4 In which 1959 film did Cliff Richard play the part of a pop singer?

5 Which horror-film actor was the narrator on Michael Jackson's 1982 single *Thriller*, his first UK Number 1 as a solo performer?

6 By what name is the Welsh singer Gaynor Hopkins better known?

7 Which singer recorded the single *Birthday* and the album *Life's Too Good* with the Sugarcubes in 1988?

8 Which singer's death in 1951 was the inspiration for Don McLean's 1971 record *American Pie*?

9 Which US disc-jockey coined the term 'rock 'n' roll' in about 1953?

10 What was the name of Sylvia's mother in the eponymous 1972 record by Dr Hook and the Medicine Show?

11 Which song by Adge Cutler and the Wurzels was adopted by Bristol City football club supporters as their theme song?

12 Who wrote Cilla Black's 1964 chart-topper, *Anyone Who Had a Heart*?

13 In which film did Elvis Presley sing *Wooden Heart*?

14 Which two singers formed the Righteous Brothers?

15 Who was the sculptor of the Beatles' *Eleanor Rigby* in Stanley Street, Liverpool?

16 Which group recorded many songs composed by one of their members, Hugh Jones, which are frequently and mistakenly labelled 'traditional', such as *The Ellan Vannin Tragedy*, *The Marco Polo* and *The Fairlie Duplex Engine*?

17 'Who Breaks a Butterfly on a Wheel?' was the headline in *The Times* of a defence of Mick Jagger and Keith Richards after their arrest for possessing cannabis in 1969: who wrote the article?

18 Which singer began her career in the chorus of the musical *High Button Shoes* (with Audrey Hepburn), had her only UK Number 1 hit with *Dreamboat*, and went on to make idiosyncratic hits such as *Just Couldn't Resist Her With Her Pocket Transistor* and *Never Do A Tango With An Eskimo*?

19 Which two singers teamed up to make the humorous record *There's A Hole In My Bucket* in 1961?

20 Which singer (with the comedy actor Ronald Shiner) co-hosted *Calling Malta* for British troops in Malta in 1942?

P is for Pop and Rock Music Answers

1 **ABBA**. The members of the group were Agnetha Faltskog (b 1950), Björn Ulvaeus (b 1945), Benny Andersson (b 1945) and Anni-Frid ('Frida') Lyngstad (b 1945).

2 **Chuck Berry** (b 1926).

3 **Synthesiser**. With Donald Buchla, Moog developed a system of voltage control in which each note on a synthesiser keyboard produced a different voltage. The instrument gained public recognition through the 1968 recording by Walter (later, Wendy) Carlos, *Switched on Bach*.

4 *Expresso Bongo*.

5 **Vincent Price** (1911–93).

6 **Bonnie Tyler** (b 1951).

7 **Björk** (Björk Guðmundsdóttir, b 1966).

8 **Buddy Holly** (1936–59), who died in a plane crash along with the singers Big Bopper and Richie Valens.

9 **Alan Freed** (1922–65). Like many terms used in music, it was African-American slang for sexual intercourse.

10 **Mrs Avery**. *Sylvia's Mother*, written by Chicago songwriter, poet and cartoonist Shel Silverstein, was intended as a send-up of country music, but country music fans took it to be the real thing and it reached Number 5 in the USA and Number 1 in the UK charts.

11 *Drink Up Thy Zider* (1966). Adge Cutler died in 1974, but the group has retained his name. They describe their music as 'scrumpy 'n' western'.

12 **Burt Bacharach** (b 1928).

13 *GI Blues* (1960). Elvis Presley had served in the US Armed Forces in Germany from 1958 to 1960.

14 **Bobby Hatfield** (b 1940) and **Bill Medley** (b 1940).

15 **Tommy Steele** (Thomas Hicks, b 1936). While he was appearing in a show in Liverpool, Tommy Steele approached the City Council and offered to make the sculpture for a fee of threepence (an allusion to the show *Half a Sixpence*), and the *Liverpool Echo* donated £4,000 for the casting. To make Eleanor Rigby's shopping bag, Tommy Steele put a collection of objects into a sack and dropped it into the molten bronze for the statue 'to imbue it with magical qualities': a four-leafed clover for good luck, a page from the Bible for spiritual help, a sonnet for lovers, an adventure book for excitement and old football socks for action.

16 **The Spinners**: Tony Davies (b 1930), Mick Groves (b 1936), Hugh Jones (b 1936) and Cliff Hall (b 1925). In 1988, after a thirty-year career, they decided to retire and produced their last album, *Final Fling*.

17 **William Rees-Mogg**, quoting Alexander Pope's *Epistle to Dr Arbuthnot* (1735).

18 **Alma Cogan** (1932–66).

19 **Harry Belafonte** (b 1927) and **Odetta** (Odetta Holmes, b 1930).

20 **Anne Shelton** (1923–94).

General Knowledge

1 Who was the lead singer (who died in 1991) of a UK rock band with musicians Brian May, John Deacon and Roger Taylor, and what was the group's name?

2 The name of which strong tidal current between the Lofoten Islands off northern Norway was introduced to English by both Jules Verne and Edgar Allan Poe and came to be used both literally and figuratively for a large whirlpool which destroys everything entering it?

3 Which actress, born in Swindon, was originally named Diana Fluck?

4 In the playing area for which sport are there a short line, a service line and a telltale or tin?

5 By what collective name were comedy films such as *Whisky Galore* (1949), *The Lavender Hill Mob* (1951) and *The Titfield Thunderbolt* (1953) known?

6 What is meant by the Latin phrase *caveat emptor*?

7 Which puppet (which pronounced 'r' as 'w') of ventriloquist Terry Hall had his own show on BBC children's television between 1957 and 1963?

8 Prickly pear and organ pipe are species of which plant?

9 In French history, what was the Oriflamme?

10 Which Swiss artist painted *The Twittering Machine* in 1922, now in the Museum of Modern Art, New York?

11 The name of which of the 'noble' gases means 'strange'?

12 Who was the first female US astronaut?

13 What colour is the pigment gamboge?

14 Tchaikovsky's 1879 opera *Eugene Onegin* is based on a novel in verse written in 1828 by which Russian writer?

15 The title of which BBC radio programme, in which public figures answered questions submitted by listeners, was originally coined by James Kiernan of the *New York Times* for the group of advisers to US President F. D. Roosevelt during his 1932 election campaign?

16 Which US intermediate-range ballistic missile (IBM), deployed in Western Europe in 1983 to counter the threat from Soviet missiles, was named after a First World War general nicknamed Black Jack?

17 Who was the first wife of Dickens' David Copperfield who died two years after they were married?

18 Which sporting calendar was begun by James Weatherby in 1733?

19 Where in Cumbria are the World Gurning Championships held?

20 Which record was Number 1 in the first singles chart published in *New Musical Express* on 14 November 1952?

General Knowledge Answers

1 **Freddy Mercury** (Faroukh Bulsara, 1946–91) of **Queen**. The group was formed in 1971 and disbanded after the death of Mercury, but produced the album *Made in Heaven* (on which Mercury had worked) in 1995.

2 **Maelstrøm**. It is about eight kilometres wide with a current of up to eleven kilometres per hour; its ferocity is much exaggerated.

3 **Diana Dors** (1931–84).

4 **Squash**. A served ball has to bounce from above the service line on the front wall on to the floor beyond the short line. The telltale (tin) indicates 'out-of-play'; it is a sheet of metal across the base of the front wall which makes a distinct sound when hit.

5 **Ealing Comedies**. They were all produced by the Ealing Studios in London and typically feature a downtrodden group rebelling against authority. In *Whisky Galore* a freighter with a large cargo of whisky is wrecked on a Hebridean island which has run out of whisky; the islanders help themselves and outwit the Home Guard captain who attempts to find the loot. In *The Lavender Hill Mob* a timid clerk plans and carries out a bullion robbery, and in *The Titfield Thunderbolt* villagers take over a railway branch line threatened with closure.

6 **Let the buyer beware.**

7 **Lenny the Lion.**

8 **Cactus**. The Mexican prickly pear (*Opuntia ficus-indica* or *Opuntia megacantha*) resembles a tree with a woody trunk. The organ pipe cactus (*Lemairocereus*, or *Cereus*, *thurberi*) has tall columns rising candelabra-like from the base of the plant.

9 **The standard of Saint-Denis**, which was carried into battle. It was usually kept with the relics of the saint in the cathedral of St Denis. It was last present in the field at Agincourt (1415).

10 **Paul Klee** (1879–1940).

11 **Xenon**. It is used in flash-lamps. The gases were named 'noble' because they are inert to all the usual chemical reactions.

12 **Sally Ride** (b 1951). She was a mission specialist on Space Shuttle flight crews, including a six-day flight of *Challenger* in 1983.

13 **Yellow**. The pigment (sometimes called camboge) is a hard, brittle gum resin from trees of the genus *Garcina*, which are native to Kampuchea. The resin is orange to brown in colour and turns bright yellow when powdered.

14 **Alexander Pushkin** (1799–1837).

15 *The Brains Trust* (first broadcast in 1942).

16 **Pershing**, named after General John Pershing (1860–1948).

17 **Dora Spenlow**, the daughter of Francis Spenlow, partner in Spenlow and Jorkins, with whom David Copperfield was articled as a clerk.

18 *The Racing Calendar*. Horse races in the seventeenth and early eighteenth centuries were match races between two or three horses, whose owners provided the purse. A third party (the keeper of the match book), with no money at stake, would record the agreement. In 1727 a Newmarket keeper, John Cheny, began publishing a consolidation of match books – *Cheny's Horse Matches*. In 1773 James Weatherby established it as the *Racing Calendar*.

19 **Egremont** (at the Egremont Crab Fair, first held in 1267). The contestants place their head in a braffin (horse collar) and pull grotesque faces.

20 *Here in My Heart* by Al Martino, on the Capitol label.

Q is for **Quotations**

1 Which credit card was advertised, from 1981, as 'your flexible friend'?

2 In a speech to the Royal Institute of British Architects in 1984, how did the Prince of Wales, describe the proposed extension to the National Gallery?

3 In Harriet Beecher Stowe's *Uncle Tom's Cabin*, what was Miss Ophelia's question which Topsy answered with: 'Nobody, as I knows on . . . I 'spect I grow'd'?

4 At the 1963 Royal Variety Performance who said to the audience, 'Will the people in the cheaper seats clap your hands? All the rest of you, if you'll just rattle your jewellery'?

5 Who wrote, in his *Critique of the Gotha Programme* in 1875, 'From each according to his abilities, to each according to his needs'?

6 Which line from a 1972 Wonderloaf advertisement did supporters of Tottenham Hotspur adopt as an anthem for one of the players?

7 Which BBC television character's catchphrase was 'I have a cunning plan'?

8 Which event was celebrated by the *Sun*'s exultant headline 'GOTCHA!'?

9 Who, in the poem by Alfred Noyes, told Bess that he would come to her by moonlight, 'though hell should bar the way'?

10 What are the words engraved on the head of the silver mace which the Queen presented to the new Scottish Parliament on 1 July 1999?

11 To what did D. H. Lawrence address the following questions:
> *When did you start your tricks,*
> *Monsieur?*
> *What do you stand on such high legs for?*
> *Why this length of shredded shank,*
> *You exaltation?*

12 Which 1959 film ended with the following lines:
> Gerry: *We can't get married at all . . . I'm a man.*
> Osgood: *Well, nobody's perfect.*

13 Who wrote the following lines and in which poem:
> *The grave's a fine and private place,*
> *But none, I think, do there embrace.*

14 Which poet wrote to his publisher: 'The poem will please if it is lively – if it is stupid it will fail – but I will have none of your damned cutting and slashing'?

15 What did Samuel Johnson say he would do if it rained knowledge?

16 Who said 'History is more or less bunk'?

17 Which journalist wrote, in 1926, 'Comment is free, but facts are sacred'?

18 To whom are the following last words attributed, spoken to his physician who had just told him a risqué story: 'That is indeed very good. I shall have to repeat that on the Golden Floor!'?

19 Who wrote, 'He wrapped himself in quotations – as a beggar would enfold himself in the purple of emperors'?

20 What is the line which comes after the following, in *Bagpipe Music* by Louis MacNeice:
> *It's no go the merrygoround, it's no go the rickshaw,*
> *All we want is a limousine and a ticket for the peepshow.*
> *Their knickers are made of crêpe-de-chine, their shoes are made of python,*

Q is for **Quotations**

1 **Access.**
2 **'A monstrous carbuncle on the face of a well-loved friend.'**
3 **'Do you know who made you?'**
4 **John Lennon** (1940–80).
5 **Karl Marx** (1818–83).
6 **Nice one, Cyril.** Cyril Knowles (1944–91) played for Spurs from 1964 to 1975, having joined them from Middlesbrough. He played in four England internationals. The Spurs team made a record of the song *Nice One, Cyril* with Cockerel Chorus in 1973. It reached Number 14 in the charts.
7 **Baldrick** (played by Tony Robinson), in *Blackadder*, written by Richard Curtis and Ben Elton.
8 **The sinking of the *General Belgrano*** during the Falklands War in 1982.
9 **The Highwayman** in the poem of the same name.
10 **There shall be a Scottish Parliament.** They are the opening words of the parliament's founding statute (the Scotland Act 1998).
11 **A mosquito** (*The Mosquito*, in *Collected Poems*, 1957).
12 *Some Like It Hot*, spoken by Jack Lemmon and Joe E. Brown.
13 **Andrew Marvell** (1621–78) in *To His Coy Mistress*. The poem continues:
   Now, therefore, while the youthful hue
   Sits on thy skin like morning dew,
   And while thy willing soul transpires
   At every pore with instant fires,
   Now let us sport us while we may;
   And now, like amorous birds of prey,
   Rather at once our Time devour,
   Than languish in his slow-chapt power.
14 **Lord Byron** (1788–1824) in a letter to his publisher John Murray in 1819.
15 **Hold out his hand** – but 'I would not give myself the trouble to go in quest of it.' (In *The Life of Samuel Johnson* by James Boswell, 1791).
16 **Henry Ford** (1863–1947), in an interview in 1916.
17 **C. P. Scott** (in the *Manchester Guardian*, 6 May). Charles Prestwich Scott (1879–1970) is revered as one of the greatest journalists of his era. He was appointed editor of the *Manchester Guardian* at the age of 26, and developed it into a serious, liberal rival to *The Times*. He was a Liberal MP from 1895 to 1906.
18 **A. E. Housman** (1859–1936).
19 **Rudyard Kipling** (in *The Finest Story in the World*, 1893).
20 *Their halls are lined with tiger rugs and their walls with heads of bison.*

General Knowledge

1 Which twentieth-century artist said, 'In the future everybody will be world famous for fifteen minutes'?

2 What is the common name for the blue garden flower myosotis?

3 In William Hanna and Joseph Barbera's cartoon *The Flintstones*, which animal does Wilma use as a vacuum cleaner?

4 Which were the six original member countries of the EEC?

5 In which musical do Sharks and Jets appear?

6 In which sport did Ulrich Salchow win the first Olympic gold medal, in the 1908 Games in London?

7 Which American astronomer discovered the planet Pluto in 1930?

8 What is the habitat of 'benthic' organisms?

9 Which football club is nicknamed 'the Seals'?

10 Which book opens with the words, 'The American handed Leamas another cup of coffee and said, "Why don't you go back and sleep? We can ring you if he shows up"'?

11 Who was the first Scottish National Party MP?

12 What are the three main ingredients of a Harvey Wallbanger cocktail?

13 What is the unit of currency of the United Arab Emirates?

14 Which fifteenth-century Italian artist painted *The Agony in the Garden*, which is now in the National Gallery, London?

15 In nineteenth-century haberdashery what was a 'marabou'?

16 In which abbey in Scotland was the heart of King Robert the Bruce reburied on 24 June 1998, the 684th anniversary of the Battle of Bannockburn?

17 Which poem by Hilaire Belloc begins:
Do you remember an inn,
Miranda?
Do you remember an inn?
And the tedding and the spreading
Of the straw for a bedding,
And the fleas that tease in the High Pyrenees,
And the wine that tasted of tar?

18 Which Shawnee chief was killed in 1813 at the Battle of the Thames in Canada leading a force of Native Americans in support of the British against a US force led by William Henry Harrison?

19 What is the Standard International Unit for measuring luminous intensity?

20 In 1945, which British politician said: 'This island is made mainly of coal and surrounded by fish. Only an organising genius could produce a shortage of coal and fish at the same time'?

General Knowledge Answers

1 **Andy Warhol** (1927–87).

2 **Forget-me-not.**

3 **A mastodon** (an extinct elephant-like mammal). Wilma steers the baby mastodon, which is mounted on a trolley, by a handle made from the forked branch of a tree.

4 **Belgium, France, Italy, Luxembourg, the Netherlands** and **West Germany.**

5 *West Side Story* (1957) by Leonard Bernstein, Arthur Laurents and Stephen Sondheim. Tony and Maria, the lovers in this modern 'Romeo and Juliet' story, are from rival gangs in New York's West Side: the white Jets and the Puerto Rican Sharks.

6 **Men's figure-skating.** Ulrich Salchow (1877–1949) of Sweden originated the Salchow jump: the skater takes off from the rear inside edge of one skate, makes one full turn in the air and lands on the rear outside edge of the other skate.

7 **Clyde Tombaugh** (1906–97). Other astronomers had calculated that a ninth planet existed; Tombaugh carried out a systematic search, based on their work, until he located the planet.

8 **The seabed.** 'Benthos' means the collection of organisms which inhabit the seabed.

9 **Chester City.** The nickname derived from the ground at which the club played between 1906 and 1997 – Sealand Road (their new ground is the Deva Stadium).

10 *The Spy Who Came in from the Cold* by John Le Carré.

11 **Robert McIntyre** (1913–98), a chest consultant at Stirling Royal Infirmary, who won the Motherwell and Wishaw by-election in 1945 but lost his seat in a General Election six weeks later. He was chairman of the SNP from 1945 to 1956 and president from 1958 to 1980, and in 1998 was made honorary president of the party's parliamentary group.

12 **Orange juice, Galliano and either gin or vodka.** It was named after its creator in the United States in the 1960s.

13 **Dirham.** The coin has the Muslim declaration of faith on the obverse and around it the marginal legend 'In the name of God; this dirham was struck at . . . in the year . . .' On the reverse there is a quotation from the Qur'an.

14 **Andrea Mantegna** (*c* 1430/1–1506). The painting, completed in about 1460, shows Christ at prayer and angels appearing in the sky (one of them carrying a cross) while the disciples sleep in the foreground. In the background Judas Iscariot is visible with soldiers.

15 **A down feather** from the marabou stork (*Leptoptilos crumeniferus*), used as an adornment for women's hats.

16 **Melrose.** Donald Dewar, then Secretary of State for Scotland, unveiled a stone marker on the lawn of the abbey to mark the reburial of a small lead casket which had been unearthed by archaeologists two years previously from under the chapter house of the abbey. Inside it was another, unmarked lead casket, and a note written by archaeologists who had dug it up during an earlier excavation in 1921.

17 **Tarantella.**

18 **Tecumseh** (1768–1813).

19 **Candela** (cd).

20 **Aneurin Bevan** (1897–1960).

R is for Religions

1 Which of the disciples did not believe the others when they told him they had seen Jesus alive after the crucifixion?

2 In Hinduism which flower symbolises purity?

3 What is the name of the holy city of Sikhism, founded in 1577 by Guru Ram Das, the fourth Guru?

4 In Judaism what is the literal meaning of *Bat Mitzvah*?

5 What was the name of the Leicestershire cobbler's apprentice and Puritan who became a preacher and founded the Society of Friends (Quakers)?

6 What name is given to the head of a Muslim community, who leads the prayers at a mosque?

7 In Buddhism what is the word given to Enlightenment, or the release from the constant cycle of birth and rebirth, which people achieve when they become free from human desires?

8 What is the name of the Holy Book of Sikhism?

9 What is the literal meaning of *Kyrie eleison* in Christian church services?

10 Who led the Jews against the Greeks who had seized their Temple in Jerusalem and whose story is now commemorated by the festival of Hanukkah?

11 In Islam what is the name of the festival which immediately follows the end of Ramadan?

12 What are the Five Joyful Mysteries of Christianity (mainly in Roman Catholicism)?

13 In which religion were Sidney Rigdon and Brigham Young prominent leaders in the nineteenth century?

14 One of the five Ks of Sikhism is *Kara*; what is it?

15 What name is given to the scroll inserted in a small case and placed on the doorposts of the homes of Jews?

16 During the *Hajj* how many times are Muslim pilgrims required to circle the *Ka'bah* in the courtyard of the Great Mosque at Makkah (Mecca)?

17 What name was given to the open-air religious meetings held by the outlawed Covenanters in Scotland in the late seventeenth century?

18 What was the name of the Sun God (also the god of justice, contracts, mutual obligations and war), worshipped as the most important god in the Iranian pantheon during the second and third centuries?

19 The name of which Jewish festival means 'tabernacles'?

20 On which Buddhist festival, which marks the end of the rainy season in India, do lay people traditionally present monks with gifts, including new robes?

R is for **Religions**   Answers

1 **Thomas.** He said to them, 'Unless I see in his hands the print of the nails, and place my finger in the mark of the nails, and place my hand in his side, I will not believe.' (John 20:24).

2 **Lotus.**

3 **Amritsar.** It is the site of the principal place of worship, the *Harimandir* (Golden Temple).

4 **Daughter of the Commandments.** *Bar Mitzvah* (Son of the Commandments) and *Bat Mitzvah* are boys and girls after they take part in the ceremony (usually soon after their thirteenth birthday) during which they accept responsibility for keeping the Ten Commandments.

5 **George Fox** (1624–91).

6 *Imam.* It means 'leader' or 'pattern'.

7 *Nirvana.*

8 **The *Guru Granth Sahib*.** It was compiled in 1604 as the *Adi Granth* or *Granth Sahib* (Lord Book) by Guru Arjan Dev (1563–1606), the fifth Guru and the first Sikh martyr. The Mughal emperor, Jahangir, had him arrested, tortured and put to death. After the death of the tenth (and last human) guru (Gobind Singh, 1666–1708) the book came to be revered as the 'living guru'.

9 **Lord have mercy.** *Kyrie* is the vocative case of the Greek *kyrios* (lord). *Kyrie eleison* is a preliminary petition made before a formal prayer and as a congregational response.

10 **Judas Maccabeus** (in about 170–160 BC).

11 *Id-ul-Fitr.* Id means 'festival' or 'holiday'. *Id-ul-Fitr* is the 'Festival of Breaking Fast'. It begins with the new Moon at the end of Ramadan and extends over the first three days of the tenth month, *Shawwal*.

12 **The Annunciation, the Visitation** (of Mary to Elizabeth), the **Nativity,** the **Presentation** (of Jesus in the Temple) and the **Finding of the Boy Jesus in the Temple.**

13 **The Church of Jesus Christ and Latter Day Saints (Mormonism)** Sidney Rigdon (1793–1876) was an early convert to Mormonism and the first counsellor to its founder, Joseph Smith, but he became estranged from Smith. When Smith was murdered (in 1844), Rigdon tried to take over leadership of the Mormon Church, but was defeated by Brigham Young and excommunicated. Brigham Young (1801–77) led the Mormon emigration of 1848 to Utah, where he founded Salt Lake City.

14 **A steel band worn on the right wrist.**

15 **Mezuzah** (Hebrew for 'doorpost'). It is a small folded parchment inscribed by a qualified calligraphist with verses from the Torah (Deuteronomy 6:4–9 and 11:13–21).

16 **Seven.** They kiss and touch the Black Stone at the corner of the building each time they pass it.

17 **Conventicles.**

18 **Mithra** (or Mithras). Most Iranians were polytheistic until the advent of Zoroaster in the sixth century.

19 *Sukkot.* A *sukkah* was a shelter built by the Israelites when they encamped near an oasis. *Sukkot* celebrates the harvest, represented by the 'Four Species' (*lulav* – palm branch, *etrog* – citron fruit, *hadassim* – branches of myrtle, and *aravat* – sprigs of willow).

20 **Kathina Day.**

General Knowledge

1 In Christianity and Judaism what is the fifth Commandment?

2 In 1977 who instigated the breakaway World Series cricket and introduced innovations such as different coloured clothing for the teams, evening floodlit games, a hidden camera in the middle stump and logos painted on the turf?

3 The ruins of ancient Babylon and its Hanging Gardens are in which modern Middle Eastern country?

4 Where did Anita Roddick open the first Body Shop in 1976?

5 In the 1960s which doctor walked from John o'Groats to Land's End to publicise vegetarianism?

6 Who in the seventeenth century designed the gardens of the Palais de Versailles, near Paris, and Kensington Gardens, London?

7 What was suppressed by comstockery?

8 What is the medical term for a balloon-like swelling in the wall of an artery?

9 Ophidiophobia is the fear of what?

10 In 1743 Charles III of Naples founded a porcelain factory in the gardens of his palace; what is the name of the palace?

11 Which Gilbert and Sullivan operetta has the sub-title *The Peer and the Peri*?

12 A tinchel is a group of what?

13 In which Welsh mine was the gold for the wedding rings of Prince Edward and Sophie Rhys-Jones mined?

14 Which German writer won the Nobel Prize for literature in 1999 for his 1959 novel *The Tin Drum* (*Die Blechtrommel*)?

15 Of which country did Hugo Chávez become president in 1998?

16 In a Church of England diocese which member of the clergy has an alternative name, '*oculi episcopi*', meaning 'eyes of the bishop'?

17 Which dynasty of former slave-soldiers ruled Egypt from 1250 to 1517?

18 What was the name of the French inventor who was awarded a prize of 12,000 francs in 1810, offered by the French government to find a way of preserving food during the Napoleonic Wars?

19 Which mammals belong to the group known as lagomorphs?

20 In Buddhism what is the name of the festival which commemorates the birth, Enlightenment, and death of the Buddha?

General Knowledge   Answers

1 **Honour your father and your mother**, that your days may be long in the land which the Lord your God gives you. (Exodus 20:12)

2 **Kerry Packer.** His television company had failed to obtain the broadcasting rights for the major matches in Australia. Instead, he signed up players from Australia, the West Indies and several other countries, including England, to play in a separate World Series.

3 **Iraq.** The gardens at the royal palace in Babylon were roof gardens on a series of ziggurat terraces, irrigated by water pumped from the Euphrates. According to classical sources, the terraces had stone balconies layered with reeds, bitumen and lead to stop water seeping through. The gardens are thought to have been created by either the semi-legendary Queen Sammu-ramat or Nebuchadnezzar II (c 605–c 561 BC).

4 **Brighton.** In 1998, with franchises in more than 36 countries, Anita Roddick stepped down as chief executive and Patrick Gournay took over.

5 **Barbara Moore.** The walk took 23 days; later that year she walked from San Francisco to New York in 85 days.

6 **André Le Nôtre** (1613–1700), who also redesigned the Tuileries gardens and extended the main avenue (Les Champs Élysées).

7 **Literature which was thought to have a corrupting influence.** The word 'comstockery' was coined by George Bernard Shaw in 1905; he named it after Anthony Comstock (1844–1915), a moral crusader and member of the New York Society for the Suppression of Vice.

8 **Aneurysm.**

9 **Snakes.**

10 **Capodimonte** (Palazzo Reale di Capo di Monte), which means 'royal palace of the top of the mountain'. Porcelain was produced there until 1759, when Charles became King of Spain, and the factory was moved to Madrid.

11 *Iolanthe* (first performed in 1882).

12 **Hunters**, especially of deer. The word derives from the Gaelic *timchioll*, and is used in Scotland to describe a group of hunters driving together a number of deer by gradually closing in on them.

13 **The Prince Edward Mine.** The mine used to be called *Moel Croesau* (Welcome Hill), but was renamed after gold from the mine was used to make the regalia for the investiture of Edward, Prince of Wales (later Edward VIII) in 1911.

14 **Günter Grass** (b 1927).

15 **Venezuela.**

16 **Archdeacon.**

17 **Memluk** (Mameluke). The original slaves had been brought from the Caucasus and Asia Minor to form a bodyguard for the sultan, a descendant of Saladin. They set up one of their number as sultan in 1250.

18 **Nicolas Appert** (c 1750–1841), a Paris chef, confectioner, and distiller who invented canning. He boiled foods for different lengths of time in corked glass containers reinforced with wire and sealing wax, and found that he could preserve soups, fruits, vegetables, juices, dairy products, marmalades, jellies and syrups.

19 **Rabbits and hares** (also pikas).

20 **Wesak**, on the day of the full moon in the month of Vesakh (April/May in the Gregorian calendar).

S is for **Ships and Shipping** Questions

1 Who led the mutiny on the *Bounty* in 1789 during its voyage to the South Seas to collect breadfruit for trade in the West Indies?

2 In the 1993–96 ITV series *SeaQuest DSV*, for what did the letters DSV stand?

3 At the instigation of which merchant and shipping reformer did the British Parliament, in the Merchant Shipping Act 1876, introduce the marking of a load line on the hull of every cargo ship, indicating the maximum depth to which the ship could be safely loaded?

4 What name was given by seafarers to the winds which blow westward and towards the equator from the high-pressure belts at latitudes around 30° north and 30° south?

5 On a sailing ship, what are halyards and jeers?

6 What name was given to the old maritime craft of carving or engraving on shells, whalebone and walrus tusks to while away the time on long voyages?

7 Which 1925 film, directed by Sergei Eisenstein, was based on a real-life mutiny which took place on a battleship lying off Odessa during the failed 1905 revolution against Tsarism in Russia?

8 Who wrote the following verse:
> *A baby Sardine*
> *Saw her first submarine:*
> *She was scared and watched through a peephole.*
> *'Oh, come, come, come,'*
> *Said the Sardine's mum,*
> *'It's only a tin full of people.'*

9 What name was given to a viking ocean-going cargo ship?

10 Which 1951 opera by Benjamin Britten is set on the warship HMS *Indomitable* during the Napoleonic Wars?

11 Which 32,000-ton British ocean liner was torpedoed and sunk by a German submarine on 7 May 1915, during a voyage from New York to Liverpool?

12 What name is given to the luminous phenomenon caused by electrical fields, which is sometimes seen around the tops of ships' masts and church spires (often accompanied by a crackling or fizzing noise) during storms?

13 Which was the first steamship to have an all-iron hull?

14 What is a jury mast?

15 Who wrote the words of the hymn *Eternal Father, Strong to Save*?

16 What is the name of the world's first nuclear-powered surface ship?

17 Which cold sea-current off South America was named after the German naturalist and explorer who wrote the popular science book *Kosmos*?

18 On a small craft, for what purpose was a killick used?

19 In 1824 who founded the National Institution for the Preservation of Life from Shipwreck (in 1854 re-named Royal National Lifeboat Institution)?

20 For what purpose did medieval navigators use a portolano?

S is for Ships and Shipping

1 **Fletcher Christian** (1764–*c* 1790/3). The *Bounty* arrived in Tahiti in October 1788, where it stayed for several months before sailing to the West Indies. Because of the alleged tyranny of Captain William Bligh, Fletcher Christian seized the ship with 25 petty officers and seamen. They set Bligh and 18 of the crew adrift in a lifeboat and tried to form a settlement in the Austral Islands. Christian, eight seamen and some Tahitians sailed away and were not heard of again until 1808, when one survivor was found, with the mutineers' descendants, on Pitcairn Island.

2 **Deep Submergence Vehicle**. It was a submarine which patrolled the sea on behalf of the 'United Earth/Oceans Organisation'.

3 **Samuel Plimsoll** (1824–98).

4 **Trade winds**. They were named by the crews of sailing ships which depended on the winds during westward ocean crossings.

5 **Ropes in the rigging**.

6 **Scrimshaw**. The word is of uncertain derivation. The designs were carved with either a sail needle or a jackknife and then emboldened with a black pigment, usually lampblack.

7 *Battleship Potemkin*. The crew had protested about poor food and, as an example, ten of them were lined up to be shot. The soldiers in the firing squad refused to shoot, and mutiny broke out. All the officers were shot or thrown overboard. The sailors heard that the entire Russian fleet was on its way to subdue them; they sailed towards it to die a heroic death. When the *Potemkin* reached the fleet, the ships parted and allowed it through without a shot being fired. The crew found refuge in a Romanian harbour.

8 **Spike Milligan** (b 1918) in *A Book of Milliganimals*.

9 *Knörr*. A *knörr* was discovered, almost entire, in 1962 in the Roskilde Fjord. It is now in the Roskilde Ship Museum in Denmark.

10 *Billy Budd*. The text, by E. M. Forster and Eric Crozier, was based on an unfinished novel written by Herman Melville just before his death in 1891.

11 **The *Lusitania***. 1,198 of the 1,959 passengers and crew lost their lives.

12 **St Elmo's Fire** or **corposant**. Elmo is a corruption of Erasmus, a fourth-century Syrian bishop who came to be regarded as one of the patron saints of seafarers. Corposant comes from the Portuguese *corpo santo* (holy body).

13 **The *Great Britain***, which was launched 1843 by the Great Western Steamship Company. The *Great Britain* is now on display in the dry dock in which it was constructed in Bristol.

14 **An improvised mast to replace one which has been broken**. 'Jury-rigged' has come to mean anything which is set up in a makeshift manner.

15 **William Whiting** (1825–78).

16 *Lenin*, a large icebreaker built in St Petersburg (Leningrad) in 1957.

17 **The Humboldt Current**. It was named after the German scientist and naturalist Alexander von Humboldt (1769–1859), who went on a five-year exploratory voyage (1799–1804) to South America.

18 **As an anchor** (it was a large stone).

19 **Sir William Hillary** (1771–1847), an equerry to Prince Augustus Frederick, son of George III.

20 **Finding harbours**. It was a manual which gave directions in terms of halves of the angles determined by a 32-point compass (particularly for the Mediterranean).

General Knowledge

1 What is the name given to the cylindrical pedestal in which a ship's compass is housed?

2 What is the name of the Tibetan mountain retreat in James Hilton's (1933) novel *Lost Horizon*?

3 Which Norwegian athlete set world records for the women's 5,000 and 10,000 metres and won the women's marathons in London in 1985 and 1987, Chicago in 1985 and Boston in 1989?

4 In the dish 'Egg Florentine', which vegetable is served with the egg?

5 Which artist designed the windows of Coventry cathedral?

6 On which African river are the Victoria Falls?

7 In the old ballad what was borrowed by Bill Brewer, Jan Stewer, Peter Gurney, Peter Davy, Daniel Whidden, Harry Hawk and Uncle Tom Cobbleigh and all?

8 By what name is the 1983 Lockheed F-117A aircraft known because of its virtual immunity to detection by radar?

9 What name was given to the Children's Temperance Societies in Britain in the mid-nineteenth century?

10 Where in the body is the gastrocnemius muscle?

11 In Greek mythology which nymph changed herself into a reed to evade the amorous advances of the god Pan?

12 What was the name of the faith healer employed by Glen Hoddle during the preparations for the 1998 World Cup?

13 What French word describes a ballet dancer's leap during which the heels meet several times in the air?

14 What is the meaning of Kaur, the name taken by many Sikh women?

15 For the measurement of what did Harry O. Wood and Frank Neumann devise a scale in 1931?

16 Which conductor founded Scottish Opera and became its artistic director in 1962?

17 Who was the author of the 1956 novel *The Talented Mr Ripley*, on which the 1999 film of the same title was based?

18 What term is used for a 'telescoped word' – a word made from combinations of more than one word: for example, 'motorcade' from 'motor cavalcade', 'travelogue' from 'travel monologue' and 'slithy' from 'slimy' and 'lithe' (coined by Lewis Carroll in *Through the Looking Glass, and What Alice Found There*)?

19 What characterises glabrous animal tissues or parts of plants?

20 In navigation, what does 'shooting the Sun' mean?

General Knowledge   Answers

1 **Binnacle**. It contains magnets and pieces of steel arranged to cancel the magnetic effects of the metal of the ship.

2 **Shangri La**. The name was also given to President F. D. Roosevelt's mountain retreat in Maryland (renamed Camp David in 1953 by President Dwight D. Eisenhower, after his grandson).

3 **Ingrid Kristiansen** (b 1956).

4 **Spinach**.

5 **John Piper** (1903–1992).

6 **Zambezi**. The 108-metre-high waterfall is near the border between Zambia to the north and Zimbabwe to the south; it spans the Zambezi River at one of its widest points (about 1,700 metres). Its mean flow is almost 935 cubic metres per second.

7 **Tom Pearce's grey mare** (to ride to Widecombe fair, in Devon).

8 **Stealth fighter**. Its shape is designed to reduce radar reflection: it has a short, pyramid-shaped fuselage and sharply swept wings.

9 **Bands of Hope**. They were temperance organisations for working-class children, which began in Leeds in 1847. Their young members, enrolled from the age of six, took a pledge of total abstinence. They met once a week to listen to lectures and participate in activities which taught them that alcohol was harmful. The movement spread across the country and the Band of Hope Union was formed in 1855. Musical competitions were held between different Band of Hope choirs, and local Temperance Societies organised outings for the children.

10 **The calf**.

11 **Syrinx**. The syrinx, or panpipes, was said to have been invented by Pan as a result.

12 **Eileen Drewery**.

13 *Entrechat*.

14 **Princess**. During the Amrit ceremony Sikhs make a promise to honour the five Ks of Sikhism, established by Guru Gobind Singh at the first festival of Baisakhi in 1699. Women take the name Kaur and men take the name Singh (Lion).

15 **The intensity of an earthquake** (the strength and effects of the vibrations). They devised the Mercalli scale, named after the Italian geologist Guiseppe Mercalli (1850–1914). The other scale used in the measurement of earthquakes, the Richter scale, measures the magnitude of an earthquake (ie the energy released).

16 **Sir Alexander Gibson** (1926–95).

17 **Patricia Highsmith** (1921–95). She was awarded the Edgar Allen Poe Scroll for Mystery Writers of America for *The Talented Mr Ripley*, which was also the basis for the 1960 film *Plein Soleil*.

18 **Portmanteau word**. A BBC Radio 4 programme in 1990 invited listeners to make up new words; they supplied portmanteau words such as 'bagonise' (from 'baggage' and 'agonise') to describe waiting for luggage at an airport, 'fagony' for a smoker's cough and 'aginda' for a pre-conference drink.

19 **They are smooth and hairless**.

20 **Taking the altitude of the Sun with a sextant**.

T is for Textiles

1 From which fibre is calico made?

2 What is the familiar name for a tracksuit which has a lightweight cotton inner layer covered by a waterproof nylon outer layer?

3 From which heavy canvas-type material were jeans originally made, before the development of denim?

4 In which fabric-making technique are purl, garter stitch, stocking stitch and cable used?

5 The lightweight, durable fleece of which grazing animal, originally from the Andes in Peru, is sometimes known as 'the fibre of the gods'?

6 The name of which popular craft, developed from a coarse lace made by knotting cords or thick threads, comes from a Turkish word meaning 'napkin' or 'towel'?

7 Which tartan was adopted as the 'government' tartan in Scotland after the 1745 Jacobite Rising?

8 From a fibre from which plant is hessian (also known as burlap) made?

9 What name is given to the method of creating a pattern on cloth in which a design is painted on to the fabric with wax to mask areas which are to be left undyed when the fabric is immersed in dye?

10 What was the first artificial fibre, created by Louis-Marie-Hilaire Bernigaud, comte de Chardonnet, in 1889?

11 In which Cheshire town is there a working silk museum?

12 The name of which wrinkled fabric, which can be woven from various natural and manufactured yarns, is a French word meaning 'wrinkled'?

13 What distinguishes crêpe de Chine from other crêpes?

14 What name is given to the sewing or gluing of patches of fabric on to a garment or piece of material for decoration?

15 Lycra and Spandelle are trademarks for forms of which highly elastic polyurethane-based fibre?

16 What name is given to the embroidery on white cotton in which the pattern is made from small punched holes whose cut edges are over-stitched and the surrounding material is embroidered in white?

17 What is mercerised cotton?

18 What kind of material is maud?

19 What name, from the Hindi word for 'spotted', is given to a plain-woven, printed or solid-colour cotton fabric?

20 In garment-making, what are flat-felled, Hong Kong, French and serges?

T is for Textiles Answers

1 **Cotton**. Calico originated in Calicut, on the Malabar coast of India, where it was being made by the eleventh century.

2 **Shell suit**.

3 **Gene fustian**. It was originally made at Genoa in Italy, and first used in 1850 for working clothes. Levi Strauss (1830–1902), a Bavarian immigrant to the USA, made trousers (jeans) out of the gene fustian material intended for wagon covers. Thus, they became known as Levis.

4 **Knitting**.

5 **Alpaca** (*Lama pacos*), a South American member of the camel family and closely related to the llama. During the Incan civilisation (1100–1530), only royalty and nobility were permitted to wear robes of alpaca wool.

6 **Macramé** (from the Turkish *makrama*). In the nineteenth century, macramé was a speciality of Genoa, where towels decorated with knotted cord were popular. It developed from a sixteenth-century technique of knotting lace, known as *punto a groppo*.

7 **The Black Watch**, a dark green, blue and black tartan. After the Battle of Culloden in 1746, Highland dress was proscribed (1746–82); during that time the Black Watch tartan, worn by the government regiment of that name, was the only one which could be worn legally – and only by members of the armed forces.

8 **Jute**, also known as allyott (*Corchorus capsularis* and *olitorius*).

9 **Batik**.

10 **Rayon**. It was developed in an attempt to produce artificial silk. Chardonnet made rayon fibres by squeezing a nitrocellulose solution through nozzles and hardening it. He set up a factory to produce this 'Chardonnet silk' in 1891. By 1905 Courtaulds was producing viscose rayon (shortened to 'viscose') made from a different cellulose compound.

11 **Macclesfield**. In 1966 we recorded *Mastermind* there in the Heritage Centre, in the beautifully restored Assembly Hall of the Macclesfield Sunday school, which was opened in 1814 as a Sunday School 'to lessen the sum of human wretchedness by diffusing religious knowledge and useful learning among the lower classes of society'.

12 **Crêpe**.

13 **It is made from silk or artificial silk**.

14 **Appliqué**.

15 **Spandex**. Spandex fibres can be stretched by more than 600 per cent without breaking and quickly return to their original length.

16 **Broderie anglaise** (French for 'English embroidery'). Broderie anglaise originated in Europe (not in England) in the sixteenth century.

17 **Cotton which has been treated to look like silk**. The process of mercerising is named after its inventor (in 1844), John Mercer. The material is treated under tension with aqueous sodium hydroxide (caustic soda), which makes it swell and increases its strength and its absorption of dye.

18 **A grey woollen plaid**, which originated in Scotland in the eighteenth century. In his 1831 novel *Count Roland of Paris*, Sir Walter Scott wrote:
   A grey maud, . . . completed such an equipment as, since Juvenal's days, has been the livery of the poor scholar.

19 **Chintz**.

20 **Seam finishes**.

General Knowledge

1 Which Hebridean island has given its name to a patterned knitwear, believed to be of Moorish origin, derived from contact with sailors from the Spanish Armada of 1588 who were shipwrecked there?

2 Which of the Teletubbies has a triangular antenna?

3 Which British coin weighs exactly 5 grams?

4 For what do the initials BMW, the car manufacturer, stand?

5 Of which French colony did the former penal settlement of 'Devil's Island' form a part?

6 What is the common name for trees of the genus *Melaleuca* of the myrtle family, whose oil is used in medicine for its antiseptic properties and for treating fungal infections?

7 In the French delicacy *marrons glacés*, what are peeled, boiled and preserved in vanilla-flavoured sugar?

8 The identifying mark on which porcelain is a pair of crossed swords?

9 How did the American female boxer Margaret ('the Tiger') MacGregor make sporting history in Seattle in October 1999?

10 Which term for the colouring of a cat is derived from a cloth of the same name, which originated in Baghdad?

11 Who played the role of Sherlock Holmes in the 1959 film version of *The Hound of the Baskervilles*, with Andrew Morrell as Watson?

12 Which bird is commonly known in North America as the 'goatsucker'?

13 Which sixteenth-century artist painted *Sacred and Profane Love*, now in the Borghese Gallery, in Rome?

14 Which composer wrote the music used for the Christmas carol *Hark the Herald Angels Sing*?

15 Which English clergyman invented the power loom in 1785?

16 Which 1897 poem by Henry Newbolt begins:
   Take my drum to England, hang et by the shore.
   Strike et when your powder's runnin' low;
   If the Dons sight Devon, I'll quit the port o' Heaven.
   An' drum them up the Channel as we drummed them long ago.

17 Who was the 'special correspondent' of *The Times* who sent back despatches about the Crimean War in 1854–5 and in 1858 published *The British Expedition to the Crimea*?

18 What is the first route in 'The Knowledge', the test which London taxi drivers have to pass before they get their badge?

19 Which English humanist, physician to Henry VIII, founded the Royal College of Physicians in 1518?

20 Grades of which plain-woven cotton fabric are known as book, mull, Swiss, and sheeting?

General Knowledge Answers

1 **Fair Isle.**

2 **Tinky Winky.**

3 **The twenty-pence piece.**

4 **Bavarian Motor Works** (Bayerische Motoren Werke). The company was founded in 1916 as a manufacturer of aircraft and built the world's first jet aeroplane engines, used by the Luftwaffe during the Second World War.

5 **French Guiana** (Guyane Française). In about 1852 the French began to deport convicts to the colony. Captain Alfred Dreyfus (c 1859–1935) of the French Army, who was found guilty of betraying military secrets to Germany, was imprisoned there in the 1890s. The penal colony on Devil's Island was abolished after Albert Londres (1884–1932) drew attention to the dreadful conditions in which prisoners were kept.

6 **Tea tree.**

7 **Chestnuts.**

8 **Meissen.** It is named after the town of Meissen in Saxony on the Elbe where it is made. The company opened in 1710 as the Royal Polish Electoral Saxonian Porcelain Manufactory of Meissen. In 1722 it adopted the swords of the electoral coat of arms of Saxony as its trademark.

9 **She boxed against a man** (Loi Chow) – and beat him! It was the first sanctioned mixed-gender fight, which Dale Ashley (Washington's former Boxing Commissioner) had campaigned against 'for Margaret MacGregor's safety'.

10 **Tabby.** It is a silk material whose surface is 'watered' (marked with wavy lines which resemble watermarks). The term came to be used for cats whose coats have various shades of brown in a similar pattern to that of the cloth. The word derives from *al-'attabiya* (quarter of Attab), the district in Baghdad where the cloth was first made.

11 **Peter Cushing.**

12 **Nightjar.** Its name arises from the common belief that it sucks milk from the udders of goats. In fact it feeds on insects, which it catches in flight.

13 **Titian.** He painted *Sacred and Profane Love* in 1512–15.

14 **Felix Mendelssohn** (1809–47). The music was adapted from a chorus in Mendelssohn's *Festgesang* by William Cummings, who had sung as a choirboy under Mendelssohn's direction. He matched the music to words written by Charles Wesley (1709–78).

15 **Edmund Cartwright** (1743–1823), rector of Goadby-Marwood in Leicestershire. The loom incorporated three motions: shedding, picking and winding the woven cloth on to the cloth beam.

16 *Drake's Drum*.

17 **Sir William Russell** (1821–1907). He criticised military mismanagement and the insanitary living conditions of the soldiers. In 1855 the photographer Roger Fenton was sent from London to the Crimea to collect visual evidence to counter Russell's reports.

18 **Manor House to Gibson Square** (Finsbury Park to Islington). The *Blue Book* (which is actually pink) contains details of no fewer than 468 runs. Fred Housego, the 'gabby cabby' who won *Mastermind* in 1980, told me that he thinks it is probably the hardest examination in the world.

19 **Thomas Linacre** (c 1460–1524).

20 **Muslin.** The fabric derived its name from Mosul (now in Iraq), where it was first made.

U is for **United States of America** Questions

1 Who has been the only presenter of the world's longest-running radio series, BBC Radio 4's *Letter from America*, since it began in 1946?

2 Which US state was once known as 'Russian America'?

3 In the USA, what is the only word on triangular traffic signs instructing drivers to give way at a junction?

4 What was the original motto of the USA *before* the present 'In God We Trust'?

5 Which was the first state to be admitted to the Union, in 1787?

6 Which American poet wrote the sonnet *The New Colossus* in 1883, the following lines from which were later inscribed on the base of the Statue of Liberty in New York Harbour:

> *Give me your tired, your poor,*
> *Your huddled masses yearning to breathe free,*
> *The wretched refuse of your teeming shore,*
> *Send these, the homeless, tempest-tossed, to me:*
> *I lift my lamp beside the golden door.*

7 What is the American equivalent word for a 'guard's van' (on a train)?

8 Whose was the first signature on the American Declaration of Independence in 1776?

9 Which State is nicknamed 'America's Dairyland'?

10 During the American Civil War who were known as 'bushwhackers'?

11 Which notorious American outlaw was killed by lawman Pat Garrett in 1881?

12 Which dam on the Colorado River in Nevada was called Boulder Dam between 1933 and 1947?

13 Which American television character was the equivalent of Britain's Alf Garnett?

14 Which proprietor of the *Washington Post* was awarded the Pulitzer Prize in 1997 for her autobiography *Personal History*?

15 Who was known as 'the Angel of the Battlefield' during the American Civil War, and founded the American Red Cross in 1881?

16 Which English writer wrote the following:

> *Like so many substantial Americans, he had married young, kept on marrying, springing from blonde to blonde like the chamois of the Alps leaping from crag to crag.*

17 Who was the last Dutch governor of New Amsterdam (now New York)?

18 In the 1940s which New York street was given the official name 'Avenue of the Americas' to honour the Latin American countries?

19 By what name was the nineteenth-century leader of the Chiricahua Apaches, Goyathley ('One who yawns'), better known?

20 In 1975 who was the first person born in America to be canonised?

U is for United States of America Answers

1 **Alistair Cooke** (b 1908). He continues to present his weekly *Letter from America* at the age of 91.

2 **Alaska**. The US Secretary of State William H. Seward negotiated the purchase of Alaska from Russia in 1867. It became the 49th state on 3 January 1959 and increased the nation's size by nearly 20 per cent.

3 **Yield**.

4 *E Pluribus Unum* ('One out of Many'). The phrase was taken from *Moretum* ('The Salad', a mock-heroic poem attributed to Virgil about a farmer preparing a meal).

5 **Delaware**.

6 **Emma Lazarus** (1849–87). She wrote the poem in support of immigrants to America. The inscription was put in place in 1903, after her death from cancer.

7 **Caboose**.

8 **John Hancock** (1737–93). From 1775 to 1777 he was President of the Continental Congress; he remained in the Congress until 1780, when he was elected Governor of Massachusetts.

9 **Wisconsin**. Of all the States it is the major producer of milk, butter and a huge variety of cheeses.

10 **Confederate guerrillas**.

11 **Billy the Kid** (William H. Bonney, 1859–81), whose nickname arose from his 'baby' face. He committed his first murder at the age of twelve.

12 **Hoover Dam**. When construction began in 1931 it was named after President Herbert Hoover (1874–1964), but its name was changed to Boulder Dam (after the nearby Boulder City) two years later. Construction was completed in 1936. It was renamed Hoover Dam in 1947.

13 **Archie Bunker**. He was the central character in the 1971–9 CBS comedy series *All in the Family*, which was based on *Till Death Us Do Part*. Carroll O'Connor played the part of Archie Bunker in that series and in the spin-off *Archie Bunker's Place* (1979–83).

14 **Katharine Meyer Graham** (b 1917). She succeeded her husband, after his death in 1963, as president of the Washington Post Company and remained president until 1973.

15 **Clara Barton** (Clarissa Harlowe, 1821–1912). She was a school teacher from Boston, Massachusetts, who became a clerk in the Patent Office in Washington DC (1854–7). She also assisted on the battlefields of Europe during the Franco-Prussian War (1870–1).

16 **P. G. Wodehouse** (1881–1975) in *Summer Moonshine*.

17 **Peter Stuyvesant** (1592–1672). He became governor of New Amsterdam in 1647, but was forced to surrender it to the English in 1664; the English changed the name of the city to New York. A brand of American cigarettes was named after him, and the Bowery, part of Manhattan, was named after his *bouwerie* (farm).

18 **Sixth Avenue**.

19 **Geronimo** (1829–1909).

20 **St Elizabeth Ann Seton** (1774–1821). She founded the American Sisters of Charity, the first order of nuns in the United States.

General Knowledge

1 In which US city was the American Declaration of Independence signed and given its first public reading in 1776?

2 Which British engineer designed the *Great Western*, the first regular transatlantic steamer, whose maiden voyage was in 1838?

3 Which Shakespearean heroine disguised herself as a man and took the name of 'Ganymede', after 'Jove's own page'?

4 Which two roles were played in the 1944, 1971 and 1996 versions of the same film by Joan Fontaine and Orson Welles, Susannah York and George C. Scott, and Charlotte Gainsbourg and William Hurt?

5 In culinary terms what is ghee?

6 In which town is the University of Ulster?

7 What is the name of the clerical directory of the Church of England?

8 What kind of establishment did William Crockford found at 50 St James's Street, London, in 1828?

9 What is the present name of the seaport on the Adriatic coast formerly called Ragusa?

10 Which cartoon character made his debut with the name of Ham Gravy in E. C. Segar's *Thimble Theatre* in 1919 with the words 'D'ya think I'm a cowboy?'

11 What was the name of the wife of George Talbot, 6th Earl of Shrewsbury ('jailer' of Mary Queen of Scots), from whom the Duke of Devonshire is descended?

12 Which Scottish philologist was the first editor of the Oxford English Dictionary?

13 In 1997 which agent was the first MI6 officer to be tried under the Official Secrets Act since George Blake in 1961, and the first person to be prosecuted under the 1989 Official Secrets Act?

14 Which 1916 musical was based on *Ali Baba and the Forty Thieves* from *The Thousand and One Nights*?

15 The name of which seabird comes from its habit of spitting a foul-smelling oil at intruders to its nest?

16 From which poem did Mary McCarthy take the title of her 1964 novel *Cast a Cold Eye*?

17 The substance which Franz Joseph Müller von Reichenstein named 'metallum problematicum' in 1782, because it defied his attempts at analysis, was later found to be an element; what name was given to it?

18 Which eighteenth-century German-born English artist and founder-member of the Royal Academy was known for his 'conversation pieces' (groups of people in their customary surroundings), such as *The Tribuna of the Uffizi Gallery* (1780) and *Charles Towneley Among His Marbles* (1790)?

19 In a synagogue, what is the *Ner Tamid*?

20 Which settlement near Los Angeles was created in 1887 by Horace Wilcox, a prohibitionist from Kansas, as a community based on his sober religious principles?

General Knowledge   Answers

1 **Philadelphia**. On 2 July 1776, Congress resolved that 'these United Colonies are, and of right ought to be, free and independent states'. The separation was officially voted on 2 July but not announced until 4 July.

2 **Isambard Kingdom Brunel** (1806–59). The *Great Western* took fifteen days to sail from Bristol to New York (half the time of most sailing ships).

3 **Rosalind** in *As You Like It*. In Greek mythology Ganymede was a handsome young Trojan hero whom Zeus abducted and took up to Olympus to be cup-bearer to the gods.

4 **Jane Eyre** and **Edward Rochester**, in adaptations of Charlotte Brontë's *Jane Eyre*.

5 **Clarified butter** (butter from which the milk solids and salt have been removed). Ghee is burned in holy lamps – for example, at Divali.

6 **Coleraine** (*Cúil Raithin*, meaning 'ferry corner'). The University of Ulster was established in 1984 by the merger of the New University of Ulster (at Coleraine) and the Ulster Polytechnic.

7 **Crockford** (Crockford's Clerical Dictionary). It was first compiled by John Crockford in 1838.

8 **A gambling club** (Crockford's). Crockford's closed down in 1848 because of changes in the Gaming Laws, but in 1928 a new Crockford's opened at 21 Hertford Street (as a bridge club).

9 **Dubrovnik**. It was founded as Rausa or Ragusium in the seventh century by Roman refugees from the Slav and Avar sack of Epidaurus. A group of Slavs joined the Romans at Rausa, and the Slav name Dubrovnik ('Oak Forest') was adopted; the Italian name for the city is still Ragusa.

10 **Popeye the Sailor**. He was answering Olive Oyl's brother Castor, who had asked him 'Are you a sailor?'

11 **Bess of Hardwick** (1518–1608).

12 **Sir James Murray** (1837–1915). It was begun in 1879 by the British Philological Society as the *New English Dictionary*. Murray edited about half of the work. It was published by the Oxford University Press in 1928 as *A New English Dictionary on Historical Principles*; it contained 400,000 words and phrases, in ten volumes.

13 **Richard Tomlinson**. At his trial he pleaded guilty to having passed an outline of the book he was writing about his experiences with MI6 to a publisher in Australia. He was sentenced to a year in prison.

14 *Chu Chin Chow* by the actor Oscar Asche (John Stanger Heiss, 1871–1936).

15 **Fulmar**, from the Old Norse *fúll már* ('foul mew' or 'foul gull').

16 *Under Ben Bulben* (1939) by W. B. Yeats (it was also his epitaph):
> Cast a cold eye
> On life, on death.
> Horseman, pass by!

17 **Tellurium**. Müller had obtained the substance from an ore described as 'German gold'. In 1798 Martin Heinrich Klaproth confirmed that the substance was an element. He named it after the Earth (*tellus*).

18 **Johann Zoffany** (1734–1810).

19 **The everlasting light** (kept burning to symbolise the presence of God).

20 **Hollywood**. Hollywood became a suburb of Los Angeles in 1910 and in 1911 Columbia Pictures set up Hollywood's first motion-picture studio.

V is for Villains

1 The skeleton of which 'resurrectionist' (body-snatcher) is on display in the Anatomy Department of Edinburgh University, where it had been publicly dissected in 1829?

2 Which cat from T. S. Eliot's *Old Possum's Book of Practical Cats* was 'the hidden paw', 'the master criminal who can defy the Law'?

3 The perpetrators of which crime were put to death at Execution Dock in Wapping?

4 Which murderer was arrested in 1910 on board the *Montrose*, bound for Canada, by means of the newly introduced telegraph system?

5 In Conan Doyle's *The Memoirs of Sherlock Holmes*, whom did Sherlock Holmes describe as 'the Napoleon of crime'?

6 What was the name of the Palestinian immigrant who assassinated Senator Robert Kennedy on 5 June 1968, outraged by Kennedy's pro-Israeli attitude?

7 What nickname did journalists give to Carlos Martinez (Ilich Ramirez Sanchez), the Venezuelan sentenced to life imprisonment in 1975 for three murders he carried out for terrorist organisations?

8 The name of which London landlord came to be used to refer to any kind of extortion by landlords after his exploitation of tenants in Paddington was investigated in 1962–3?

9 What was the name of the New York serial murderer of 1976–7 who called himself 'Son of Sam'?

10 What was the real name of the US bandit Butch Cassidy, whose story was told in the 1969 film *Butch Cassidy and the Sundance Kid*?

11 What was the name of the steeplechaser which the highwayman Dick Turpin stole, and which led to a reward of £200 being offered for his capture?

12 What was the name of the legendary brigand of Eleusis who used to lay travellers on a bed and, if they were too long for it, cut short their legs but if they were too short, stretch them?

13 Who were the five Cambridge graduates recruited as Soviet agents in the 1930s and referred to as 'the Magnificent Five' by the KGB?

14 In 1976 which English art dealer admitted to having forged more than 2,000 paintings and sold them as originals by Gainsborough, Turner, Rembrandt and others?

15 What is the name of the evil Lord of the Rings in J. R. R. Tolkien's novel of that title?

16 In the First World War which member of a European royal family was nicknamed 'the Laughing Murderer'?

17 What was the name of the fictional criminal-turned-detective, created by Maurice Leblanc in 1907, who first appeared in *The Seven of Hearts*?

18 What was the name of the man convicted of murder and sentenced to death after the bombing of the Alfred P. Murrah building in Oklahoma City in June 1997, in which 168 people died?

19 Which Scottish serial killer in the 1950s conducted his own defence but was found guilty of seven murders in 1958 and hanged in Glasgow?

20 In *Othello* Iago says, 'I had rather be a toad/And live upon the vapour of a dungeon' – rather than what?

V is for **Villains**

1 **William Burke** (1792–1829). With his accomplice, William Hare (1790–1860), who turned King's Evidence at his trial, Burke murdered people and dug up bodies for sale (at £10 each) to the Edinburgh anatomist Dr Robert Knox for dissection.

2 **Macavity** (The Mystery Cat).

3 **Piracy**. The pirates were hanged and then, to deter others, their bodies were chained in the dock until three tides had washed over them.

4 **Dr Crippen**. Dr Hawley Harvey ('Peter') Crippen poisoned his wife Belle Elmor, cut up her corpse and buried it beneath the cellar of their home. He sailed (under the name of Robinson) with his mistress Ethel le Neve, who was disguised as his 'nephew'. The ship's captain became suspicious and telegraphed Scotland Yard.

5 **Professor James Moriarty**, a brilliant mathematician turned criminal.

6 **Sirhan Bishara Sirhan** (b *c* 1943).

7 **The Jackal**. The name was taken from Frederick Forsyth's 1970 novel *The Day of the Jackal* about a professional assassin hired by Algerian War veterans to kill President de Gaulle.

8 **Peter Rachman** (1920–62).

9 **David Berkowitz**. He was sentenced to 25 to 30 years for each murder, running concurrently, so that he would serve the full term for only one murder.

10 **Robert Le Roy Parker** (1886–1909). His nickname came from his former occupation (he was a butcher).

11 **White Stocking**. Dick Turpin used to rob race-goers on their way to Newmarket. The horse was recognisable because of its white feet, and was quickly spotted after Turpin stole it. When one of Turpin's gang went to collect it from the stables of the Red Lion in Whitechapel where Turpin had left it, the police were waiting. They found out from the man where Turpin was but, after an exchange of shots, failed to catch him.

12 **Procrustes**. He was killed by Theseus.

13 **Guy Burgess** (1911–63), **Donald Maclean** (1913–83), **Harold ('Kim') Philby** (1912–88), **Anthony Blunt** (1907–83) and **John Cairncross** (1913–95). Burgess and Maclean defected to the Soviet Union in 1951 after a warning from Philby (the 'third man'). Philby followed in 1963 and Blunt, a distinguished art historian and surveyor of the Queen's pictures, confessed to being the 'fourth man' in return for immunity from prosecution. Cairncross (the 'fifth man') confessed in 1991.

14 **Tom Keating** (1918–84).

15 **Sauron**. To gain control of the Rings of Power, Sauron had sacrificed much of his magical power to create one ruling ring, which he later lost.

16 **Friedrich Wilhelm, Crown Prince of Germany**, the eldest son of Kaiser Wilhelm II. He was Commander of the German forces at Verdun.

17 **Arsène Lupin**.

18 **Timothy McVeigh**.

19 **Peter Manuel** (1931–58). His victims included three members of the Watt family in Rutherglen.

20 *Than keep a corner in the thing I love*
    For others' uses.
    (*Othello*, Act III, Scene iii).

General Knowledge

1 What was the popular name for the Dutch dancer and courtesan Margaretha MacLeod (née Zelle), who was shot by the French in 1917 on charges of spying for Germany?

2 Which former curate and rector wrote the children's classic *The Water Babies* in 1863 and *Hereward the Wake* in 1866?

3 Which volunteer force was founded in 1908 by the 1st Viscount Haldane, Secretary of State for War from 1905 to 1912?

4 In 1991, addressing the Institute of Directors at the Royal Albert Hall, who said of his jewellery shops, 'We even sell a pair of earrings for under £1, which is cheaper than a prawn sandwich from Marks and Spencers. But I have to say the earrings probably won't last as long'?

5 What was the name of the snail in the BBC television series *The Magic Roundabout*?

6 In shipping for what do the initials ULCC stand?

7 By what names are the frequently combined green salad ingredients *Sinapis alba* and *Lepidum sativum* better known?

8 What device is used for measuring the pressure of liquids or gases?

9 In Greek legend who cut the Gordian knot?

10 Which battle between the English and the Scots was fought near the village of Branxton in Northumberland on 9 September 1513?

11 What was the name of the founding president of modern Croatia who died on 13 December 1999?

12 By what name was the US blues singer, composer and guitarist McKinley Morganfield better known?

13 The 1988 memoirs of which actor and producer, who died in May 2000, the star of more than 80 films including *The Prisoner of Zenda*, *Sinbad the Sailor* and *Gunga Din*, were entitled *Salad Days*?

14 For what does the acronym ZIP (as in zipcode) stand?

15 After visits to the East which pre-Raphaelite artist painted *The Finding of the Saviour in the Temple* and *The Scapegoat*?

16 In legal terms what is the meaning of the Latin term *ignoramus*?

17 What does Candlemas, celebrated on 2 February, commemorate?

18 What are listed in Messier's catalogue?

19 Which daily periodical was founded by Richard Steele and Joseph Addison in March 1711?

20 Who created the gentleman crook A. J. Raffles, who appeared in a series of short stories first published in the 1890s in the *Strand* and other popular magazines and then in novels, beginning with *Raffles, The Amateur Cracksman*?

General Knowledge

1 **Mata Hari** (1876–1917).

2 **Charles Kingsley** (1819–75). Under the name 'Parson Lot' he published numerous articles on social issues. He also wrote influential social novels such as *Alton Locke* (1850) and *Yeast* (1851) and a dramatic poem, *The Saint's Tragedy, or The True Story of Elizabeth of Hungary* (1848).

3 **The Territorial Army.**

4 **Gerald Ratner**, chief executive of Ratner's.

5 **Brian.** The series made use of a mixture of animation and marionettes. It was created by the French animator Serge Danot and written and narrated for British television by Eric Thompson.

6 **Ultra Large Crude Carrier.** These vessels are described in terms of their deadweight which is a measure not of the weight of the ships themselves but of the oil they can carry.

7 **Mustard and cress.**

8 **Manometer.**

9 **Alexander the Great** (356–323 BC). According to the legend, Gordius, the King of Phrygia (now part of Anatolia in Greece), had dedicated his cart to Jupiter. He tied its yoke to a beam with a knot so intricate that no one could untie it, and the oracle foretold that whoever undid it would rule Asia. When Alexander arrived at Gordium, the capital of Phrygia, during his invasion of Asia and heard the story, he said, 'Well then, it is thus I perform the task' and cut the rope in two with his sword.

10 **Flodden.** Henry VIII had invaded France, and Louis XII of France had asked his ally James IV of Scotland to create a diversion by invading England. James led an army of about 35,000 to 40,000 into Northumberland and the Earl of Surrey, Henry VIII's lieutenant in the north, gathered an army of 26,000 men and went to meet the Scots. Surrey's army defeated the Scots, killing James and about 10,000 men.

11 **Franjo Tudjman** (1922–99).

12 **Muddy Waters** (1915–83). His band's recordings include *Hoochie Coochie Man* (1954) and *I've Got My Mojo Working* (1957).

13 **Douglas Fairbanks Junior** (1909–2000).

14 **Zone Improvement Plan.**

15 **Sir William Holman Hunt** (1827–1910). In 1848 he founded the 'Pre-Raphaelite Brotherhood' with Dante Gabriel Rossetti and John Everett Millais.

16 **We take no notice.** A jury would scribble this on the back of indictments which were not considered worthy of sending to court. The literal meaning is 'we do not know', and '*ignoramus*' came to be used as a noun for an ignorant person.

17 **The Presentation of Christ.** It used to be called The Purification of the Virgin Mary. In Roman Catholic churches all the candles to be used during the year are consecrated on Candlemas day. Candlemas is a Quarter Day in Scotland.

18 **Star clusters, nebulae and galaxies.** Messier's catalogue lists more than a hundred of them. It was compiled in 1781 by the French astronomer Charles Messier (1730–1817), who discovered many of them.

19 *The Spectator.*

20 **E. W. Hornung** (1866–1921).

W is for Weather

1 What is the name of the cold, dry, strong wind which blows from the north down the Rhône valley to the Mediterranean coast of France?

2 From which 1939 musical film is the song *Over the Rainbow* by E. Y. Harburg?

3 What is the origin of the American saying 'to take a rain check'?

4 What is the unit of measurement of atmospheric pressure?

5 What kind of weather did Dickens refer to as 'a London particular'?

6 Which BBC television weather forecaster announced on 15 October 1987, 'A woman rang to say she heard there was a hurricane on the way. Well, don't worry, there isn't'?

7 What kind of clouds produce a 'mackerel sky'?

8 What name is given to a system of winds which blows around an area of high atmospheric pressure in a clockwise direction in the northern hemisphere and in an anticlockwise direction in the southern hemisphere?

9 What shape is the road sign which warns that a road is liable to icing, and what is depicted on it?

10 What is measured by a udometer?

11 After which animal is 2 February named in the USA, from the folklore idea that if it does not see its shadow when it emerges from its burrow after hibernation it retreats and hibernates for a further six weeks?

12 What term is used in meteorology for a warm front which has been quickly overtaken by a cold front moving rapidly around a low-pressure centre?

13 In Greek mythology what names were given to the personifications of the north, south, east and west winds?

14 What kind of weather has features named 'leaders', 'stepped leaders' and 'dart leaders'?

15 Which English meteorologist, the first professor of meteorology at Imperial College of Science and Technology, London, wrote *Manual of Meteorology* in 1926–31 and introduced the tephigram (a graph of temperature changes)?

16 Which American poet wrote the following lines in 1916:

> *The fog comes*
> *on little cat feet.*
> *It sits looking*
> *over harbour and city*
> *on silent haunches*
> *and then moves on.*

17 What is the term for the fog caused by the horizontal passage of warm moist air over cold land?

18 In mountainous areas what type of wind blows down slopes at night when high ground radiates heat gained during the day, and is cooled?

19 What is recorded on a Campbell-Stokes recorder?

20 Which English meteorologist invented a pressure-tube anemometer, the first device to measure both the velocity and direction of wind?

W is for **Weather**

1 **The Mistral.**

2 *The Wizard of Oz*, which was based on the children's story of the same title by L. Frank Baum. The song, sung by Judy Garland, won an Academy Award for Best Original Song.

3 It is a **counterfoil of a ticket for a baseball game** which can be used for entry to watch another if the first one is cancelled through bad weather.

4 **Bar** (divided into **millibars**).

5 **Fog**: 'This is a London particular . . . A fog, miss.' (Said to Esther Summerson by Richard Carstone, *Bleak House*, Chapter 3.)

6 **Michael Fish**. That night there were severe gales across southern England.

7 **Cirrocumulus.**

8 **Anticyclone**. The system is the reverse of that of a *cyclone*, in which the winds blow around an area of low pressure.

9 **It is triangular with a six-pointed snowflake (or ice crystal)**:

10 **Rainfall**. It is a rain gauge.

11 **The groundhog**. The day is named 'Groundhog Day'.

12 **Occluded front**. It is characterised by low temperatures, thick clouds and widespread precipitation, often in the form of snow.

13 **Boreas, Notus, Eurus** and **Zephyrus**.

14 **Lightning**. A 'leader' is a luminous electrical discharge from a cloud to the ground, followed by a brighter return stroke to the cloud. The first leader in a lightning flash is called a 'stepped leader' because it descends in a series of rapid steps. It forms an electrically conductive path along which the return stroke travels. Subsequent leaders (which might be stepped) are called 'dart leaders'.

15 **Sir William Napier Shaw** (1854–1945). He also introduced the millibar as a unit of measurement of air pressure. He was elected to the Royal Society in 1891 and in 1900 became secretary of the Meteorological Council (the governing body of the Meteorological Office). He set up the reorganisation of this office and was its director from 1905 to 1920.

16 **Carl Sandburg** (1878–1967) in *Fog*.

17 **Advection fog**.

18 **Katabatic wind** (also called 'downslope wind' or 'gravity wind'). The air in contact with the high ground is cooled, and so becomes denser than other air at the same elevation but not in contact with the slope. It begins to move downwards beneath the warmer, less dense air. This process is less noticeable in windy weather, when the air is mixed and therefore cold pockets do not form.

19 **Hours of sunshine**. A Campbell-Stokes recorder consists of a glass sphere arranged to focus the Sun's image on to a bent strip of card on which the hours are marked. The focused heat burns through the card (but does not set it on fire) and the duration of sunshine is read from the length of burnt track.

20 **William Dines** (1855–1927). Dines pioneered the use of kites and balloons for upper-air measurement and designed a meteorograph (for taking upper-air soundings) which weighed only about 60 grams.

General Knowledge

1 In 1752 who showed that the luminescence of lightning is caused by electric discharge through the atmosphere, and invented the lightning conductor?

2 Which former Head of Current Affairs for BBC Northern Ireland, and later Editor of Thames TV News, wrote the Sharpe novels?

3 What is the English name for Llyn Tegid, the largest natural lake in Wales?

4 What is the official language of Bangladesh?

5 Which spring festival on the full-moon day of the month of Phalgun (February/March) do Hindus celebrate by throwing coloured water or powder over one another?

6 Which two vegetables are the main ingredients of *vichyssoise*?

7 What is the term applied to the increase in mineral and organic nutrients which reduces the dissolved oxygen in a lake or other body of water, providing an environment which favours plant over animal life?

8 Which were the original Cinque Ports?

9 Which Czech athlete (nicknamed 'the bouncing Czech' because of his ungainly running style) won the 5,000 and 10,000 metres races as well as the marathon at the 1952 Olympics?

10 In which city is the Topkapi Palace Museum?

11 What was the name of the first nuclear-powered submarine?

12 At which establishment did the £25 million Brinks Mat gold bullion robbery take place in 1983?

13 Which 'new romantics' band, formed in 1979, whose hits included *True*, *Gold* and *Only When You Leave*, took its name from a West Berlin prison in which Nazi war criminals were confined?

14 In which British city did the Porteous Riots take place in 1736?

15 What is the collective noun for moles?

16 In 1934 which author created Mary Poppins?

17 Which Dutch artist painted the rectilinear composition *Broadway Boogie-Woogie* in 1942–3?

18 In about 1712 which Scottish physician, mathematician and writer popularised the name John Bull for a quintessentially English character?

19 In the saying 'Possession is nine points of the law', referring to the advantages a person can have (short of actual right, which is the tenth point), what are the nine points of the law?

20 On a weather map, what are linked by isohyets?

General Knowledge

1 **Benjamin Franklin** (1706–90). The lightning conductor consists of a metal rod (usually copper) linked to the ground by a metal strip, to conduct electricity (from lightning) away from the building to the ground.

2 **Bernard Cornwell** (Bernard Wiggins, b 1944). Several of the Sharpe novels have been made into television series, starring Sean Bean as the promoted-from-the-ranks Major Richard Sharpe of South Essex.

3 **Lake Bala** in the Snowdonia National Park.

4 **Bengali.** Use of Bengali is compulsory in all government departments, but English is used widely as an unofficial second language.

5 **Holi.** The frivolity of the festival imitates the play of the god Krishna with the *gopis* (female cowherds). The *Dolayatra* (swinging of the god) festival takes place during Holi, when images of the gods are set on decorated platforms and swung to the accompaniment of singing and music.

6 **Leek and potato.**

7 **Eutrophication.**

8 **Dover, Hastings, Hythe, Romney** and **Sandwich**. Later Winchelsea and Rye were awarded Cinque Port status, as were 32 other, less important, ports. The Cinque Ports were granted special privileges through their provision of ships and men for the defence of the English Channel.

9 **Emil Zátopek** (b 1922), who had also won the 10,000 metres at the London Olympics in 1948. He set Olympic records in each race and watched his wife Dana Zátopková win the women's javelin.

10 **Istanbul.** The palace was built in the 1470s by Mehmed II (1432–81), Sultan of Turkey, and was turned into a museum in 1892. Its collection includes classical antiquities, manuscripts, ceramics, armour and textiles.

11 *Nautilus*, a US Navy vessel which was named after the submarine in Jules Verne's *Twenty Thousand Leagues Under the Sea* (1873) and launched in 1954. *Nautilus* was decommissioned in 1980.

12 **Heathrow Airport.**

13 **Spandau Ballet** (Gary Kemp, Tony Hadley, John Keeble, Steve Norman and Martin Kemp).

14 **Edinburgh.** The riots began when a popular smuggler, Andrew Wilson, was hanged. Captain John Porteous ordered the town guard to fire on the mob. He was himself condemned to death for murder but was granted a reprieve, after which the mob dragged him from the jail to the Grassmarket, where they hanged him from a barber's pole.

15 **A labour.**

16 **P. L. Travers** (Pamela Lyndon Travers, 1899–1996).

17 **Piet Mondrian** (1872–1944).

18 **John Arbuthnot** (1667–1735). He did not invent the name but used it in his political allegory about the political jockeyings of the British, French, Spanish and Dutch before the Treaty of Utrecht (1713). Published in five pamphlets from 1712, it was collected in 1727 under the title *Law is a Bottom-less Pit or The History of John Bull*.

19 **A good deal of money, a good deal of patience, a good cause, a good lawyer, a good counsel, good witnesses, a good jury, a good judge** and **good luck.**

20 **Places with the same total precipitation** during a given time period or a particular storm.

Y is for Yesterdays

1 Which line precedes the following, from the second verse of the Beatles 1976 song *Yesterday*, written by John Lennon and Paul McCartney:
   There's a shadow hanging over me
   Oh, yesterday came suddenly.

2 In which year were the Coronation, the first ascent of Everest and Gordon Richards' first Derby win?

3 Which Hungarian professor of design at the Academy of Applied Arts and Design in Budapest built a model which he used as a tool for teaching algebraic group theory, and which was marketed worldwide in 1977 as a puzzle?

4 How did Ian Hamilton, Kay Matheson, Alan Stuart and Gavin Vernon make news on 25 December 1950?

5 Which Berkshire town was the meeting point for the Easter marches of the Campaign for Nuclear Disarmament between 1958 and 1963?

6 What was the name of the massive oil tanker which was wrecked on the Seven Stones reef off the Scilly Isles in March 1967?

7 What was the popular dance of the 1980s, a mixture of Latin American and Caribbean styles, which consisted of embracing very tightly and gyrating the hips in a fluid manner?

8 Which minister of education was responsible for the 1944 Education Act, in which he reorganised the secondary education system and introduced the eleven-plus examination for selecting grammar school pupils?

9 Who was the producer of the satirical 1962–3 BBC television series *That Was The Week That Was*?

10 What was the name of the 'Butcher of Lyons' who had about 4,000 people put to death while he was head of the German Gestapo there from 1942 to 1944, and who was extradited from Bolivia in 1987?

11 By what collective name were the slapstick comedians of the 1930s to 1950s Larry Fine, Moe Howard and Jerry (Curly) Howard known?

12 What is the name of the unofficial club started by the Irvin Parachute Company for RAF airmen who had baled out in action?

13 Which Chinese nationalist leader was briefly kidnapped in the 'Xi incident' or 'Sian incident' in 1936?

14 What was a 'Sloppy Joe', which was popular from the 1940s to 1960s?

15 From which pre-war show did the dance the Lambeth Walk, first performed by Lupino Lane, come?

16 In which city was the first Allied summit conference of the Second World War held between 28 November and 1 December 1943?

17 In which country was the Eurovision Song Contest first staged in 1956?

18 During the First World War what kind of animal was posthumously awarded the Légion d'Honneur for services to the French army during the battle of Verdun in 1916?

19 Disturbances during a strike among members of which trade in November 1910 became known as the Tonypandy riots?

20 Which country was occupied by British forces on 10 May 1940, the day on which Germany launched its blitzkrieg invasion of the Low Countries and Winston Churchill took over from Neville Chamberlain as Britain's wartime Prime Minister?

Y is for **Yesterdays**   Answers

1 *Suddenly, I'm not half the man I used to be.*

2 **1953.** Sir Edmund Hillary and Tenzing Norgay reached the summit of Everest on 29 May. Gordon Richards was taking part in his 28th Derby on Pinza, which beat the Queen's colt Aureole by four lengths.

3 **Erno Rubik** (b 1944). Rubik's Cube was marketed by Konsumex, Hungary's state trading company. It sold more than 100 million authorised units by 1980, with an estimated 50 million unauthorised imitations.

4 **They removed the Stone of Destiny from the Coronation Chair in Westminster Abbey.** They brought the Stone back to Scotland, but returned it by placing it in the ruins of Arbroath Abbey on 11 April 1951.

5 **Aldermaston.** It was the location of the Atomic Weapons Research Establishment.

6 *Torrey Canyon.*

7 **The lambada.** It was thought to have originated among sailors and prostitutes in the shanty towns of Rio de Janeiro.

8 **R. A. Butler** (Richard Austin Butler, 1902–82), who was Minister of Education from 1941 to 1945.

9 **Ned Sherrin.** David Frost led a team of presenters including John Cleese, Dennis Potter and Keith Waterhouse, with Millicent Martin singing and taking part in the sketches.

10 **Klaus Barbie** (1913–91). He was brought back to France for trial and sentenced to life imprisonment for crimes against humanity.

11 **The Three Stooges.** Their real names were Louis Fienberg (1902–75), Moses Horwitz (1897–1975) and Jerome Horwitz (1903–52).

12 **The Caterpillar Club.** The Irvin Parachute Company presented a small gold caterpillar pin to the airmen in memory of silkworms, which produced the material for the parachutes.

13 **Chiang Kai-shek** (1887–1975).

14 **A very loose-fitting sweater,** often worn with tight-fitting trousers.

15 *Me and My Girl.* The dance purported to imitate the strutting walk of the typical Lambeth Cockney. Lambeth Walk is a thoroughfare leading from Black Prince Road to Lambeth Road.

16 **Tehran.** The second summit conference was at Yalta in the Crimea.

17 **Switzerland** (at the Teatro Kursaal in Lugano). It was developed as an offshoot of the San Remo Song Festival in Italy by Marcel Baison from France. The winner in 1956 was Switzerland's Lys Assia with *Refrain.*

18 **A pigeon.** Pigeons played an important part in the Allied communications network. 'The Verdun Pigeon' was noted for its persistence despite artillery fire, and it was greatly mourned when it died from wounds sustained during one of its missions.

19 **Coal miners.** The Chief Constable of Glamorgan had requested the local army commander to take action to control the situation. When Winston Churchill heard that a small force was on its way to Tonypandy in the Rhondda Valley, he insisted that it be kept in reserve and that extra unarmed police constables should be sent instead.

20 **Iceland.** After Germany invaded Denmark in April 1940, it had laid claim to Iceland (which was then in union with Denmark under the Danish Crown). The British occupying troops were replaced by American forces in July 1941.

General Knowledge

1 Who produced the Whitehall Farces in the 1950s and 1960s (and starred in many of them)?

2 In coinage what was the value of the groat, which was introduced during the reign of Edward I?

3 In the ITV series what was the name of the eponymous palomino horse which talked to its owner, the architect Wilbur Post?

4 In about 1800–5, which Spanish artist painted *Naked Maya* and *Clothed Maya*?

5 What name has been given to the collection of eleven medieval Welsh tales based on mythology, folklore and heroic legends which includes *Kulhwch and Olwen*, *Lludd and Llefelys*, *The Dream of Macsen* and *The Dream of Rhonabwy*?

6 What was the ancient name of the Dardanelles, the strait between the Sea of Marmara and the Aegean Sea?

7 Coeliac disease is an intolerance to what?

8 From which plant does vanilla come?

9 Crewel, tapestry and chenille are different types of which implement?

10 The website of which British publisher is fireandwater.com?

11 In the early eighteenth century what was the occupation of Anne Bonney and Mary Read?

12 Who was the only British swimmer to win a gold medal at the 1980 Olympics in Moscow?

13 The first novel of which Polish-born British author and former shipmaster was *Almayer's Folly*, published in 1894?

14 To whom were the following lines addressed in a poem by John Betjeman:
   Love-thirty, love-forty, oh! weakness of joy,
   The speed of a swallow, the grace of a boy,
   With carefullest carelessness, gaily you won,
   I am weak from your loveliness . . .

15 Which German composer, regarded by many as the liberator of German music from Italian influences with his adaptations of folk-music, wrote *Invitation to the Dance* in 1819?

16 What are the names of the eight Ivy League universities, the oldest in the United States?

17 In Scots law, what is a poinding (pronounced 'pinding')?

18 The love-story of which Oxford don and which American poet was the subject of the 1985 BAFTA award-winning BBC television drama, *Shadowlands* (starring Joss Ackland and Claire Bloom), and the 1993 film of the same name (starring Anthony Hopkins and Debra Winger)?

19 Which song was sung as the 'anthem' at the royal opening of the new Scottish Parliament on 1 July 1999?

20 What name was given to the woman who represented the American ideal of femininity at the turn of the century, created in 1896 by an American cartoonist based on his wife, Irene Langhorn, and her sisters?

General Knowledge

1 **Brian Rix** (b 1924). They were named after the Whitehall Theatre in London, where they were produced.

2 **Fourpence.** Previously most silver coins had been referred to as 'groats', but the term was later restricted to the fourpenny coin introduced by Edward I. Issue of the groat ceased in 1662, but it was reintroduced as the Britannia Groat in 1836. Fourpenny coins are still struck for the sovereign to distribute on Maundy Thursday.

3 **Mr Ed.** The voice of Mr Ed was provided by Allan 'Rocky' Lane, and Alan Young played the part of Wilbur Post.

4 **Goya** (Francisco José de Goya, 1746–1828). The eroticism of the paintings caused such outrage that he was interrogated by the Spanish Inquisition.

5 *The Mabinogion.* The title *Mabinogion* was given by Lady Charlotte Guest to her translations of the stories in 1838–49, but the word *Mabinogi* (matters concerning [the family of] Maponos) appears only in the four linked stories known as *The Four Branches of the Mabinogi*, or *The Four Branches*.

6 **Hellespont.**

7 **Gluten.**

8 **Orchid** (*Vanilla planifolia*). The traditional method of curing the beans begins with nightly sweating and daily exposure to the sun for about ten days until they are a deep chocolate brown. Then they are spread on trays in an airy shelter to dry. Curing and drying takes about four or five months.

9 **Needle.** They are of different thicknesses and suitable for use with different weights of fabric and sewing thread.

10 **HarperCollins.**

11 **They were pirates.** They disguised themselves as men and sailed on the ship of Captain 'Calico' Jack Rackham. When the ship was attacked by a British Navy sloop near Jamaica in 1720 they drew their pistols and fought alongside the men. They were captured, however, but at their trial they both escaped the death sentence because they were pregnant.

12 **Duncan Goodhew** (b 1957). He won his gold medal in the 100 metres breast-stroke, and a bronze medal in the 4 × 100 metres mixed relay.

13 **Joseph Conrad** (Józef Teodor Konrad Nalecz Korzeniowski, 1857–1924).

14 **Joan Hunter Dunn** (in *A Subaltern's Love-song*, published in *New Bats in Old Belfries*, 1945).

15 **Carl Maria Weber** (1786–1826).

16 **Harvard** (established 1636), **Yale** (1701), **Pennsylvania** (1740), **Princeton** (1746), **Columbia** (1754), **Brown** (1764), **Dartmouth** (1769) and **Cornell** (1865). The name Ivy League originally referred to the universities' sporting league and came from the ancient ivy on the walls of the buildings.

17 **A warrant-sale** which impounds the property of a debtor. 'Poind' is a Scottish verb meaning to impound. The word is derived from the Old English *pyndan* (impound).

18 **C. S. Lewis** (1898–1963) and **Joy Gresham** (née Davidman, 1915–60).

19 *A Man's a Man for a' That* by Robert Burns (sung by folk-singer Sheena Wellington).

20 **Gibson Girl.** Charles Dana Gibson (1867–1944) produced a series of black and white line drawings of the 'Gibson Girl', which were published in *Collier's* magazine.